W9-AEP-999

Gosnell, Harold
Boss Platt and his
New York machine

DATE DUE

#47-0108 Peel Off Pressure Sensitive

BOSS PLATT AND HIS NEW YORK MACHINE

THOMAS COLLIER PLATT
(Photograph by Van der Weyde)

BOSS PLATT AND HIS NEW YORK MACHINE

A STUDY OF THE POLITICAL LEADERSHIP
OF THOMAS C. PLATT, THEODORE
ROOSEVELT, AND OTHERS

By

HAROLD F. GOSNELL

With an Introduction by

CHARLES E. MERRIAM
Professor of Political Science in the University of Chicago

NEW YORK / RUSSELL & RUSSELL

FIRST PUBLISHED IN 1924
REISSUED, 1969, BY RUSSELL & RUSSELL
A DIVISION OF ATHENEUM PUBLISHERS, INC.
BY ARRANGEMENT WITH HAROLD F. GOSNELL
L. C. CATALOG CARD NO: 74-75466
PRINTED IN THE UNITED STATES OF AMERICA

TO
MY MOTHER

PREFACE

In this study the author has endeavored to describe the social background, the personal qualities, and the technique of a typical state political boss. The boss system was in a particularly flourishing condition during the late nineties in the northeastern part of the United States. Thomas Collier Platt of New York was selected for this analysis because there is a wealth of material available upon New York politics. In calling Senator Platt a "boss" the author does not wish to pass judgment upon the man. The endeavor is to give some objective meaning to the term. Platt happened to be the man who was recognized as the leader of the Republican party in the state of New York at the time when Theodore Roosevelt was coming into national notice. Platt's relations with Roosevelt would make an intensely interesting biographical study. The author has attempted to touch upon some of these relations. But only in part of this book is the chronological method followed. The organization of the book sometimes does violence to the sequence of events, but it is hoped that the arrangement adds to the understanding of the boss and the machine in actual operation.

In gathering material for this analysis, the writer was aided by the following New Yorkers: Hon. Frederick M. Davenport, state senator from Clinton, Col. D. A. Alexander, former congressman from Buffalo, Hon. C. H. Betts, state assemblyman from Lyons, Hon. B. B. Odell, former governor of New York, Hon. Chauncey M. Depew, former United States senator, Hon. Herbert P. Parsons, former

congressman from New York, Professor R. C. E. Brown
of Columbia University, formerly on the *New York Tribune,* Mr. W. T. Arnt, secretary of the New York Citizens'
Union and formerly on the *New York Evening Post,* Mr.
E. G. Riggs, formerly on the *New York Sun,* Mr. L. J.
Lang, of the *New York American,* and Mr. Hagedorn and
Mr. R. W. G. Vail, of the Roosevelt Memorial Association.
These men and the many others, librarians, newspaper men,
and politicians, who rendered valuable assistance to the
author are in no way responsible for statements made in
this book.   In organizing the material, the writer is under
great obligations to Professor C. E. Merriam, of the University of Chicago.   Valuable counsel was also furnished by
Professors A. C. McLaughlin and W. E. Dodd, also of the
University of Chicago.   In spite of this help, the author is
aware that many imperfections remain for which he alone
is accountable.

HAROLD FOOTE GOSNELL

UNIVERSITY OF CHICAGO
NOVEMBER, 1923

TABLE OF CONTENTS

LIST OF ILLUSTRATIONS

INTRODUCTION

The most widely known study of a political leader or boss is Machiavelli's *Prince,* which has stood for four hundred years as the classic type of a critical analysis of political character and methods. The work of the observing Florentine was anticipated, however, by the remarkable analyses made by Aristotle in his *Politics,* nearly 2000 years in advance of the Italian; and Aristotle was in turn anticipated by his great teacher, Plato, in his attempt to make a psychological pattern of the despot and the just man in the political world. By mathematical calculations, the basis of which I confess I am unable to follow, the great Greek philosopher reached the conclusion that the despot was precisely 729 times less happy than the just ruler, this figure being the cube of nine. We cannot say that the study of leaders was not begun early by the students of government, or deny that it was well begun by these illustrious inquirers.

In the meantime, however, new types of leaders have appeared, and new forms of analysis and appraisal. Modern democracy has produced novel situations under which leaders may develop, and modern political science and psychology are developing new modes of more critical and accurate analysis of the traits of the leaders and the habits of those who are led. In every part of the field of social science, there is beginning a wide movement toward the more intimate understanding of those qualities of human nature that underlie social and political control. The economic man, the social man, the political man cannot continue to be the product of arm-chair speculation or a type of general reasoning with chief regard to logical consistency in the line of arguments, but in increasing the degree the political man submits to the more objective tests of actual observation of behaviour and to specific measurement and analysis.

Using the new tools of survey and comparison, of statistics and psychology, the modern investigator is penetrating farther and farther into the recesses of that "human nature," which for a long time stood guard at the end of the world, barring the way to further discovery. Long ago we ceased to believe that rulers governed because they were the sons or blood relations of gods; or even that they ruled by special divine right. "The mystery that doth hedge about" a king has largely been dispelled, and with it the lesser mysteries that were worn by the lesser lights around the throne. It may still be assumed, however, that there is some other kind of a mystery that surrounds a leader of men, some magic that grows out of mysterious "human nature," and defies human analysis and understanding. Political leaders, some believe, are super-men, inscrutable, insoluble types, to be accepted as in the earlier times earthquakes, volcanoes, storms, or other works of nature were accepted.

"Human nature," however, is no more of a defense against modern science than "divine right" in the earlier period of human development, for the whole trend of modern social science is toward the discovery of the secrets or rather the sequences of "human nature." We no longer look upon the human beings who may be our masters with superstitious awe, but rather with scientific curiosity as to how they are constructed and how they operate, and with determination to reduce the mysterious to its very lowest terms. The "great man" is not merely a hero to be worshipped, as if in some occult way endowed with semi-divine attributes, but he (or she) presents a problem, a situation to be analysed and explained. His biological inheritances, his social environment, his social training, his life experience, his developed traits and characteristics, measured as closely as may be and with increasing precision;—these are the factors from which the great man may be understood; and with them the less great and the near great. This is as true of the great man or the leader in the political world as in any other field of the larger social world.

In the last generation increasing attention was given to the examination of the social origins and environment of leaders, following Carlyle's period of hero worship and great man adoration. In the present generation increasing attention is being given not only to the social *entourage* out of which the leader comes, but also to the analysis of the individual qualities of the leader, and finally to the interrelation of these qualities to the environment. We want to know what sort of an environment makes a Lincoln or a Roosevelt, and also what the special qualities of these types are, as they may have come out of inheritance or been shaped by environment and experience, and to know how these special traits or types of behaviour react upon the environment.

Inevitably the study of leaders involves the study of followers as well, and, indeed, the whole question of the political interests of man. How these interests originate, develop and decline; what determines their strength and direction; within what limits they may be adapted and adjusted;—these are all questions which must be answered before we can solve the riddle of leadership. For the attractiveness of the leader and the attraction of the follower are the same phenomena, viewed from different sides. They are types of reciprocal forces, producing political tropisms, which are the worthy subjects of scientific inquiry, however difficult the precise approach may be. Why men obey or do not; why they incline toward conformity or dissent; why they tend to lead or follow in certain circumstances;—these are fundamental questions of politics, and they are likely to be given the most thorough examination within the next few years. They are problems lying at the basis of any system of government, whether aristocratic, democratic, or communistic, and only upon a thorough understanding of the political side of human nature can a science of politics or a prudent art of government and statesmanship be built.

It is true that party leadership is not a thing apart, and that it has many intimate relationships with other types of leadership in other fields of social life. Perhaps there is much of kin in the general, the cardinal, the magnate, and the political leader or boss. The development of psychology is likely to throw much light upon this subject in the next few years, and, of course, the literature of political leadership will be correspondingly enriched. But the special study of the political types of leadership will always remain an object of inquiry by the political scientists.

The problem of leadership has not been wholly neglected, although very imperfectly considered thus far.[1] Notably Robert Michels[2] in an inquiry based chiefly upon social democratic leaders in Italy and the Germanic states, made a brilliant study of the "metamorphosis" of party leaders, and of some of the typical characteristics of political leadership. As significant traits of leaders he enumerated the following: 1. Force of Will; 2. Wider extent of knowl-

[1] See my *American Party System*, pp. 32–49, for a summary of the literature on this subject; see also Park and Burgess, *Introduction to Sociology*, pp. 854–55.

[2] *Political Parties.*

edge than ordinary; 3. Catonian strength of conviction; 4. Self-sufficiency; 5. Reputation for goodness of heart and disinterestedness; 6. Some form of celebrity. In my volume on the *American Party System* (1922) I traced in passing some of the qualities of leaders and outlined some of the high points in the subject. But that analysis was not designed to be an exhaustive examination of the topic, but suggestive of the possibilities of more minute research in this field. In addition to the possession of certain other qualities I suggested the following as a working list of the attributes of the political leader.

1. Unusual sensitiveness to the strength and direction of social and industrial tendencies with reference to their party and political bearings.

2. Acute and quick perception of possible courses of community conduct with prompt action accordingly.

3. Facility in group combination and compromise—political diplomacy in ideas, policies and spoils.

4. Facility in personal contacts with widely varying types of men.

5. Facility in dramatic expression of the sentiment or interest of large groups of voters, usually with voice or pen—fusing a logical formula, an economic interest and a social habit or predisposition in a personality.

6. Courage not unlike that of the military commander whose best laid plans require a dash of luck for their successful completion.

This was intended, however, only as a temporary scaffolding, and has been so used by others and by me. It will be necessary to accumulate many individual studies before much substantial progress can be made. A series of careful studies would make possible much more minute analysis than has hitherto been possible and would pave the way for more careful comparison. Such studies will make possible the construction of categories that may be more definitely applied than is now the case. What these tests or traits of types of behavior may be we do not know, but we shall be in the way of finding out, if we project a long series of these inquiries and watch carefully for similarities and dissimilarities.

We need to know the hereditary influences affecting the individual. We need to have the most thorough knowledge of the social environment in which the phenomena of leadership develop. We need to have the most careful data regarding the physical organization of the leader, an organic survey which we are likely to have available in the near future, and which may contain the explanation of many types of leadership. We need to have a thorough survey of the intellectual qualities of the leader. We need to have an analysis of the social qualities of the leader. We need to have traced the patterns of his traits and dispositions in which may be found some of the springs of his power. It is clear that leadership lies not only in intelligence, but in sympathy, in determination, in social *savoir faire*, in a set of traits which we are just beginning to appraise and very roughly to measure. The interesting attempts of Moore to measure aggressiveness, of Downey to measure will or persistence, of the army authorities to evaluate the character qualities necessary to military leadership; all these and others are interesting illustrations of the types of inquiry that are likely to give us within the next generation the necessary mental and temperamental measurements of individuals on the basis of which we understand the situation we term leadership. When these patterns are completed, it may easily be found that leadership is a relative term, and that the same individual will be found a leader in this field and a follower in that.

It will also be found useful to examine the achievement record of the leaders in various walks of life, and to find

the relations between these achievement records and political leadership, for here again in the experience of the
individual, and the circumstances under which he has developed political interests and prestige may be found part of
the secret. Another significant field is the decline and
disintegration of leadership, and the circumstances under
which this occurs, using again the same categories and
standards of equipment, achievement, situation or qualification.

Likewise, the study of various kinds of groups will develop much material of value for the understanding of
leadership. In the midst of the group arise those who appeal
with greatest magnetic attraction to its members, and in
proportion to our intimate knowledge of the processes of
collective behaviour will come insight into the nature and
limits of the leader's pre-eminence. Leadership is a function of collective action, and cannot be fully understood
outside of its special setting. Possibly some persons of unusual force or versatility would be leaders anytime or any-
where, but most are peculiar to their particular social situation, and all are conditioned by the surrounding social and
political forces which they express and interpret. In this
connection we may look for interesting analyses of groups
among the forthcoming studies of the sociologists. Moreover, social psychology, thus far little developed and maintaining a precarious existence, is likely in the not distant
future to come to the aid of the student of government by
making clearer the nature of the interaction that goes on in
the complex social process. There can be no doubt that
political attractions and aversions are intimately related to
the elaborate cycles that appear and disappear in the shifts
of social behaviour, and which can be fully understood only
when the group process and social psychology are more
thoroughly studied and more fully comprehended.

I have no doubt that the development here suggested may be deemed by some fanciful and impossible of realization, at any rate in the near future. A reviewer of my *American Party System* raised his eye-brows at my use of the phrase "psycho-biological" qualities of party leaders, especially, said he, "coming from one who has sat in the City Council of Chicago." Curiously enough, however, my analysis of party leaders on a scientific basis began precisely under these circumstances, by watching the behaviour and traits of city hall leaders, and by observing the insufficiency of the analyses ordinarily made by those who abhor the scientific terminology. It is common practice to classify party leaders as "good" or "bad," and let the analysis stand there. I am quite capable of making such classifications and have frequently done so, although often with many misgivings as to just what was "good" or "bad." In many instances the "worst" type of party leaders are breaking one commandment, but are keeping others broken by their critics; and on the whole it may be difficult to decide in some cases whether the critic or the culprit is the more anti-social in his conduct, judged by the broader standards of social progress. Genuine progress will be made by more intensive study of the situations under which so-called "good" and "bad" leaders develop and operate, and by the most minute analysis of the qualities of the leaders and the followers, including the psycho-biological qualities that sound so strangely in the ear of the unsophisticated.[3] There is to be sure no magic in terminology, but there is distinct scientific value in the development or more precise analysis and the beginnings of accurate measurement.

Dr. Gosnell's study is *sui generis* among the examinations of political leaders, a novel attempt at closer analysis. Past

[3] See my article in the *National Municipal Review* on "The Next Step in the Organization of Municipal Research," September, 1922.

studies of policital leaders have usually been built upon treacherous ground. They are likely to be the work either of the enthusiastic adherent or of the bitter foe, and both are likely to distort the facts and twist the conclusion. In any event the student of one particular person cannot make a scientific appraisal of him without reference to a considerable number of like persons, and for this work the material has been lacking, or more accurately the detailed analysis of comparative qualities has been wanting. Accordingly the intensive study of the comparative qualities or traits of leaders has not been developed to anything like its full possibilities.

The autobiographies of political leaders are always interesting and generally useful if taken with care. But the political leaders who can successfully analyse his own traits is unusual. Like other successful men, it is quite probable that he will be unable to appreciate the very causes that have contributed most to his advancement, but will find the sources of his strength in some trivial circumstance little connected with the real springs of power. The leader's rationalizations of his power are not safe guides.

Two notable examples of this are the autobiographies of Platt and Roosevelt. Senator Platt's story of his own political life is obviously a crude explanation of what happened—a wholly inadequate study of the character and tactics of a powerful political manager. President Roosevelt's study is the best of the kind ever written, by reason of the dramatic life of the author and his scholarly and literary qualities. However, there are many very notable omissions in the record, as the mayoralty campaign of 1886 and the presidential campaign of 1912, both of which are passed over with only a few words, although they were both significant events in his career. As a study in motives and interests, it is likewise very incomplete. In short we

xxii INTRODUCTION

can scarcely expect from the leader a volume of confessions; we are more likely to find the material for epitaphs—
gilded. This is not intended to disparage the use of autobiographies. Quite the contrary, they are immensely
valuable sources of information, and could be used much
more effectively than they have been, with the necessary
care in interpretation, and avoidance of the spell of hero
worship. Dr. Gosnell has used all of such material that is
available (and much more has been published regarding
New York State than in most of our commonwealths) and
has gleaned from it many suggestions of great value. But
he has gone farther in the direction of analysis than any
one has before.

In the present study, Dr. Gosnell has blazed a new trail.
He has examined the social, economic, and political background of Mr. Platt; he has studied as carefully as material
permitted his personal equipment; he has traced his training
and his achievements; he has examined the weapons at his
command, and the strategy and the tactics of his political
warfare; he has shown how the power that was so built up
began to decline and disintegrate; and he has made an
estimate and appraisal of this particular leader from the
point of view of individual technique and social significance.

This is pioneer work of the very greatest value and
significance to every student of party phenomena. It is the
kind of solid investigation that must underlie the advance
of genuinely scientific politics, and as such it is worthy of
the most careful study by the observer of American political
life as well as by the special student of technical political
science.

The list of leaders yet to be studied might well include
the greater national figures of the type of Tilden, Blaine,
Garfield, Reed, Cleveland, Pettigrew, LaFollette, Debs; the
types of political bosses, rural and urban, such as Croker,

Tweed, Ruef, Cox, Quay, Brayton, Penrose, and many others of the same type; and in addition to this scores of key men in the local situations who manifest exactly the same qualities of leadership except upon a smaller and perhaps more familiar scale. An adequate inquiry would of course include all the varied types of leaders developed in different situations and under different backgrounds, the effect of the urban, the rural, the racial, the religious, the economic, environment in shaping the type of leader and determining his tactics. There is indeed no more fascinating field in the study of American political life, or in the development of modern democracy in fact; and in none is there greater need for an objective attitude and for scientific methods of inquiry, yet to be shaped and developed.

It goes without saying that inquiries in the field of leadership cannot well be isolated expeditions apart from other advances in political science. Leadership is in the last analysis a cross section of human nature on its political side, and it cannot be studied with entire success except as a part of the whole political process. Only a new era of scientific inquiry in which more sweeping studies of the political nature and behaviour of men based upon more fundamentally scientific methods are employed can make completely successful investigations of leadership possible. There are many indications that a revival of genuinely scientific interest in politics is likely to develop in the near future, and that we are drawing near to a new epoch in the study of the political nature of man.[4]

Government is weak today because it has lost the power that once rose because force or unreflecting custom was its

[4] See my article on "The Present State of the Study of Politics" in the *American Political Science Review,* May, 1921, also "Progress Report of the American Political Science Assn's Committee on Political Research." Ibid., May, 1923.

base, or because of the assumed divinity that hedged about the throne, or from the easy generalizations of the natural law philosophy that ruled the minds of men in the Revolutionary period. The future security of government lies in the introduction of a measure of science that will give government the recognition accorded to other obviously useful agencies, and further in scientific inquiry into the fundamental bases of government as they are found in the constitution of human nature. Neither custom, nor religion, nor logic, nor force will supply the future basis of obedience and command, of leadership and following. The roots of political organization will be found in general appreciation of the scientific basis and uses of the governing process.

CHARLES E. MERRIAM.

CHAPTER I

SOCIAL AND ECONOMIC BACKGROUND

Thomas Collier Platt and Theodore Roosevelt had political relations with each other from the middle of the eighties until well on toward the end of the first decade in the twentieth century. These relations can hardly be understood apart from the social and economic changes which were taking place in the state of New York during that period. Both Platt and Roosevelt took great pride in having something to do with the politics of the "Empire State," the state which surpassed all the other states in population, wealth, commerce, finance, industry, and the arts.[1]

The most outstanding social change in the state during the period under discussion was the great increase in population. In 1890 there were some six million people in the state; ten years later there were seven and a quarter million; and in another decade there were over nine million. Thus, in twenty years the state added to its population a number of people equal to the entire population of Switzerland in 1900 or that of the entire United States in 1790. Startling as these figures are, even more striking was the shift of population from the rural to the urban communities. In 1890 sixty-five per cent of the population lived in cities and towns of 2,500 inhabitants or more and two decades later nearly seventy-nine per cent of the population was

[1] There is no satisfactory social history of the state for this period. The chief sources here used are: New York State Department of Labor, *Growth of Industry in New York*, 1904; *Statistical Abstract of the United States*, 1912; and the Eleventh, Twelfth and Thirteenth Censuses of the United States.

1

classed as urban. The greatest contributing factor to the growing preponderance of the urban population was the rapid expansion of New York City. The population of the metropolis nearly doubled during the two decades and in 1910 it comprised over half of the population of the entire state. Aside from New York City, the state would have taken medium rank with the other states in population, but nevertheless the forty-eight cities north of the Bronx increased in the aggregate about one and a half times during this period. This meant that the population of the state outside of New York City was losing its predominant rural character with the passing of the century. In fact, in twenty-two of the sixty-one counties of the state there was an actual decline in population resulting from the shift of population from the country to the cities. It was a vague dread of this change which led a rural delegate to the New York State Constitutional Convention of 1894 to say:

But numbers are not the only things to be considered in making a just and right apportionment. Territory has something to do with it. . . . I cannot look with complacency upon the fact that a little territory in the southern part of the state is likely to have in the near future a preponderance in the legislation of this state.[2]

The deep rooted antagonism between the urban and the rural sections of the state was more clearly expressed by another delegate to the same convention who said: "The average citizen in the rural district is superior in intelligence, superior in morality, superior in self-government to the average citizen in the cities."[3] It is little wonder that the inhabitants of the up-state regions, with their Protestant faith, their native parentage and their local traditions running back a hundred years or more, looked with condescen-

[2] *Record* (unrevised), IV, 1882.
[3] *Ibid.*, p. 1984.

sion upon the polyglot population of the great city. By reason of its natural advantages and the peculiar character of its site, New York City had long been the chief gateway for the immigrant tide which flowed into the entire nation. In 1890 about two-fifths of the inhabitants of New York County and one quarter of the state's entire population were foreigners. Chief among the immigrant groups at that time were the Germans, the Irish, the English and the Swedes. During the next twenty years a million and a sixth persons of foreign birth were added to the state's population, for the most part of Slavic or Latin origin.[4] These newer immigrant hordes, from Russia, Poland, Bohemia, Bulgaria and other parts of southeastern Europe, settled in the slums of the great city where their old habits tended to break down. Scarcely any of them owned their own homes and many of them could neither read nor write. Since the newer immigrants presented more difficult problems of assimilation than those which arose in connection with the earlier immigration and since the addition their numbers made to the ranks of the Catholic and Jewish worshippers undermined the primacy of Protestantism in the state, the gulf between the inhabitants of the metropolis and the up-state grew constantly wider during the period under discussion.

The abundance of cheap, unskilled labor, in consequence of the large immigrant population, partially explains the rapid industrial development of the state during this period. It was to be expected that an increase in the urban population would make possible greater industrial activity, but who, in 1890, would have prophesied that during the next twenty years the number of wage earners in the manufacturing industries of the state would increase one and a half

[4] *Report of the New York State Commission of Immigration,* 1909, Appendix V.

times, the value of the products manufactured annually in the state would double, and the amount of capital invested in the industries of the state would increase two and a half times? In 1909, the 44,935 manufacturing establishments in the state, representing practically every industry found in the country, gave employment on the average to 1,203,241 persons during the year, and paid out in salaries and wages $743,263,000. The significance of these changes was pointed out by Governor Roosevelt in his annual message to the legislature in 1900:

For almost every gain there is a penalty, and the great strides in the industrial upbuilding of the country, which have on the whole been attended with marked benefit, have also been attended by no little evil. Great fortunes are usually made under very complex conditions both of effort and of surrounding, and the mere fact of the complexity makes it difficult to deal with the new conditions thus created. The contrast offered in a highly specialized industrial community between the very rich and the very poor is exceedingly distressing, and while under normal conditions the acquirement of wealth by the individual is necessarily of great incidental benefit to the community as a whole, yet this is by no means always the case.[5]

A characteristic feature of this industrial expansion was the growth of the corporate form of business organization, a device which greatly facilitated large-scale production and the concentration of control in the hands of a few men. While the larger trusts were engaged in exploiting the resources of the nation, their interests within the boundaries of the state itself were not insignificant. One after the other, the railroad kings, the oil magnates, the steel monarchs and the other leaders of industry, went through the experience which the great steel magnate, Andrew Carnegie, has described:

[5] *Public Papers of Governor Roosevelt*, 1900, p. 20.

Our business continued to expand and required frequent visits on my part to the East, especially to New York, which is as London to Britain—the headquarters of all really important enterprises in America. No large concern could very well get on without being represented there.[6]

The industrial leaders were attracted to New York in part by the facilities which the city and the state furnished for manufacturing. Thus, some of the more important trusts, like the American Sugar Refining Company, the Standard Oil Company, the United States Steel Corporation, and the American Tobacco Company continued and expanded their manufacturing operations in the state during the period of plant consolidation. Another cause for the attractiveness of New York was its importance as a commercial center. In 1901, the foreign commerce of New York, imports and exports combined, equalled that of the rest of the country.[7] The rapid growth of giant industrial and commercial combinations within the state during these years inevitably presented a series of highly complex political problems. New adjustments in the taxation system of the state were needed, and there was a demand for the elimination of unfair methods of competition. In the solution of these and other problems the directors of the great corporations demanded and secured a prominent part.

The transportation system of the state developed during the period to keep pace with the progress in manufacturing and commerce. Although the increase in railroad mileage in the state was not as great as that of some other states, the total number of passengers carried annually upon the steam roads more than doubled during the years from 1890

[6] Andrew Carnegie, *Autobiography of Andrew Carnegie* (Boston, 1920), p. 149.
[7] New York State Department of Labor, *op. cit.*, p. 10.

to 1906 and the total number of tons of freight carried each
year increased one and a half times during the same years.[8]
As a result of a policy of consolidation, nearly one-third of
the 8,416 miles of railroad in the state in 1910 was owned by
the New York Central and Hudson River Railroad (the
Vanderbilt system). Along the line of this railroad were
to be found the most populous cities of the state and during
the period under consideration the company spent vast sums
of money improving its terminal in New York City, one of
its most valuable assets. In this and other ways the railroad
increased the lead it had gained over the Erie Canal, a rival
system of transportation, and strengthened its grip upon the
industrial and agricultural interests of the state. The other
railroads of importance in the state were the Erie, the Pennsylvania, the Lehigh, and the Lackawanna, all of which ran
through the southern counties of the state and were engaged
for the most part in the transportation of coal and steel
from Pennsylvania. The men who controlled these railroads, although they were constantly seeking government
favors, were loath to come under government control. On
the other hand, increasing demands were made on the part
of the shippers, the farmers and the merchants for adequate
railroad regulation. To adjust these conflicting views was
one of the tasks of the politician and the statesman.

While there were no railroad scandals in the nineties like
those which had occurred during the "Erie War" of the
seventies, there were traction scandals which aroused the
public and paved the way for more thorough regulation of
municipal utilities. The growing population of the urban
centers created a need for better facilities for transportation,
lighting and communication. Thus, in 1890 there were only
1140 miles of municipal railway in the entire state; twenty

[8] New York Railroad Commissioners, *Report*, 1890, II, 64, and
Report, 1906, II, 60.

years later this mileage had nearly quadrupled. During the year, 1910, the traction lines of New York City alone carried over a billion and a half passengers, double the number carried in the city during 1898.[9] The growth of gas companies, electric lighting and power companies, the ramifications of the American Telephone Company, were all equally phenomenal. Since the private corporations which operated these utilities were dependent for their very existence upon franchise privileges granted by the government, they were banded together into state associations for the protection and furtherance of their interests in dealing with the government. The conflict between the private and public interest in the operation and management of these utilities furnishes the background of many of the political struggles described below.

This rapid expansion of the industrial and transportation facilities in the state demanded unprecedented amounts of capital and credit, and the concentration of these necessities occurred in New York City. The money lenders, the promoters, the underwriters, and the investment bankers became the most "articulate" element in the economic life of the state. This group, perhaps more clearly than any other group, knew what it wanted and it was able to command the best professional brains of the country in carrying out its schemes. The remarkable career of J. P. Morgan illustrates the strategic position which an influential member of this group came to occupy. A recounting of a few of Morgan's financial connections will show the tendency of the times. In the eighties he became a director and the sole fiscal agent of the New York Central Railroad; in 1895 he became one of the three voting trustees of the Erie Railroad; in 1901 he helped organize the United States Steel Corporation;

[9] New York State Public Service Commission, First District, *Report*, 1910, I, 22; Second District, 1910, I, 67.

and so on, his affiliations with producing, trading, utility, insurance, trust and banking companies might be multiplied at great length. Another powerful financial group was the Rockefeller or Standard Oil group which extended its operations into the railroad, the utility, and the banking fields. Among the lesser lights of Wall Street were the Havemeyers of the Sugar Trust and the group headed by William C. Whitney and Thomas F. Ryan which controlled the Tobacco Trust and many municipal utilities. A congressional committee investigating the "money trust" in 1912–13 came to the conclusion that "there is an established and well-defined identity and community of interest between a few leaders of finance, created and held together through stock ownership, interlocking directorates, partnership and joint stock transactions, and other forms of domination over banks, trust companies, railroads, and public-service and industrial corporations, which has resulted in great and rapidly growing concentration of the control of money and credit in the hands of these few men." [10]   While these few men were not always united among themselves, most of them came to think with Morgan that the immediate future of the country was safer in the hands of the business men than in those of its politicans and chosen representatives.[11]

The growing dependence of labor upon capital for the tools and machinery of production and the growing centralization of control among producers and merchants in part led the workingmen of the state to organize for protection. It was perhaps this developing group consciousness among certain classes of workers found in the great cities which caused the rural voters and representatives to view

[10] U. S. Congress, House, *Committee to Investigate the Concentration of Control of Money and Credit,* 1913 (Pujo Committee).

[11] W. S. Rainsford, *Story of a Varied Life, An Autobiography* (New York, 1922), p. 290.

with alarm their own declining numbers. In 1894, the low water mark for organized labor in many sections during the nineties, the membership of all trade unions in the state totalled some one hundred and fifty thousand.[12] This was about ten per cent of these gainfully employed in transportation and industry. One third of these trade unionists were in the building trades, one fourth in the clothing and textile industries, while less numerous but still powerful unions were found among the railway employees, in the machine shops, in the printing trades, and among the cigarmakers. Nearly three fourths of all these organized workers were found in New York City. Seventeen years later the membership of labor organizations in the state had more than trebled. Most of this increase occurred in the clothing trades which were changing over from the deplorable sweatshop basis of the early nineties to a factory basis. Although in comparison with the total number of wage earners, the number of trade unionists was still comparatively small, politically, the labor organizations became more and more important factors. Following the example of Samuel Gompers in national affairs, the Workingmen's State Federation confined itself to exerting pressure upon the existing party organizations. A careful student of labor organization in New York came to the conclusion that "in securing the enactment of the labor laws of the state, labor organizations have taken a very active interest and that as compared with other organizations, they have exercised the greatest and in most cases the determining influence."[13]

In contrast with the tendency among industrial workers to combine, the farmers of the state seemed disinclined to

---

[12] New York State Department of Labor, *Annual Report of the Bureau of Labor Statistics,* 1910, p. xlix.

[13] G. G. Groat, *Trade Unions and the Law in New York* (New York, 1905), p. 39.

abandon their old individualistic and patriarchal system. To be sure there were county agricultural societies, but these societies did not work out any schemes for group co-operation nor make the farmer any less of an individual producer, each competing against his neighbor. In disposing of his products, the farmer came more and more to occupy a disadvantageous position. He had to meet not only the sharp competition of the western farmers but also the united front of the so-called "Beef Trust," [14] the Consolidated Milk Exchange,[15] the New York Poultry Dealers' Protective Association.[16] and other combinations of merchants and users of farm products. In spite of these conditions, the total value of the farm products produced annually in the state did increase about fifty per cent from 1890 to 1900 and about twenty-five per cent during the next decade. While this increase was not as great as the corresponding increase made in industry, it was sufficient to keep the farmers in a fairly complacent mood. Although only thirteen per cent of those engaged in gainful occupations in the state in 1900 were engaged in agricultural pursuits, the farmers still made up an important group as far as political affairs were concerned. Living in similar environments, their views on such matters as the tariff, taxation and the control of transportation tended to be alike. Long accustomed to political power, they successfully asserted their claim to territorial representation.

There were many other social groups of political importance with which Platt and Roosevelt had to reckon. The chambers of commerce, the real estate dealers' associations, the merchants' associations, the educational societies, the

[14] U. S. Commissioner of Corporations, *The Beef Industry*, 1905.
[15] N. Y. Legislature, *Sen. Doc.*, No. 45, 1910 (Report of the Attorney General in the Matter of the Milk Investigation).
[16] *People* v. *Dwyer*, 145 N. Y. Supp. 748.

philanthropic clubs, the sporting clubs, and an infinite number of other more or less coherent groupings all had some stake in the activity or inactivity of the government. While the combinations of capital and labor were probably the most active in bringing pressure to bear upon the government, these other associations were not inactive when their particular interests were involved. The task of the politician and statesman was confined largely to the adjustment of the demands, often conflicting, which these various groups made upon the party organization which controlled the government. In a political community of seven millions of inhabitants, of great wealth, of widely varied industries and with a population singularly diversified, not merely in occupation but in race origin, in religious beliefs, in habits of life and ways of thought, this task was not an easy one.

CHAPTER II

NEW YORK SCHOOL OF POLITICS

In the late eighties when Thomas C. Platt attained a position of leadership in the Republican party of the state of New York, he was in his fifties, while Roosevelt was just past thirty. Platt's leadership rested not only upon the geographical, racial, economic, and social conditions outlined in the previous chapter but also upon the fact that he had had a long period of rigorous political training. The methods which the older man used to maintain his control over the Republican party organization were not new. From the time of Burr and Van Buren, party organizations in the state had been compact centrally dominated bodies.[1] Platt was primarily a keeper and guardian of a set of political traditions, to which by a natural process of selection he had fallen heir. Practically every device that he used in 1888 when his political star was on the ascendency, he had seen tested and exploited at some time during the previous thirty-two years of his political schooling. At this time Roosevelt, as one of the most vigorous representatives of the new generation, had already shown himself to be somewhat of an iconoclast.

In his *Autobiography,* Platt wrote that he "drifted into politics—just drifted." [2] He came to his majority at a time

[1] H. L. McBain, *DeWitt Clinton and the Origin of the Spoils System in New York* (New York, 1907), *passim.*
[2] T. C. Platt, *The Autobiography of Thomas Collier Platt* (compiled and edited by Louis J. Lang, New York, 1910), p. xxi. Mr. Livingston Platt, Platt's grandson, informed the writer on Septem-

when it was extremely easy for a young man of his training and temperament to drift into politics. Thomas Collier Platt was born in the village of Owego, Tioga County, on July 15, 1833. This meant that the election of 1856 was the first national election at which he voted. This election came two years before Theodore Roosevelt was born. John C. Fremont, the first Republican candidate for president, aroused peculiar enthusiasm in the country towns of central New York like Owego. As early as 1854 "Republican" mass meetings had been held in all the old Whig counties of the state.[3] During the next two years the Republican cause was aided by the climax of the Kansas struggle and by the appeals of the clergy and the religious press. Platt's father, William Platt, a lawyer of local importance whose forebears "fitted into the Revolution," was a rigid Presbyterian and especially susceptible to these influences. It was William Platt's ambition to make his son Thomas a clergyman and to this end Thomas was sent through the local academy and later to Yale. Although the dutiful son said in his later years, "I had such a surfeit of church going in my youth that if it could be averaged up and spread out, it would do for all my life,"[4] and although he was compelled to leave Yale at the end of his freshman year in 1850 on account of ill health, he did take his schooling seriously, for he was awarded a copy of Scott's works inscribed by President Woolsey for winning third prize for translation from Latin into Eng-

ber 27, 1922, that the *Autobiography* was not entirely satisfactory to the family. The writer has found many inaccuracies in the book, but the book is valuable for the light it throws upon Platt's motives and point of view.

[3] G. S. P. Kleeberg, *The Formation of the Republican Party as a National Political Organization* (New York, 1911), p. 18.

[4] *New York Sun*, March 7, 1910. This obituary was written by Edward G. Riggs, a political correspondent who had friendly relations with Platt.

lish.[5]   At Yale, the slavery question in all its phases was the subject of discussion on the campus, in the literary societies, and in frequent lectures in the halls.[6]   In 1856 it was therefore the most natural thing for Platt to take an active part in the national campaign as an organizer of the new party in his county.   He was not an orator but he had "developed some ability as a writer" at Yale and he "could sing some," so he composed campaign ditties and appeared upon the stump as the chief of the Owego Campaign Glee Club.[7] The excitement of those days made a deep impression upon his mind and furnished the root of that unquestioning loyalty to the Republican party which he displayed in later life. In 1856 Fremont carried the state and two years later a Republican governor was elected.   In both of these elections Platt could point with pride to fact that two-thirds of the voters in Tioga County had endorsed the Republican ticket.[8]

Thomas C. Platt started his business career as a clerk in a drug store, and this occupation as well as his later vocations became closely linked with his political education.   Regarding this period of his life, he wrote: "While at the drug counter I studied assiduously the speeches and acts of Thurlow Weed, William H. Seward and Horace Greeley, about whom the New York State Whigs and the ·'Conscientious Democrats' rallied, and longed to be in their confidence." [9] In studying the methods of Thurlow Weed, a young politician had special advantages in that Weed's paper, the *Albany Evening Journal,* was the leading Whig and later

[5] Platt, *op. cit.,* p. 3.
[6] C. M. Depew, *My Memories of Eighty Years* (New York, 1922). p. 15.   Depew was three classes behind Platt at Yale.
[7] Platt, *op. cit.,* p. 8.   On page 25 some of his verses are reproduced.   See also C. M. Depew, *Speeches, Orations and Addresses* (New York, 1910), II, 194.
[8] *New York Tribune Almanac for 1858,* p. 45.
[9] Platt, *op. cit.,* pp. 7–8.

the most influential Republican organ of the up-state. By 1860 Weed was rounding off thirty years of political leadership, during which he had been a maker of senators, governors, and state officers, a dictator of all but three state conventions, a distributor of state and federal patronage, and a director of legislation. Weed's personal magnetism was so great that Samuel Bowles regarded him in 1860 as "one of the most remarkable men of our time—one whom I had rather have had such an interview with than with any president of our day and generation." [10] County leaders who went to Albany during those days looked with longing eyes at the members of the legislature gathered around the editor of the *Evening Journal* for counsel and advice, and careful readers of the *Evening Journal* made mental notes of such things as the confession, appearing in the issue of August 27, 1860, that funds for the presidential campaign had been made available because Weed had been instrumental in securing the passage of certain city railroad bills.[11] Knowing observers in New York City during the Civil War glanced with awe and admiration at Room No. 11, Astor House, where Weed presided over the conferences which made and unmade measures and men.

Platt was fitted by his natural endowments to play a rôle similar to that of Thurlow Weed. In Owego, as in many other small towns of New York, saloons were frowned upon in the fifties and the drug store or the general store was the center where the "elder statesmen" congregated to discuss politics and the questions of the day. By 1856 Platt and a friend of his named Hull had established a drug store of

[10] G. S. Merriam, *Life and Times of Samuel Bowles* (New York, 1885), I, 302.
[11] Cited by S. D. Brummer, *Political History of New York State During the Civil War* (New York, 1911), p. 23. See also T. Weed, *Autobiography* and *A Memoir of Thurlow Weed* by T. W. Barnes (Boston, 1883), pp. 105, 584.

their own. From then on until 1872 most of the political work of the county was done in a little office in the rear of this drug store.[12] The success of this institution, which was made possible because of the universal acquaintance, fellowship, and confidences of village and country life, was evidenced by the fact that Platt was chosen as county clerk in 1858. It was from this office that he managed the torch light parades which took part in the Lincoln campaign of 1860. When the war broke out, he was not able to enter the Union forces as an active fighter because of a stomach trouble which clung to him the remainder of his life, but as an auxiliary member of the war committee of the state, he was active in raising funds for the maintenance of the troops, his drug store being the headquarters for this work.[13] He followed the course of the war closely and in the latter part of the sixties he was made chairman of the Tioga County Republican Committee. In a small way he was playing the part of a Thurlow Weed.

Because of his position as the recognized political leader of Tioga County, Platt took great interest in the course of reconstruction after the Civil War. When he perceived the overthrow of Seward, Weed and Raymond as the supporters of the conservative policy of President Johnson by the alliance between Reuben E. Fenton, the Radical Republican governor, and Horace Greeley, the editor of the *New York Tribune,* he hastened to get upon the winning side along with the other discerning county leaders.[14] Fenton, like Weed, was primarily a political strategist. He was gracious in his manner, keen in his analysis of party sentiment,

[12] *New York Sun,* March 7, 1910. See also Depew, *My Memories,* p. 13.
[13] Platt, *op. cit.,* p. 340, citing the letter of I. S. Catlin. See also the *New York Sun,* March 7, 1910.
[14] Platt, *op. cit.,* p. 52.

and wise in his distribution of the patronage. His administration of the canal system of the state furnished many lessons for aspiring young political managers. While some of the up-state Fenton men were alleged to be members of the "canal ring" and while some of the New York City followers of Fenton were called "Tammany Republicans" because of their relations with the notorious Tweed, there was little demand for reform within the ranks of the Republican party. The chief danger that Governor Fenton faced was the rise of a rival leader within the party.[15] The election of Roscoe Conkling as United States senator in 1867 was the biggest cloud on Fenton's political horizon.

"It was in 1870," wrote Platt in his *Autobiography*, "that I really began to know Roscoe Conkling." "Conkling was then," he added, "one of the handsomest men I ever met. . . . His noble figure, flashing eye and majestic voice made one forget that he was somewhat foppish in his dress."[16] By this time Platt had become important enough politically in the Southern Tier of counties to command the attention of the new leader. In business and politics Platt had prospered. He was president of the Tioga County National Bank, a director of the Southern Central Railroad of New York, and a holder of large lumber interests in Michigan. He was known at Albany and was already a dictator of local nominations in his own district. At the Republican State Convention held in September, 1870, Conkling and Platt came together. Two months earlier Senator Conkling had waged a battle with his junior colleague, Senator Fenton, over the appointment of a collector for the port of New York. Senator Conkling successfully backed up the choice of President Grant and thereby won the president's favor

[15] H. A. Stebbins, *A Political History of the State of New York 1865-1869* (New York, 1913), pp. 150, 411.
[16] Platt, *op. cit.*, p. 55.

and confidence, which had been previously shared by Fenton.[17] The Senior Senator, then, at the request of the President, used his newly gained control over the federal patronage to influence the election of the temporary chairman of the state convention. Delegates were won over by offers of patronage or threats of removal.[18] "Conkling whipped Fenton to a finish," said the admiring Platt. Platt had joined the forces of the victorious senator at the crucial moment, so he could say, "I helped him to do it." [19] This convention secured to Conkling the control of the state committee and one of his lieutenants, Alonzo B. Cornell, also Platt's friend, was made chairman. At the next state convention, Cornell, "risking grave bodily injury," refused to put a motion which was favorable to the Fenton faction, and again Conkling dictated the work of the convention. As a delegate and a member of the inner ring which ran these two state conventions, Platt was learning the formal and informal rules which governed the operation of the state nominating machinery.

Platt was especially interested in the presidential campaign of 1872, because he himself was running for Congress that year. He had refused to accept a nomination for Congress in 1870 because he had pledged his support to Mylo W. Goodrich. When Goodrich turned Liberal Republican and accepted the Democratic endorsement on a ticket which was headed by Horace Greeley, Platt felt absolved from all obligations. Conkling was always hostile toward "independents," and in 1872 his contempt for Greeley knew no bounds because the federal patronage and his leadership depended upon the re-election of General Grant.

[17] *Nation* (New York), July 14, 1870.
[18] A. R. Conkling, *Life and Letters of Roscoe Conkling* (New York, 1889), p. 328; *New York World*, September 8, 1870; Depew, *My Memories*, pp. 77–79.
[19] Platt, *op. cit.*, p. 56.

During the campaign the *New York Sun* hinted a gross
and wholesale briberies of congressmen in connection with
the building of the Union Pacific Railroad. After the election, these charges were investigated by the outgoing Congress. It was into this atmosphere that Platt entered as a
member of the House of Representatives. "Statesmanship
in Congress," wrote Thurlow Weed toward the close of
1873, "is now so low that it will take many years to build it
up to a higher tone." [20]   In 1874 the disclosures of the
Whiskey Ring, involving United States internal revenue
officers and even the president's private secretary, necessi-
tated careful treatment by the congressional investigating
committees. Shortly afterward a cabinet officer was im-
peached because of his connections with the notorious Indian
frauds. As a member of Congress, Platt also had an opportunity to hear that remarkable burst of emotional oratory in
which Blaine defended himself against the accusations that
he had used his official position to aid questionable railroad
transactions. Platt's attitude toward these matters is well
illustrated by his eulogy of Blaine, who was then speaker of
the House of Representatives: "What I liked about him
then, as always, was his bold and persistent contention that
the citizen who best loved his party and was loyal to it, was
loyal to and best loved his country." [1]   Regarding Platt's
loyalty to his party in Congress, there can be no doubt. During his first term he was on the Committee on Post Offices
and Post Roads and in his second on the Pacific Railroads
Committee. In 1874 he was made a member of the National
Republican Congressional Campaign Committee, a committee whose methods were so partisan that they later
aroused agitation for reform. Platt performed his political

[20] *Op. cit.*, p. 501.
[1] Platt, *op. cit.*, p. 185.

tasks in Congress so well that Blaine could later write of him :

> Thomas C. Platt came from the Binghamton district of New York. He had been an active man of business and had gained personal popularity. He developed an aptitude for public affairs and soon acquired influence in his state. He was not a trained debator, nor had he when he entered Congress, official experience of any kind. But he was gifted with strong common sense, and had that quick judgment of men which contributes so essentially to success in public life.[2]

In 1876, the year that Roosevelt went to Harvard University, Platt attended his first Republican national convention as a delegate from the "Southern Tier" of New York. The main feature of this convention was the rivalry between Conkling and Blaine. Both men were candidates for the presidential nomination, Conkling being the first choice of the Stalwarts or that faction of the Republican party which had held Grant's favor, while Blaine was the candidate of the Half-Breeds, the group which had become dissatisfied with Grant's administration. Resolutions had been adopted by the New York delegates in a preliminary state convention presenting Conkling as the choice of New York for president, but after the first ballot it was apparent that Conkling had no chance of winning the nomination. Blaine's lead over the other candidates was considerable but he did not have the necessary majority. Conkling, mindful of the day when Blaine referred to his "haughty disdain, his grandiloquent swell, his majestic, supereminent, overpowering, turkey-gobbler strut," [3] combined with Cameron from Pennsylvania and with the other Stalwart leaders to prevent the nomination of Blaine. The sixty-one delegates from New

[2] J. G. Blaine, *Twenty Years of Congress* (Norwich, 1886), p. 542.
[3] *Cong. Globe*, April 20, 1866, Vol. XXXVII, Part 3, p. 2298.

York were brought in line for Hayes, who proved to be the "dark horse" of the convention. In this convention Platt was learning the methods by which the national nominating process could be controlled; in the campaign which followed he was edified by the novel devices employed by Tilden, the Democratic candidate. Blaine's claim to the Republican nomination and Tilden's claim to the presidency made little impression upon the loyal young Stalwart.[4]

At the Republican State Convention held in Rochester in September, 1877, Platt gained wide-spread notice as a faithful follower of Senator Conkling. The Senator had taken his defeat for the presidential nomination "much to heart." The first events of the Hayes administration did not improve his temper. The appointment of William M. Evarts as secretary of state was regarded as a "straight-arm blow at the regular organization" not only because of Mr. Evarts' independence but also because the friends of Conkling had urged that Conkling be offered the appointment.[5] Furthermore, Conkling had suggested Platt for postmaster-general, but the proposition had been "rather contemptuously declined."[6] The crowning offense of the Hayes administration, from the standpoint of the New York Stalwarts, was the investigation of the New York Customs Office, supervised by John Sherman, the secretary of the treasury. This inquiry was digging at the foundations of the Conkling organization in New York, and the executive order that no federal officer should participate in party politics seemed to be directly aimed at Alonzo B. Cornell, who was both the naval officer of the port of New York and chairman of the Republican

[4] In Congress, Platt made a speech in favor of the Electoral Commission Bill: *Cong. Record*, January 25, 1877, Vol. V., Part 3, App., p. 59.
[5] C. R. Williams, *Rutherford B. Hayes* (Boston, 1914), I, 514–15 Governor Hayes' diary for December 17, 1876.
[6] Platt, *op. cit.*, p. 83.

state committee.[7] The views of the New York "regulars" regarding these matters had not been expressed at the time that Platt was selected as temporary chairman of the convention. There was a story that he prepared two speeches for the occasion, one full of vindicative hostility and the other mild and non-committal. Conkling read them both and selected the "Stalwart" speech.[8] Platt referred to the speech which he delivered as a "scorcher." In it, he put the eminent secretary of state in a class with "demagogues" and referred to those who disagreed with him as "political pecksniffs and tricksters." Civil service reform was called a "shibboleth," a "sweet morsel," which a certain journalist (George William Curtis) "rolled under his tongue and daily blurted in the face of a nauseated public."[9] While the *New York Nation* called the speech "silly and abusive" and some partisan organs doubted its propriety,[10] the Stalwart delegates applauded it loudly and Conkling indicated his satisfaction by making Platt the permanent chairman of the convention. The second feature of this convention was the reply which Conkling made to Curtis' attack upon the report of the resolutions committee. In his recollections, Platt wrote that "Conkling was rarely in more superb form."[11] Curtis was one of the advisers of the President who had stood for the principle of civil service reform. In the course of his speech, Conkling turned toward his opponent and exclaimed: "When Dr. Johnson defined patriotism as the last refuge of a scoundrel, he was unconscious of the then under-

7 V. L. Shores, *The Hayes-Conkling Controversy*, 1877–1879, *passim*.

8 *Utica Press*, March 7, 1910.

9 Platt, *op. cit.*, pp. 85–93.

10 D. S. Alexander, *A Political History of the State of New York* (New York, 1909), III, 376.

11 Platt, *op. cit.*, p. 85.

veloped capabilities and uses of the word reform." [12]   The similarity in tone between Platt's speech and Conkling's invective shows how well the former had caught his chief's spirit, and it is needless to say that as presiding officer of the convention, Platt followed the customary rules and carried out the prearranged plan.

About a year and a half after the Rochester Convention, President Hayes succeeded in removing Chester A. Arthur and Alonzo B. Cornell from the New York Custom-house, but this Stalwart defeat made little impression upon Platt.[13] Conkling, in a fit of insolence had forced the nomination of Cornell as the Republican candidate for governor in 1879 and had made Platt national committeeman from New York in Cornell's place.   Political and business success was coming to Platt.   On August 1, 1879 he was elected general manager and secretary of the United States Express Company, an association which had been created in 1854 to do the express business of the Erie Railroad.[14]   Upon assuming his new duties with this company, he moved to New York, although retaining for voting purposes his Owego residence.   This move was characteristic of his usual astute ness, for he knew that he would still be a powerful figure politically and commercially in Owego long before he gained influence in the great metropolis.   The following year he was made president of this express company, a position which he retained until his death in 1910.   From this strategic center, he became one of the chief dispensers of favors to rural editors, politicians and legislators in those counties touched by the Erie Railroad.   As his fortunes rose, his relations with Conkling grew more close and confidential; he was first made chairman of the executive committee of the state committee

[12] Conkling, op. cit., pp. 538–49.
[13] This fact is not mentioned in the Autobiography.
[14] Platt, op. cit., pp. 548 ff.

and later chairman of the committee proper. Both of these positions were high up in the committee hierarchy of the party and required the services of a man who was sensible, close-mouthed, devoted, always useful and never troublesome. Evidently Conkling regarded Platt as such a man.

The chairman of a state committee in a doubtful state like New York was a most important figure during a national campaign. In the Republican National Convention of 1880, the Stalwarts had suffered a signal defeat; their attempt to gain control of the national administration by renominating Grant for a third term had not met the approval of a majority of the delegates. Although Conkling made a stirring speech for Grant and although the Stalwart managers exhibited great skill in lining up the "Old Guard" solidly for Grant, James A. Garfield, a Half-Breed, was nominated. Conkling's disappointment was great, and it seemed in no way to be alleviated by the nomination of Chester A. Arthur, a New York Stalwart, for vice-president. What would the attitude of the New York organization be during the campaign? The state committee remained inactive in the campaign until Garfield "came down" to make terms. Platt claimed that Garfield promised in return for the Stalwart support to consult the Conkling organization and to regard its wishes as "paramount with him touching all questions of patronage." [15] Whatever the agreement, Platt took an active part in the campaign after the Garfield conference. Levi P. Morton, who was close to Wall Street, took charge of the main finances of the campaign, but Platt sent a letter to the federal employees in the state, suggesting that they would doubtless consider it a "privilege and a pleasure" to contribute to the

[15] Platt, op. cit., p. 131. The claim is also made here that Garfield offered Morton a high office in return for his campaign services.

campaign fund.[16]   A special train over the Erie was arranged, from which Garfield addressed enthusiastic thousands; business men's parades were organized and the work-
shops flooded with "arguments."   Garfield carried New
York and was elected president of the United States.   No
one could accuse Platt of not being "regular."   This same
year, young Theodore Roosevelt, a Republican by bringing
up and convictions, cast his first ballot for the Republican
ticket.[17]

In the meantime Platt was not neglecting his own political
fortunes.   One contemporary account asserted that in the
handling of the campaign funds he had put at least thirty
members of the Assembly under implied obligation to him.
This account goes on to describe his patronage dispensing
activities as follows:

He puts men under obligation to him and commands their
friendship and services.   Why, he has secured places for not
less than seventy-five persons in public offices.   He has appointees in the New York Custom House, in the New York
Postoffice, and in the New York City government.   He has
practically 'run' Cornell's administration; and the canal officials, from Superintendent Dutcher down to the boat in-
spector at Syracuse are under obligations to him.   He made
Jones the agent and warden of Auburn prison, and he put
another Tioga County man as clerk in the assistant superintendent of public work's office at Syracuse.   And so it is
all along the canals and in the government offices.   Platt
men are plenty in all the state departments at Albany. [18]

Soon Platt heard himself "talked about for the United
States Senate."   At least we have his word that "friends insisted" he should declare himself a candidate.[19]   Richard

[16] C. R. Lingley, *Since the Civil War* (New York, 1920), p. 157.
[17] *Theodore Roosevelt: An Autobiography* (New York, 1919,
p. 55.
[18] *Syracuse Journal*, January 13, 1881.
[19] Platt, *op. cit.*, p. 139.

Crowley was the candidate of Vice-President Arthur, Speaker Sharpe and the other confirmed Conkling men for this position. Rumors were whispered that Platt was "setting up house for himself." Chauncey M. Depew, the Half-Breed candidate, came to Platt and said, "You can have my strength if as senator you will support the President." The story goes that Platt replied, "I have done my best to elect a Republican president and as senator I will support him." [20] When this was told to Depew's backers, one of them asked, "Even if Judge Robertson's name should be sent in?" To this inquiry Platt was said to have given an affirmative answer.[1] At any rate, Depew withdrew and Platt became the choice of the Republican caucus for United States senator.

Platt's first election to the United States Senate had a stormy and calamitous finish. President Garfield, without consulting Conkling or Platt,[2] sent the name of William H. Robertson for that seat of patronage and power, the collectorship of the port of New York. Judge Robertson was the Half-Breed who had let the revolt in the New York delegation against Grant the year before and he was "thoroughly detested by Conkling." Conkling at once appealed to the long established custom known as "senatorial courtesy." Platt was in a difficult position; whichever way he turned he would subject himself to criticism and ridicule. He had hoped to avoid such a dilemma by invoking the pre-election pact which guaranteed a consultation on all New York appointments. The president's action made it necessary for him to face either Conkling's fury or the Half-Breeds' scorn.

[20] Depew, Orations, II, 213.
[1] Alexander, op. cit., III, 468.
[2] R. Cortissoz, The Life of Whitelaw Reid (New York, 1921), II, 62.

THE SENATORIAL SUICIDE

(Cartoon by Thomas Nast, *Harper's Weekly,* July 2, 1881, Harper and Brothers)

According to Depew,[3] he braved the former by stating that if Robertson's name came up he would vote for it. However, while Conkling was using every means he had to make a deal with the Democratic senators to refuse consent, Platt patiently sought to avoid the issue by arranging matters between Conkling and the President. After a two months' struggle, Garfield sent a message to the Senate withdrawing all the nominations for positions in New York except that of Robertson. When this message was read in the Senate, Platt was said to have hung his head.[4] Before a vote was taken, Platt suggested to Conkling that they both resign. It was a desperate remedy, but it would technically absolve Platt from his promises and furnish Conkling an expression for his pent up irritation. The possibility of a re-election and a "vindication" by the Republican legislature at Albany did not then seem remote inasmuch as the Stalwarts controlled a majority of the caucus. When their resignations became public, the obvious interpretation was that Conkling had forced Platt to resign with him. "I have been portrayed as a 'Me, too,' an 'Echo' and 'Dromio' of Conkling," wrote Platt. "In editorial and cartoon I was pictured as a small boy sticking out of Conkling's pocket, with a card labeled 'Me, too!' tied to one of my hands."[5] The affair was called the "senatorial suicide"[6] and the incomparable Nast pictured Conkling and Platt as having "lost their heads."[7]

In the struggle that followed at Albany, Platt and Conkling lost in the initial skirmish. It was expected that Governor Cornell would send a message to the legislature announcing the resignation at once, but by adroit action on the

[3] Statement to the writer on September 25, 1922.
[4] M. P. Breen, *Thirty Years of New York Politics* (New York, 1899), p. 656.
[5] Platt, *op. cit.*, pp. 150–59.
[6] *New York World*, May 17, 1881.
[7] *Harper's Weekly*, XXV, 357, 404, 421.

part two Half-Breed senators the Senate was adjourned before a message could be received.[8] This gave the Half-
Breeds time to organize and to agree not to enter the Repub-
lican caucus. The first ballot showed that Conkling and
Platt were playing a losing game. Louis F. Payn, one of
Platt's close advisers, prophesied defeat. Even some of the
Stalwarts did not approve of Conkling's "rule or ruin" policy
and the Half-Breeds evidently thought that Platt had not
lived up to his pledges. A majority of the legislature refused
to believe that it was "dishonest" or "dishonorable" for
President Garfield to reward Robertson for his services at
Chicago at the expense of the "regular" New York organization. However, Conkling and his friends did not give up
without a struggle. Vice-President Arthur appeared in the
lobby of the capitol on behalf of Conkling and Platt. After
a month's balloting without results, Platt withdrew his name.
The next day the *Albany Argus* made the following comment:

> Mr. Platt's withdrawal as a candidate is significant. From
> the first, Mr. Platt has known he could only be an obstacle.
> Suddenly he learned he could not continue to be even that.
> His escapade, whether he was innocent or a guilty victim,
> diverted the scales in his case to the side of ridicule, an in-
> clination which his association with Mr. Conkling alone pre-
> vented them from taking long ago.[9]

On the same day that this article appeared, President Garfield was shot by a half-crazed, disappointed Stalwart office-
seeker. It looked as though Garfield's enemies would profit

[8] C. R. Skinner, "A Memorable Senatorial Contest," *State Service*,
IV, 27.
[9] July 2, 1881. The *New York World* for the same date said:
"The gosssip of the day at Albany charges Mr. Platt with unbe-
coming conduct in a matter lying quite outside the field of politics.
The charge is reputed to rest upon evidence collected, according
to a Brooklyn contemporary, by a half-breed committee of inspec-
tion established on step-ladders in the hotel at Albany."

by his death. "Dark suspicious and angry threatenings filled the public mind," said one observer, "and for the moment there was doubt—grave doubt and imminent peril that the orderly succession of power under the Constitution might not take its peaceful course." [10] This calamity made Platt more emphatic in insisting that he had "lost all interest in the contest at Albany." [11] Finally the Half-Breeds and the Independents agreed to hold a caucus. Warner Miller was then elected to fill Platt's place and Elbridge C. Lapham, one of the first "deserters," was elected to succeed Conkling. This humiliating defeat ended a chapter in Platt's life. He had lost the friendship of Conkling,[12] he had lost the respect of the party workers, and he had become an object of general ridicule and scorn. A consuming desire upon his part to regain his old position may in part explain the indefatigable energy with which he pursued the game of politics in the ensuing years.[13]

In the hour of Platt's disgrace and temporary retirement from politics, Theodore Roosevelt was just beginning to take an active interest in "practical politics." In 1880 he had joined the Twenty-first District Republican Association in the city of New York, an act which brought him under the tutelage of Jacob Hess, a New York politician who later

[10] Elihu Root, address delivered at the unveiling of President Arthur's statue in Madison Square, New York, June 14, 1899, cited in Breen, *op. cit.*, p. 61.

[11] *Op. cit.*, p. 164.

[12] "For Conkling it was worse than defeat. The humiliation of having gone to Albany, of being deserted by friend after friend, of enduring the taunts of an inhospitable press and, finally, of having his place taken by one, who, in his opinion, had proven most faithless, was like the torture of an unquenchable fire."—Alexander, *op. cit.*, III, 482.

[13] For an elaboration of this theory, see W. A. White, "Platt," *McClure's Magazine*, XVIII, 148.

became identified with the "machine" which Platt built up.[14]
In the fall of 1881 young Roosevelt was nominated and
elected to the lower house of the New York State Legislature from his district. Although the youngest man in the
legislature, he soon displayed those qualities which later
brought him world wide distinction. He was fearless in at-
tacking the old spoils régime, even going so far as to demand
the impeachment of a judge whom he deemed guilty of
"corrupt collusion" with a wealthy stock gambler. He was
also active in suggesting reforms for the government of the
city of New York. From the start, he was tremendously
successful in getting his name upon the front page of the
newspapers.

Thoroughly discredited and neglected, Platt remained in
seclusion for a time. The State Convention which met in
September, 1881, was almost completely under the control of
the anti-Conkling wing. In the November election which
followed many of the Stalwarts "knifed" the Half-Breed
candidate for state treasurer,[15] and factional quarrels in the
assembly districts resulted in the election of a Democratic
legislature. In the following year Conkling demonstrated
how a state convention could be run in the face of adverse
circumstances. Governor Cornell sought a renomination and
his conciliatory policy and efforts toward efficient administration had been aimed in that direction. President Arthur,
however, had objected to Cornell's attitude during the senatorial contest, and Charles J. Folger was his choice for the
nomination. Conkling was "out of politics" but he was active in Folger's canvass as Jay Gould's "legal adviser."
Governor Cornell had refused to sign some bills which fa-

[14] J. L. Heaton, *The Story of a Page* (New York, 1913), p 326.
[15] All the Republicans on the state ticket were elected by plurali-
ties around 13,000 except the candidate for state treasurer who was
defeated by 20,000 votes.

vored certain Gould interests.[16] The "administration" packed the convention with federal office-holders and was aided by a forged telegram in its effort to secure control over the temporary organization of the convention.[17] Folger was nominated, but the Conkling organization had failed to read the signs of the times. A feeling of public indignation was rising against high-handed "machine" methods, the boss-despised civil service reform was gaining in popular favor, and the Democrats had chanced upon a new leader, Grover Cleveland, a man who regarded "public office as a trust" and who was not afraid to appeal over the heads of the politicians to the people. Cleveland received a majority of over 190,000, the largest majority ever given a candidate for governor up to that time. Conkling was down and out. Conkling was a man of undoubted ability, a keen lawyer, and an orator of great power but he had been caught in the meshes of the party spoils system,[18] his voice was heard with decreasing frequency in the councils of the nation,[19] and he put his intellectual powers more and more at the command of those primarily interested in pecuniary gain.[20] To Platt it seemed that these Republican disasters were the result of party discord and from then on he stood for "harmony." Roosevelt was more inclined to take the view toward politics sponsored by Cleveland, but he also recognized the "necessity of party harmony."

The stand which Platt and Roosevelt took in the Conven-

---

[16] A bill regulating the taxation of the elevated railroads in New York City. See Appleton's *Ann. Cyc.*, 1882, p. 600.

[17] *Nation*, September 28, and Oct. 15, 1882. Platt alleges that the recipient of the telegram honestly believed it to be genuine, but he does not assert that the telegram was in fact genuine. Platt, *op. cit.*, pp. 171–76.

[18] Depew, *My Memories*, p. 82.

[19] *New York World*, January 23, 1879.

[20] C. A. Beard, *Contemporary American History* (New York, 1914), pp. 51 ff.

tion of 1844 was a sign that the bitter factionalism of Conkling's day was passing. Until his dying day, Conkling maintained a hostile attitude toward Blaine. Conkling was not a delegate to the Republican National Convention of 1884, but Platt went as a delegate from his old home district after a bitter primary struggle. Roosevelt also attended this convention, having made several concessions to the organization.[1] In the convention, Platt seconded Blaine's nomination, saying: "I second this nomination, believing as I do, that his turn has come; believing as I do, that the Republican people of the Republican states that must give the Republican majorities want him."[2] Platt's grounds for changing his attitude toward Blaine were that the "organization was not disposed to forgive Arthur for refusing to get rid of Collector William H. Robertson" and that the "organization was wrathful at Arthur . . . because he did little or nothing as president to cure the sores from which the Republicans of his state were smarting."[3] In other words, he was not so set against Blaine as he was against the New York Republicans who had deserted him at Albany. Arthur could not be used to punish these "deserters"; much less could George F. Edmunds, the candidate supported by Roosevelt and other "independents." The old Stalwart forces were completely disorganized and without any outstanding leader. Platt decided to cast his lot with the dominant elements in his party. Roosevelt made a like decision, arguing that the "future of the country was safer under Republican control."[4] Platt's stand was not approved by Conkling nor was Roosevelt's by his independent friends. It was a strange

[1] J. L. Heaton, op. cit., p. 325.
[2] Official Proceedings, p. 103.
[3] Op. cit., pp. 178–80.
[4] D. S. Alexander, Four Famous New Yorkers (New York, 1923), p. 27.

coincidence that these two men of such dissimilar tastes were found on the same side of such an important issue. The conciliatory attitude which Platt and Roosevelt adopted in 1884 was not immediately successful. It is useless to conjecture what would have happened if Blaine had been elected. The Republicans were disheartened by the Democratic victory and many of the old leaders lost their interest in politics, but neither Platt nor Roosevelt lost interest in the game. In 1885 Platt was active in securing the election of G. Z. Erwin as speaker of the state Assembly. The same year Platt and Roosevelt backed different candidates for the United States senatorship. The year following the two men joined hands in the New York mayoralty campaign. Roosevelt consented to let Platt's district managers nominate him for mayor on a straight Republican ticket to run against Henry George and Abram S. Hewitt. Those who were opposed to George's theories were amazed at Roosevelt's action. In the election Roosevelt ran a poor third, probably much to his own and to Platt's chagrin.[5] In 1887 while Roosevelt was out touring the West, Platt was trying to speed up the movement to elect Levi P. Morton United States senator in Miller's place. Platt was not a member of the legislature but he was "influential" in the Southern Tier where the local organization had been loyal to him even in the dark days of 1881 and he had "helped" many legislative candidates in doubtful districts. The senatorial contest turned out in the first caucus vote to be a three cornered struggle between Miller, Morton and Frank Hiscock, with Hiscock far in the rear. When the Morton forces saw that the Hiscock supporters could not be moved, they managed to switch their entire strength to Hiscock who

[5] Neither Platt nor Roosevelt mention this campaign in their respective autobiographies.

was selected by a vote of one over Miller. Miller was at least defeated and the gratitude of the new senator secured. Platt first attained a position of what might be called recognized leadership in 1888. For the first time he was selected as one of the delegates-at-large to a Republican national convention. The New York delegation went to the convention in a harmonious mood supporting Chauncey M. Depew for the presidential nomination. Depew withdrew his name after the third ballot and suggested that the New York delegation throw its support to Harrison of Indiana.[6] In a posthumous account, Platt claimed that Stephen B. Elkins "stated he was authorized to say that if the New York delegation would give General Harrison their support, the latter would appoint Mr. Platt secretary of the treasury in case of his election and allow him to control the federal patronage in the state of New York." [7] The account goes on to state that the pledge was not made in those exact words, but everyone present so understood it. J. Sloat Fassett, one of Platt's lieutenants who was in the conference, said that the story was "substantially correct." Mr. Elkins insisted that "Tom Platt never was promised the secretaryship of the treasury." President Harrison also positively denied he had ever made any such promise to Platt.[8] Whatever the truth may be, it is clear that Platt thought he had made some such arrangement, for he devoted the remainder of his time in the convention to bringing the New York delegation solidly into line for Harrison. On the fourth ballot fifty-eight of the New York delegates gave their votes to Harrison and continued voting for him to the end. This

[6] Depew, *My Memories,* pp. 131–33
[7] *Elmira Advertiser,* March 10, 1910, citing the *Washington Evening Star's* story written by Mr. William E. Curtis.
[8] *New York Tribune,* March 10, 1910. Harrison's letter to W. H. Miller.

[20] *Op. cit.,* p. 501.
[1] Platt, *op. cit.,* p. 185.

was the "corrupt bargain" which John Sherman believed was responsible for his defeat in the convention.[9] Platt's hostility to Sherman dated back to the customs-house struggle of the late seventies, when Sherman was secretary of the treasury. While the action of the New York delegates was probably not the sole cause of Sherman's defeat, it did greatly contribute to Harrison's final success. The New York managers were then allowed to name the candidate for vice-president and they chose Levi P. Morton. Platt had become an "active operating force" in the national councils of his party.

Mathew S. Quay was the chairman of the national committee in 1888, and but for his "masterful conduct of the campaign in New York State," Platt tells us, "Harrison never would have been president."[10] Quay had been through a course of training in Pennsylvania under Don Cameron, quite similar to that which Platt had received in New York under Conkling. The friendship between Platt and Quay from this time on was very close. The first step in the New York campaign was a "harmony" move, the nomination of Warner Miller for governor. It has been alleged that Platt foresaw that "with Miller as a beaten candidate before the people, his claims of strength would be regarded as mere humbug pretensions."[11] During the campaign, Miller made some radical speeches on the liquor question which lined up the liquor interests with Hill, his Demo-

---

[9] "I believed then, as I believe now that one of the delegates from the state of New York practically controlled the whole delegation, and that a corrupt bargain was made on Sunday which transferred the great body of the vote of New York to General Harrison, and thus lead to the nomination."—J. Sherman, *Recollections of Forty Years in the House, Senate and Cabinet* (New York, 1895), II, 1029.

[10] *Op. cit.*, p. 210.

[11] *New York Sun*, September 26, 1889.

cratic opponent.[12]   Clubs were formed which floated the banner, " Harrison and Hill." All that Platt had to do was to concentrate his attention upon the national campaign. Harrison carried the state but Miller was defeated. Although Platt was not made secretary of the treasury, Benjamin F. Tracy, the law partner of Platt's son, was selected as secretary of the navy and Platt was given considerable "recognition" in the making of minor New York appointments. This blow at Miller's prestige sent the county leaders to Platt for "advice" and soon the papers were proclaiming the rise of the "Easy Boss."

Roosevelt did not attend the National Convention of 1888 nor did he take an active part in the campaign of 1888, but Harrison recognized his political talents by appointing him civil service commissioner, a position which was bound to bring him in conflict with Platt.

At the beginning of the last decade of the nineteenth century, Platt and Roosevelt both became active participants in New York politics. The older man was a seasoned politician: he had witnessed the decline of Thurlow Weed's power, he had seen Fenton come and go as a state leader, he had lived through Conkling's victories and defeats, and he had been responsible in a measure for the disintegration of Miller's influence in the Republican councils of the state. He had also learned many lessons from his political enemies, the Democrats. He studied the methods which brought success to Samuel J. Tilden and David B. Hill, and when he came to New York City he found much to admire in the efficient working of that great urban organization, the Tammany Democracy. During his years of training the technique of political management had become refined and specialized and required years of actual experience. Begin-

12 *Nation*, November 15, 1888.

ning as a county committeeman, Platt had held in turn practically every position in the committee hierarchy of his own party; chairman of his county committee, national congressional campaign committeeman, state committeeman, chairman of the executive committee of the state committee, chairman of the state committee, and national committeeman. The great number of county, assembly district, congressional district, judicial and state conventions that he had attended taught him the elements of convention strategy. Besides, he had attended four national conventions, where he had met and matched wits with leaders from all over the country interested in problems of party organization and machinery. His participation in nine presidential campaigns and in nearly four times that many state campaigns, had brought him in touch with every sort of campaign method from the ditty of the campaign glee club to the "business insurance" plea of a Wanamaker. Not only had he been interested in nominations and elections but he had also followed closely the methods of controlling legislation and administration and had put these methods in operation. The younger man had served three terms in the state legislature, he had attended one national convention and he had made an unsuccessful campaign for the mayoralty of the city of New York.

The experiences through which Platt and Roosevelt passed during their respective periods of political training determined in large part the nature and scope of their subsequent political activities. Conkling's failures had taught Platt the dangers of an overbearing attitude, and the factional quarrels between the Stalwarts and the Half-Breeds had taught him the imperative necessity of party "harmony." The passage of the Civil Service Law in 1883 had given him some conception of the power of reformers like Dorman B. Eaton, George W. Curtis and Theodore Roosevelt. Nevertheless, the great number of political victories that he had seen won by those who controlled the patronage and the party funds convinced him that he must control these sources of power. He had learned that party funds were available to those who were regarded "safe" by the big business interests. As president of an express company, he had met the railway magnates and the financial kings and he knew how to avoid offending them. All that Platt needed in 1899 was a favorable opportunity to put his expert knowledge into practice. On the other hand, Roosevelt was just gaining momentum as a popularizer of a new order. His experiences as a law maker had shown him the evils of the party spoils system, and his rather unsuccessful convention and campaign history had taught him some hard lessons in the game of "practical politics." These lessons, however, did not dampen the enthusiasm with which the younger man joined battle with the old régime.

CHAPTER III

POLITICAL UPHEAVAL IN NEW YORK.

Although in 1889 with the coming of the Harrison administration at Washington, Thomas C. Platt was elevated to a position of leadership in the Republican party of the state of New York, his control was no where nearly as complete then as it came to be in the middle of the nineties. In his *Autobiography*, Platt said: "I did contribute toward transforming a once Democratic state into an impregnable Republican stronghold."[1] A brief survey of the political history of the state from 1889 to 1896 will show that Platt's contribution to the political upheaval in the state was slight. The victories of the Republicans in 1894 and 1896 were not due so much to the efficient Republican organization as they were to the disorganization of the Democratic party, national, state and local. It is necessary to review the industrial and political events which led to the breakup of the Democracy in order to understand the rise of Thomas C. Platt to a position of undisputed leadership in the councils of his party in the state, a position which he held when Roosevelt was made governor.

It has already been pointed out that David B. Hill was re-elected governor in 1888 although Cleveland failed to carry the state as a candidate for the presidency. An analysis of this election will show the weak and strong points of the Democratic state organization. Mr. Hill, the Democratic candidate for governor, was an able man, a prominent

[1] Introduction, p. xvii.

lawyer, and a skilled political manager.[2] Like Platt, Hill had been trained in the practical school of politics. Starting at the age of twenty-one as a ward leader in the city of Elmira, he rose gradually to power, holding successively the positions of corporation counsel of Elmira, member of the state legislature, delegate to the Democratic National Convention of 1876, chairman of the Democratic State Convention of 1877, member of the Elmira Common Council, mayor of Elmira, lieutenant-governor of the state and governor. The last mentioned position he held continously from 1885 to 1892. He had studied the methods, successes, and failures of Democratic leaders like William M. Tweed, the notorious Tammany chief; Samuel J. Tilden, the reform governor and victim of the presidential "fraud" of 1876; Daniel Manning, the leader of the up-state Democrats and able manager of Cleveland's campaign in 1884; and William C. Whitney, one of the organizers of the New York County Democracy and the successor of Manning as Cleveland's campaign manager. When Cleveland became president of the United States, Hill was elevated to the governorship to fill Cleveland's unexpired term and Manning and Whitney were both called to Washington to take places in the first Democratic cabinet formed since 1860. As governor, Hill distributed the state patronage so skillfully that he attracted all the county leaders who had been dissatisfied at the way President Cleveland disregarded their recommendations for federal appointments.[3] His rapid rise to state leadership in 1885 also depended upon a close alliance between the "Big Four;" the veteran leader of the Brooklyn (Willoughby Street) Dem-

[2] G. F. Bixby, "David B. Hill, Statesman and Politician," *State Service*, IV, 89.
[3] W. C. Hudson, *Random Recollections of an Old Political Reporter* (New York, 1911), pp. 252 ff.

ocracy, Hugh McLaughlin;[4] the chief of the Tammany Democracy, Richard Croker;[5] the vigorous organizer of the Buffalo Democrats, William F. Sheehan; and the Trojan warrior, Edward Murphy.[6] Hill, himself, cared little for money, though he philosophically accepted the greed of others as a fact with which a practical politician must deal. Like Platt, he was an enemy of civil service reform and a meticulous student of the minutiae of New York politics.

The tactics of these leaders in the election of 1888 clearly illustrate the character of their party organization. Attention has already been called to the fact that Warner Miller, the Republican candidate for governor, was an advocate of high license. About that time there was forty thousand saloon-keepers in the state organized for purposes of securing legislation favorable to their business and of preventing the enactment of laws restricting it.[7] In addition there were the powerful wholesale liquor dealers and the liquor manufacturers. Those who were interested in the liquor traffic and in its perpetuation naturally turned to the Democratic party in the state, the party which drew most of its strength from the great cities where most of the liquor was made and consumed.[8] Besides appealing to the liquor vote, the Democrats also tried to attract the labor vote. Through-

[4] Hudson, *op. cit.*, p. 260.
[5] *The Democratic Party of the State of New York*, edited by James K. McGuire (New York, 1905), II, 228.
[6] Breen, *op. cit.*, p. 740.
[7] City Reform Club, *Annual Records of the Assemblymen and Senators from the City of New York*, 1891, p. 23.
[8] The *Wine and Spirit Gazette*, the organ of the wholesale liquor dealers, said on April 28, 1891: "Do you deny that the liquor vote controls the situation in this state? What defeated Warner Miller and elected Governor Hill? What gave the Democratic party its present majority in the Assembly? What elected the Tammany ticket in this last year? Was it not the united strength of the liquor vote?"

out his administrations, Governor Hill posed as the champion of the labor interests. Confronted as he was with a hostile Republican legislature, his constant recommendations for laws ameliorating the conditions of labor may have had some political if-not legal effect.[9] During this campaign, he proclaimed his famous slogan, "I am a Democrat," which was supposed to imply that he was a thorough partisan whereas Cleveland with his civil service reform notions was not.[10] After the election Hill was accused of having made a "deal" with Platt whereby the presidency was "traded" for the governorship.[11] In an interview published some years later, Cleveland denied that he ever had any idea that the presidential ticket was the victim of treachery in this election, and he further stated in effect that the disparity between his vote and that of Governor Hill could be accounted for by the liquor vote.[12] It was Hill's own opinion at the time that the result of this election would be a prejudice to his political future.[13]

Governor Hill naturally desired to have a legislature in political accord with him. On account of the rotten borough system in the state which favored the rural districts, there seemed to be little chance of this desire ever being fulfilled, but in 1891 a nation-wide reaction against the McKinley tariff resulted in the election of a Democratic Assembly with a majority sufficient to override the Republican Senate upon a joint ballot. This made it possible for the

[9] C. Z. Lincoln, *Messages from the Governors*, VIII, 35, 163, 303, 315, *et passim*.

[10] H. T. Peck, *Twenty Years of the Republic*, 1885–1905 (New York, 1907), p. 161.

[11] *Nation*, November 15, 1888, XLVII, 385.

[12] G. F. Parker, *Recollections of Grover Cleveland* (New York 1909), p. 342.

[13] *Ibid.*, p. 344. A. B. Parker's recollection of a conversation with Governor Hill in November, 1888.

Democrats to elect Governor Hill to the United States Senate. However, Hill finished his term as governor and took his seat in the Senate on January 1, 1892. At the Democratic State Convention of 1891, Roswell P. Flower, a wealthy banker who had always been a favorite of Tammany Hall,[14] was nominated for governor and William F. Sheehan was nominated for lieutenant-governor. In the fall election the Democrats carried the executive offices, a majority of the assemblymen and enough of the senatorial seats to leave the final composition of the state Senate in doubt. The way in which this doubt was resolved in favor of the Democrats was one of the events which made a deep inroad into Hill's political strength. One of the contested seats hinged upon the returns from an election district in Dutchess County. It is unnecessary here to go into the intricacies of this election tangle. The act which attracted attention was the seizure from the mails of an election certificate which favored the Republican candidate. This episode involved Isaac H. Maynard, one of Hill's lieutenants, who asserted that the seizure was legal. The Democratic officials considered that the Court of Appeals in a series of decisions supported their claims[15] and a legislative investigating committee which later met was of the same opinion,[16] but the State Bar Association severely censured Maynard and the Republican and Independent newspapers talked about the "theft of the Senate."[17] Hill was destined not to profit greatly by the

[14] McGuire, loc. cit.

[15] People ex rel. Daley v. Rice, 129 N. Y. 449; People ex rel. Sherwood v. Rice, 129 N. Y. 391; People ex rel. Nichols v. Board of Canvassers, 129 N. Y. 443.

[16] New York State Legislature, Proceedings and Testimony before the Joint Committee of the Senate and Assembly, 1892, (Investigation of certain documents and letters of Judge Maynard in regard to Senate election cases in the Fifteenth Senate District).

[17] New York Tribune, January 6, 1892 and March 22, 1892; Nation, January 28, 1892, LIV, 63.

Democratic control of the legislature. From his new position he could not keep the same watch over state affairs that he had maintained while at Albany, and Richard Croker was drawing his lines closer over the Tammany representatives at the state capitol who comprised nearly forty per cent of all the Democratic legislators.[18] "System" and "direct responsibility" were the rules which guided the Tammany chieftain.[19] The old professional lobbyists were superseded by the "boss" who delivered the party vote in return for contributions or services to the party.[20] The Democratic legislature of 1892 thus became one of Hill's stumbling blocks.

Like other governors of New York, Hill had presidential ambitions, but the method which he employed to obtain a solid delegation pledged to his support in the Democratic National Convention of 1892 reacted unfavorably upon his candidacy and political career. He gained absolute control of the state committee by un-seating the regularly elected anti-Hill delegates to the State Convention of 1891 and this committee early in 1892 issued a call for a state convention to elect delegates to the national convention. The date set for the convention was so early that protests were immediately heard from all sides. The New York Reform Club styled it a "snap" convention [1] and the *New York World,* which had been a fairly consistent supporter of Hill up to this time, printed the warning, "Don't," and furnished the Cleveland supporters with many valuable arguments.[2]   In

[18] City Reform Club, *op. cit.,* 1893, p. 11.
[19] Croker interview published in the *New York Tribune,* Dec. 17, 1893.
[20] J. B. Bishop, "The Price of Peace," *Century Mag.,* XLVIII, 668.
[1] E. P. Wheeler, *Sixty Years of American Life* (New York, 1917), p. 203.
[2] *New York World,* February 3, 1892.

spite of admonitions from his party press, Hill persisted in
carrying out his scheme. Not only was the convention
"sprung upon the party" so that the Anti-Hill elements had
no time to organize, but the caucuses were also sprung upon
the voters. Primaries were held with insufficient notice or
no notice at all regarding the time and place of meeting.[3]
As a part of his plan, Hill had recognized Tammany Hall
as the "regular" New York organization because it was opposed to Cleveland. Although Hill obtained a solid delegation from the state of New York, his high handed methods
caused unfavorable comment among the delegates from the
other states, and whatever chances he might have had to secure the presidential nomination were ruined. Cleveland's
supporters, skilfully marshalled by William C. Whitney,
won upon the first ballot.

While the year 1893 was a lean one for the Republicans in
New York, it was far from being a fortunate one for the
Democrats. The Republicans had been turned out of the
national offices in time to avoid public disapproval on account of the panic of 1893. The Democratic organization
which had to bear the brunt of this misfortune was dis-
united. The Cleveland administration had recognized the
Anti-Snappers in the distribution of the New York patronage. Democratic blunders within the state greatly increased
the party's demoralization. One of the first of these was the
promotion of Edward Murphy to the United States Senate,
where he was looked upon as the representative of the makers of collars and cuffs at Troy and an echo of Hill.[4] Another blunder was perpetrated by Lieutenant-Governor Sheehan when he "jammed through" the legislature some Buffalo
charter amendments which greatly enhanced the power of

[3] F. W. Dallinger, *Nominations for Elective Office* (New York,
1897), p. 124.
[4] Wheeler, *op. cit.*, p. 255.

his henchmen over the government of the city. The passage of these "ripper" bills caused great excitement in Buffalo and many business men's exchanges, professional societies, and political clubs held indignation meetings.[5] The next incident which injured the standing of the Democratic state organization was the nomination of Isaac H. Maynard by the state convention for the Court of Appeals. The general opinion was current that Hill forced Maynard upon the convention in order to reward Maynard for his services in securing a Democratic Senate. Many years later a letter from Hill to Maynard was revealed which showed that Hill on the eve of the convention had urged Maynard to retire,[6] but this he refused to do and his candidacy was looked upon by many of the voters as an act of brazenness and insolence on the part of the "bosses."[7] In a vituperative campaign speech Hill called those who controlled the Bar Association a "brainless set of namby-pambys."[8] These were the tactics of desperation. "Boss" McLaughlin also confronted an uprising in his domain. William J. Gaynor unearthed a scandal in connection with the purchase of the Long Island Water Supply Company by the city of Brooklyn. Many civic and business organizations united to "smash the ring" and prosecuted a vigorous and bitter campaign.[9] The election of 1893 was nearly everywhere disastrous to the "organization" Democrats. Maynard fell considerably behind his ticket and was defeated by an overwhelming majority. During the election a riot occurred in Gravesend, a town on the outskirts of Brooklyn ruled by the petty John Y. Mc-

[5] City Reform Club, *op. cit.*, 1893, pp. 106 ff. Statement of Mr. Ansley Wilcox.
[6] New York Legislature, *Memorial of David B. Hill*, p. 17. Address by A. B. Parker.
[7] J. L. Heaton, *The Story of a Page* (New York, 1913), p. 98.
[8] *New York Tribune*, Oct. 24, 1893.
[9] McGuire, *op. cit.*, pp. 252–53.

Kane. The report of McKane's high handed and fraudulent methods helped the cause of the reformers in Brooklyn. An election brawl and homicide in Troy had a similar effect upon those opposed to Senator Murphy's local nomination. The Democrats lost control of the governments of Brooklyn and Buffalo, the minor state executive officers, the constitutional convention and the state legislature. "Divine Providence did it," said Platt,[10] thus admitting that the victory was not achieved by any effort on his part.[11] The result was summarized in *Harper's Weekly* in the following words: "The selfish tyranny of the Democratic party bosses in this state has of late years been so audacious in its wickedness that at last in the most rigidly disciplined of political parties the outraged dignity of human nature asserted itself in open revolt." [12]

The Tammany Hall Democracy was not disciplined until the following year. Although the Rev. Charles H. Parkhurst had begun his crusade against the "damnable pack of administrative bloodhounds" in his famous philippic of Sunday, February 14, 1892,[13] tangible inroads upon Tammany's strength were not made until 1894. In the meanwhile, the Society for the Prevention of Crime, of which Dr. Parkhurst was president, was collecting evidence upon the open connection between the Police Department and the resorts of vice and gambling and arousing public opinion. The matter came to a head when the New York Chamber of Commerce submitted a resolution to the state legislature request-

[10] *Op. cit.*, p. 267.
[11] "The victory was won almost without organization or plan, and with so little money that the Tammany leaders jeered at the straightened circumstances of the Republican committees."—*New York Tribune*, November 9, 1893.
[12] November 18, 1893, XXXVII, 1094.
[13] C. H. Parkhurst, *Our Fight with Tammany* (New York, 1895), p. 10.

ing an investigation of the department. Four days later, Clarence Lexow, one of Platt's lieutenants, introduced a resolution in the state Senate providing for the appointment of an investigating committee. When the bill providing for the defraying of the expenses of this committee was vetoed by Governor Flower, the Chamber of Commerce came to the rescue and raised the necessary funds. Political influences were manifest in the early work of the committee. William A. Sutherland, an up-state lawyer and politican, was appointed counsel for the committee while it investigated Democratic election frauds.[14] The real work of the committee began when John W. Goff was chosen as sole counsel for the remainder of the committee's work. Goff was a Democrat who, as assistant district attorney, had thoroughly learned the devious ways of the underworld. He prosecuted his work fearlessly, relentlessly, and with wonderful astuteness. The revelations extorted from the unwilling witnesses greatly shocked the community. Certain police officials had developed a systematic method of blackmailing; they levied a ratable charge upon all saloons, houses of ill-fame, gambling dens, policy shops and green goods swindlers. In return these resorts of the criminal classes were given "police protection." Even legitimate businesses were compelled to pay tribute; hardly a contractor, a pawnbroker, or a small retailer escaped. One of the dramatic climaxes of the hearings was the confession of a police captain that he had paid $15,000 to secure his promotion.[15] The metropolitan newspapers gave wide publicity to the revelations, were practically unanimous in their condemnation of the police corruption and did not hesitate to designate the heads of Tammany

[14] *Ibid.*, p. 291.
[15] New York State Legislature, *Senate Doc.*, 1895, No. 63, I, 48 (Report of the committee to investigate the Police Department of New York City).

Hall as the chief beneficiaries of the debasing system. Although absent in Europe, Richard Croker became a target for the press.[16] It was pointed out that the corruption extended to all the city departments and that Tammany chieftains, whose only ostensible profession was politics, had amassed vast fortunes within a few years. These disclosures produced a revolt against Tammany similar to that of 1871. Even Platt was so impressed that, after some dickering, he urged the Republicans to endorse the fusion ticket made up by the citizens' Committee of Seventy.[17] William L. Strong, the fusion candidate for mayor, was elected by a majority of 45,187 over his Democratic opponent. One of Mayor Strong's first official acts was the appointment of Theodore Roosevelt as one of the police commissioners.

The popular upheaval against Tammany was one of the contributing factors in the defeat of the Democratic state ticket in 1894. Senator Hill presided over the state convention which met to nominate a candidate for governor that year. Governor Flower had been persuaded to withdraw his name from the list of possibilities before the convention. It was felt that he was not "available" for a renomination because the general impression had grown up that he had been a tool of the bosses.[18] A Democratic defeat was likely whoever the candidate might be. The financial panic and the tariff scandals were reacting against the party all over the nation, and in the state the reverses of the year before were a warning that desperate remedies were necessary. However, the Democratic managers rejected "reform" Democrats with little ceremony as they preferred defeat to a surrender of their organization. When William C. Whitney

[16] J. D. Townsend, *New York in Bondage* (New York, 1901), *passim*.
[17] *Op. cit.*, p. 271.
[18] *New York Times*, April 22, 1892; Heaton, *op. cit.*, p. 101.

withdrew his name, the Tammany Hall delegates started a stampede for David B. Hill. Hill fought the rush vigorously but in vain. It was afterward learned that the stampede had been carefully prearranged.[19] Tammany, floundering, had also dragged Hill into the mire. As one journal expressed it: "He had repeatedly ridden into power on the backs of his mercenary henchmen; now his henchmen jumped upon his back, demanding that he carry them to success, and he could not refuse." [20] All the Democratic blunders of the two previous years were heaped upon Hill's head and he went down to a defeat so overwhelming that he never regained from its effects. Thus Croker's followers played into Platt's hands by killing off the ablest of the "organization" Democrats.

The defeat of the Democratic candidates in 1894 was accompanied by the passage of several constitutional amendments which were designed to shackle the future power of the Tammany Democracy. The Constitutional Convention of 1894 which the Democrats had hoped to control was predominantly Republican and it proposed an amendment to the constitution which aimed to eliminate the fraudulent naturalizations which were so common in the great Democratic cities upon the eve of election.[1] However, one authority has said that the apportionment provision was the only partisan use of power by the majority of the convention.[2] This amendment made radical alterations in the representative system and provided that no county, however populous it might become, should have more than one-third of all the senators and that no two counties which adjoined or were

[19] *Harper's Weekly,* October 13, 1894, XXXVIII, 962.
[20] *Ibid.,* October 6, 1894, p. 938.
[1] Constitution, Art. II, Sec. 1. See also *New York Tribune,* Oct. 31, 1894.
[2] J. H. Dougherty, *Constitutional History of New York State* (New York, 1911), p. 339.

separated only by public waters should have more than one-half of all the senators.[3] The Democrats were quick to see that this proposal would reduce New York City to a condition of partial vassalage and they denounced it unsparingly. "The whole object of it," said a Tammany delegate, "is to maintain the present balance and preponderance of the rural counties of this state against the city." [4] Another Tammany delegate expressed his opposition in more picturesque words:

Should the Republicans entirely disband their organization in the three great cities of the state, and should the Republican party collapse in every county where its organization is not now controlled by Mr. Platt, Mr. Platt could continue to elect from the counties which he does control a majority of both houses of the legislature, and the dictates of the Republican machine under his able and skilful leadership would be the sole representative of "The people of the state of New York, in Senate and Assembly assembled." [5]

This amendment was ratified by the people of the state in the November election of 1894 when the Democratic party was discredited.

Some of the amendments adopted at this time imposed limitations upon both of the party organizations and must be looked upon as victories for the elements with which Roosevelt was in sympathy. Thus the prohibition placed upon the issuance of passes by railroad, telephone and telegraph companies to public officers, the various limitations placed upon the legislature, the civil service reform clause, and the provision separating municipal elections from state and national elections proved to be equally burdensome to both of the old line party organizations. Considering the

[3] Constitution, Art, III, Sec. 4.
[4] *Record,* 1894, IV, 1861.
[5] *Ibid.,* p. 1887.

general nature of the amendments and the circumstances surrounding their ratification, it is clear that both Platt and Roosevelt were benefited by the new constitution, although neither had expended much effort upon the instrument.[6]

So far in the discussion of the part which the Democrats played in making Platt and Roosevelts' rise in politics possible, the indiscretions of the leaders of the Democratic state organization have been stressed. National issues and events were quite as important, if not more so, than state issues in bringing about a political revolution in the state. In 1892 the feeling regarding national questions was so strong that the Democratic state organization was continued in power in spite of the talk about the "theft of the state Senate" and the "snap convention."[7]   On the other hand, the financial, industrial and labor unrest throughout the country contributed to the state upheavals of 1893 and 1894. The greatest blow to the state Democracy came in the national election of 1896. The New York delegation to the Democratic National Convention of 1896 looked aghast at the capture of their party by the populists and the free silverites. The importance of this election to certain powerful groups in New York had been pointed out by the able biographer of Mark Hanna : "The dominant issue endangered the national financial system, and the money must be collected in New York, the headquarters of national finance."[8]   The leaders of business and finance in the great metropolis were so frightened that over $3,000,000 was raised among them for the purpose of defeating Bryan, the "Boy Orator," and his "economic heresies."[9]   Mark Hanna, "the business man

[6] New York Tribune, May 24, 1896.
[7] Heaton, op. cit., chap. VI.
[8] H. Croly, Marcus Alonzo Hanna: His Life and Work (New York, 1912), p. 219.
[9] Ibid., p. 220.

in politics," was the guiding genius of the Republican campaign. He "organized the state bosses." [10] Platt, who had
bitterly opposed the nomination of McKinley in the Republican convention, was placated and entered wholeheartedly
into the canvass.[11] The Democrats in the state were completely disorganized. The machine Democrats and the reform Democrats were alike broken up by internal revolts.
David B. Hill had made a strong protest against the platform adopted by the Chicago Convention, and when he was
asked during the campaign whether he was a Democrat still,
he had replied, "I am a Democrat still, very still." [12] The
Reform Club led the movement for a third ticket, made up
of Sound Money Democrats. The leading independent
metropolitan newspapers which had supported Cleveland in
his three contests repudiated the Chicago platform and its
candidate.[13] Day after day the names of prominent and
wealthy Democrats who declared their intention to "bolt" the
ticket were published. One of these was the president of a
great insurance company who boasted ten years later that
he had used the policy holders' money to help the Republicans.[14] There was an enormous falling off in the Democratic campaign contributions and a general feeling of
apathy developed among the party workers. Even Tammany Hall was quiescent.[15] The result of the election was
an unprecedented Republican landslide in the state. McKinley's plurality in New York County, the stronghold of Tammany Hall, was over 20,000, and in the state, nearly 270,000.

[10] W. A. White, *The Old Order Changeth* (New York, 1910),
p. 24.
[11] *Syracuse News*, August 4, 1896.
[12] J. A. Woodburn, *Political Parties and Party Problems* (New
York, 1914), p. 208.
[13] A. K. McClure, *Our Presidents and How We Make Them*
(New York, 1905), p. 393; Heaton, *op. cit.*, p. 148.
[14] See chap. X, below.
[15] McGuire, *op. cit.*, p. 173; G. Myers, *History of Tammany
Hall* (New York, 1917), p. 281.

From this sketch of some of the Democratic dissensions, state and national, it is apparent that the assured position of the Republican party in the state at the beginning of 1897 was attained largely by accident, at least as far as any action upon the part of the Republican state organization was concerned. It was the Bar Association which started the vigorous campaign against Maynard and Hill for the "theft of the state Senate." It was Hill himself, who split the Democrats into regulars and Anti-Snappers. It was the indiscretion of his lieutenants which led to the disintegration of the parts of his up-state "machine." It was Dr. Parkhurst and the Chamber of Commerce that initiated and prosecuted the crusade against Tammany. It was the Tammany organization which proved to be the undoing of Hill in 1896. Finally, it was William Jennings Bryan, who as much as any one, helped to define the issue of 1896, and it was Mark Hanna who directed the Republican campaign of that year. Such were the influences which lay back of the Republican victories of the middle nineties in the state of New York. The Republican state organization under the leadership of Thomas C. Platt was not inactive during this period. It was in a position to reap the benefits of the revolution in public opinion. Its methods and tactics, however, were largely those of self-preservation. The organization accepted Roosevelt in 1898 in order to conserve the victories which it had done so little to earn.

CHAPTER IV

PLATT'S "SUNDAY SCHOOL CLASS"

According to a very suggestive analysis of leadership made by a prominent sociologist, the "prime condition of ascendency is the presence of undirected energy in the person over whom it is to be exercised; it is not so much forced upon us from without as demanded from within." [1] Following the withdrawal of Conkling from politics and the Republican reverses of the eighties, there was present among the Republican party workers in the state, both small and great, a good deal of "undirected energy." There were bitter and prolonged factional quarrels in various parts of the state. While these quarrels consumed energy, they defeated the main purpose of all good Republican workers, namely, Republican victories at the polls. It is possible to describe only a few of the more important political managers who finally came to look to Thomas C. Platt for guidance. Their gravitation to Platt has been described by one of them in the following words:

He came into leadership because, at a time when the party was weak, when its voters were both listless and broken into factions, when its organization was disrupted, and those who might have led had given over their opportunity and had withdrawn themselves into discouraged retirement, Mr. Platt had the motive, the interest, the ambition, and the personal force to draw to himself, first in plans to guide the leg-

[1] C. H. Cooley, *Human Nature and the Social Order* (New York, (1902), p. 285.

55

islature, and later in plans to control the state committee, a little band of trained, able and adventurous politicians; and he held the leadership because of the indifference of the party and of those who were or might have been its leaders in those days of party weakness allowed the plans of this small band of politicians to succeed.[2]

This "little band of politicans" came together at frequent intervals for purposes of consultation and conference. It was one of these conferences which set in motion Roosevelt's nomination for governor in 1898. The most common meeting place was the old Fifth Avenue Hotel in New York City, the headquarters of the Republican state committee and the New York home of Mr. Platt. In the time of Thurlow Weed No. 11 Astor House had been the common meeting place for all those who were interested in New York politics, but the Fifth Avenue Hotel, opened in 1859, soon held out rival attractions to all Republican county leaders. When Conkling was at the height of his power, the local politicians came to this new center to be informed as to the party program and to get the proper "steer." In 1889 when it looked as though Platt was going to distribute the federal patronage in New York,[3] he became the guiding spirit of these conferences.[4] In Platt's own words, "Nobody can take

---

[2] Lemuel E. Quigg, "Thomas Platt," *North American Rev.*, 1910, CXCI, 671.

[3] *Nation*, April 11, 1889, XLVIII, 295.

[4] "It was from this chaotic condition that these strong and masterful men, who were jealous of or antagonistic to each other, gradually came to recognize and defer to the judgment, the sagacity, the skill, and the judicial consideration of Thomas C. Platt. They found him always with an open ear and an open mind always ready to hear every suggestion. When the case had been fully presented by those who had formed their judgments in the different localities from different environments and different inspirations and aspirations, he, as a court of last appeal, rendered decisions which were universally accepted, and the success which followed almost invariably justified their wisdom."—C. M. Depew, *Orations*, II, 197.

away from the Fifth Avenue Hotel the fame that it for years enjoyed as the place where from every city and county in this state there came, met and conferred the strongest minds in the Republican party, and the place from which, after their combined judgment had been finally reached, there went a sentiment in accordance with which popular judgment was molded and put into effect." [5] It is true that the subleaders who came to New York City during business hours usually saw Platt at the office of the United States Express Company at 49 Broadway, but this was more or less of a continuous performance and did not have the same significance that was attached to the larger confabs at the Fifth Avenue Hotel. After Platt was elected to the United States Senate in 1897, he was compelled to spend much of his time during the week at Washington when Congress was in session. However, he returned to New York City every week end and upon Sunday important conferences were held upon the affairs of the state at the Fifth Avenue Hotel.[6] These Sunday conferences, to which the up-state leaders came from all parts of the state to join their city "brethren," were called "Platt's Sunday school class."[7] The two sofas at the end of the broad corridor of the Fifth Avenue Hotel upon which the politicians and reporters sat and gossiped acquired the significant name, the "Amen Corner."[8] The results of the Sunday executive sessions were given out to

[5] *Op. cit.* p. 492.

[6] These Sunday conferences began before 1897 of course, because Sunday was a convenient day for the up-state leaders to leave their business and legislative duties. For typical newspaper accounts of some of these meetings, see *New York Tribune,* Feb. 18, 1895; May 5, 1896; Jan. 18, March 22, and April 12, 1897; Jan. 10, 24, and Nov. 21, 28, 1898; and the *Nation,* March 18, 1897.

[7] Platt, *op. cit.,* p. 489.

[8] "It received this name because when Senator Platt, during his long leadership, after a conference with the party leaders from all over the state, would announce the conclusion at which he had

the reporters and appeared in the Monday morning papers for the edification of all those interested in state politics.

In an unguarded moment at the reminiscent meeting in the Fifth Avenue Hotel just before it was torn down, Senator Depew, a friend of both Platt and Roosevelt, described some of the meetings of the "Sunday school class" in the following terms:

During the quarter of a century of the leadership of Senator Thomas C. Platt more men in the state and nation who amounted to much consulted with him in this corner than in any other place. Here were made governors, state senators, and assemblymen, supreme court judges, judges of the Court of Appeals, and members of Congress. Governors thought the capitol was at Albany, but really took their inspiration and the suggestions for their policies from the Amen Corner. State conventions would meet at Rochester, Syracuse, or Saratoga, but the eight hundred members would wait before acting to know what had been decided upon in the Amen Corner.[9]

It may have been that on this occasion of the "wake ceremonies," April 4, 1908, the amiable Depew was paying a compliment to his colleague Senator Platt out of sympathy for Platt's position of comparative impotence at the time. However, this speech shows at least some of the things that were discussed at the "Sunday school." Another version of the same speech adds a significant detail:

I know speakers who are looked to for the make-up of committees from the lower house of the legislature. They said they would consult with the members of their families in the rural regions, and I have found that the families they consulted were Senator Platt in the "Amen Corner."[10]

---

arrived as to nominations, policies, and platforms, there never was any dissent, but the waiting magnates sitting on this sofa would all say 'Amen.' "—Depew, *Speeches,* VI, 285.

[9] *Ibid,* p. 282.
[10] Platt, *op. cit.,* p. 494.
of the liquor vote?"

One of the chief topics for discussion at these Sunday conferences was the course of legislation at Albany.[11]

A fuller understanding of the significance of these consultations can be obtained from a brief discussion of the training and interests of some of the men who attended them. The successful military commander of to-day is the one who can choose a group of officers of the same mental quality as himself and by a combination of intellectual authority, intimate intercourse, a bold delegation of function, think effectively of a large body of facts.[12] The members of the Sunday executive sessions might be looked upon as the officers of Platt's political army.

One of the oldest frequenters of the corridors of the Fifth Avenue Hotel was Louis F. Payn, of Columbia County. In a way it is an anachronism to mention Payn as a member of Platt's "Sunday school." "Lou" Payn might be regarded as one of Platt's mentors.[13] Although he was about a year and a half younger than Platt, Payn had attended every Republican national convention since 1860 with one or two exceptions, and his activity in state politics covered an even longer period.[14] While Platt was perfecting his control of the Republican organization in Tioga County in the late sixties, Payn was harbor master of New York City, a public officer of state and national connections. But "Lou" Payn's chief occupation was in the lobby of the state capitol at Albany. In a legislative investigation in 1895, he testified

[11] *Nation,* March 18, 1897; *New York Tribune,* April 12, 1897; *New York Sun,* March 7, 1910; Platt, *op. cit.,* p. 469.

[12] G. Wallas, *Our Social Heritage* (New Haven, 1921), p. 60.

[13] G. Myers, "'Boss' Platt," *National Rev.,* 1901, XXXVIII, 219; White, "Platt," *loc. cit.,* pp. 145 ff.

[14] *Leslie's History of the Republican Party* (New York, 1898), p. 207.

that he had "always, for 35 years been interested in the election of speakers, you know, and United States senators and that sort of thing."[15] In 1868 "Lou" Payn was censured by a legislative committee for his activities in connections with the passage of the notorious bills that legalized certain overissues of stock of the Erie Railroad Company.[16] Payn boasted that Jay Gould had paid him $10,000 for his "services" in connection with this bill and that Gould later gave him a "tip" on the Wall Street market whereby he made $90,000 in four weeks.[17] Payn was one of Platt's managers in the famous senatorial contest of 1881. In the consultations that followed immediately after the resignations of Conkling and Platt from the Senate, "Lou" Payn prophesied that they would not be re-elected. Payn's predictions were usually correct. In the investigation of 1895 he admitted that he was the salaried legislative agent of several undisclosed principals; that he influenced the action of members of the legislature on bills in which his employers were interested, not by arguments before committees, but solely by personal conversations of a private and confidential nature, and that he had no other remunerative occupation.[18] Payn was at the head of a "political machine" in his own congressional district [19] and he took part besides in the consultations regarding the nominations made in New York City.[20] Although Payn did not have the confidence of many Republicans in the state among whom Roosevelt was

[15] Sen. Doc. No. 56, 1895, p. 455. (Investigation of the corrupt negotiations charged by the New York "Press" in relation to the bill for an increase of salaries of the members of the New York City Fire Dept.).
[16] Sen. Doc. No. 52, 1869, p. 3.
[17] New York "Press" investigation, p. 484.
[18] Ibid., pp. 16, 476 ff.
[19] Ibid., p. 455.
[20] Ibid., p. 480.

one,[1] he was close to Platt and very influential in the Sunday conferences.[2]

Another one of the "Ameners" to whom Platt was especially attached was Colonel George Washington Dunn, of Binghamton, Broome County. Broome County adjoins Tioga County and the two counties are part of the congressional district from which Platt was elected in 1872. Colonel Dunn was one of those Civil War veterans who became the leaders of the social, political, and commercial life of their respective communities. Colonel Dunn's political training was of a continuous and rigorous sort. He started out as superintendent of public documents at Washington, but he kept in touch with Binghamton affairs and was elected sheriff of his county a few years later. At the end of his term as sheriff, he became the publisher and treasurer of the *Binghamton Republican,* the leading Republican organ in the Southern Tier.[3] It was in this capacity that he helped hold the paper in line for Conkling and Platt during the senatorial contest of 1881. In the latter part of 1881 he was appointed postmaster of Binghamton by President Arthur. It was through the efforts of Postmaster Dunn and other "tried friends" that Platt was selected as a delegate to the National Convention of 1884.[4] Colonel Dunn's prominence in business circles is shown by the fact that in the early nineties he was interested in banking, insurance, manufacturing and public utility companies located in his community. He was valuable in the Sunday conferences not only because of his

[1] Elihu Root said that Payn had been a stench in the nostrils of the people of the state of New York for many years. C. Schurz, *Speeches, Correspondence, and Political Papers* (New York, 1913), VI, 381.

[2] Platt, *op. cit.,* pp. 158–163, 514.

[3] Biographical Review, *The Leading Citizens of Broome Co.* (New York, 1894).

[4] Platt, *op. cit.,* p. 178.

experience at state conventions and on the state committee, but also because he was in close touch with the substantial men of his district.

While Platt clung to his old friends, the members of the "Old Guard," he was shrewd enough to see the advantage of recognizing rising ability.[5] In 1887 there appeared upon the state committee a promising young politician from the city of Rochester, named George Washington Aldridge. Mr. Aldridge was then about the same age as Roosevelt, and he had already established himself as an important political factor locally. Four years before he had been elected a member of the executive board of the city and during his incumbency of this office, the board had charge of extensive improvements in the departments of water, street, fire, and public works.[6] He had acquired his taste for politics and his knowledge of construction work from his father who was a contractor by profession and who had been active politically as councilman and later as mayor. Mr. Aldridge followed in his father's footsteps and was himself elected mayor of the city in 1894. While Mayor Aldridge was looked upon by some as a "machine politician and spoilsman of the Platt type," [7] there can be little doubt that he represented fairly well in the Sunday councils at New York some of predominant groups in his city, which was the most populous urban community along the line of the Erie Canal and the New York Central Railroad between New York and Buffalo.

[5] Depew, *Orations,* II, 197; *New York Sun,* Jan. 15, 1897.
[6] C. E. Fitch, *Encyclopedia of Biography of New York* (New York, 1916), "George Washington Aldridge."
[7] *Harper's Weekly,* Feb. 9, 1895, XXXIX, 122. The *New York Tribune,* Dec. 1, 1894, said: "Moreover, the people did not vote for the continuation under another name of the old spoils system of Hill and Flower. Mr. Aldridge is put forward by the element of the Republican party who wish for that kind of administration. He has been the local boss of Rochester, and has built up his power by the aid of the mercenary Democrats."

The youngest commissioned officer who appeared in Commander Platt's councils of war in the early nineties was William Barnes, Jr., of Albany. Mr. Barnes had been brought up in an atmosphere which was steeped in politics; his maternal grandfather, Thurlow Weed, had been an object of admiration and veneration in his boyhood days;[8] his father, William Barnes, was a lawyer of importance in New York and Albany who had been superintendent of insurance for many years and was thus intimately acquainted with the politics of the state;[9] and his elder brother, Thurlow Weed Barnes, was a business man who had mixed in the politics of New York City. Unlike the other Platt councilors who have been so far mentioned, Barnes had received a college education. He graduated from Harvard in 1888 (eight years after Roosevelt) with high honors in history and political science. He was prominent in a class which contained men who later achieved distinction along several lines. Thus, he won a public speaking prize in competition with E. R. Thayer [10] and R. B. Mahany,[11] he was a member of a literary club which included Charles F. Adams, and he was editor-in-chief of the *Harvard Crimson.*[12] When he left college, it seemed as though he wanted to be like his grandfather, who "secured office for ever so many friends, but never any for himself, except a public printer's place which was profitable in revenue but very modest in rank." [13] He purchased with his patrimony in 1888 the *Albany Morning Express,* a Republican paper which had represented the

[8] *Albany Evening Journal,* Nov. 15, 1897. Weed died in 1882 when William Barnes was 16 years old.
[9] 1860 to 1870.
[10] Later dean of the Harvard Law School.
[11] Later congressman and editor of the *Buffalo Enquirer.*
[12] These facts have been taken from an article by W. T. A. (William T. Arnt, now secretary of the New York Citizens' Union) appearing in the *New York Evening Post,* Sept. 24, 1910.
[13] C. Schurz, *Reminiscences* (New York, 1907), II, 177.

64   BOSS PLATT AND HIS NEW YORK MACHINE

Conkling-Platt faction. Three years later he gained control
of the *Albany Evening Journal,* the paper which had been
founded by his grandfather over sixty years before. The
Journal had been the organ of the Anti-Conkling wing, so
the opposition press in Albany called Barnes the "Boy Editor
of the combined Republican press." [14] Under Barnes' direction, the *Albany Evening Journal,* which later absorbed the
Morning Express, became one of the most outspoken representatives of the Platt policies in the state.[15] In 1892 Platt
gained the gratitude of Barnes by recognizing his delegation
to the state convention and by making him a member of the
state committee, although he was only twenty-five years old.
When Barnes started his career in politics, the city and
county of Albany were Democratic strongholds. The "Boy
Editor" was commissioned to perform a difficult task, but
he was quick to learn the lessons that were taught at the
"Sunday school." William Barnes, the man who entered
politics "for the purpose of obtaining honest elections in
Albany and elevating politics," [16] must have seen in Platt
some of the qualities which he had admired in his grandfather.

Platt's chief of staff and Roosevelt's right hand man in
organization affairs in the late nineties was Benjamin B.
Odell, Jr., of Newburgh. Odell, like Barnes and Aldridge,
acquired his interest in politics from his father and early in
life be became an important local leader. His fealty to Platt
dated from the year 1884 when Platt helped to gratify his
longing to become a member of the state committee. Odell

14 H. N. Fuller, "Albany County" in *Official New York, from
Cleveland to Hughes,* edited by C. E. Fitch (New York, 1911), III,
56.
15 See below p. 100.
16 New York State Legislature, *Report of the Special Committee
of the Senate Appointed to Investigate the City and County of Albany,* 1912, p. 116.

was known as the "business man from Newburgh" because, after spending three years at Columbia University, he became interested in various business enterprises in his home city, chiefly of a public utility nature.[17] Newburgh was a small city situated on the Hudson river near the summer home of E. H. Harriman, the railroad magnate, and as a consequence of their propinquity, Odell and Harriman became friends.[18] Because of his driving power and his business training, Odell was a respected member of Platt's Sunday councils and a valuable counsellor to Roosevelt. As Platt grew old and feeble, and Roosevelt became more interested in national politics, more and more important matters were delegated to Odell.

So far, several types of regional leaders in the Republican organization up-state have been discussed. A description of some of the other local "officers" would be more or less of a repetition. However, some of the salient features of the training of the more important "garrison commanders" may well be mentioned. In 1889 one of Platt's most promising young men was J. Sloat Fassett, of Elmira. Like Barnes, Fassett had graduated from college with high honors, he was a good speaker,[19] he was the editor and proprietor of an important party organ,[20] and he had to contend with a strong local Democratic opposition.[1] In the state Senate, in the party conventions and upon the platform, Fassett was a prominent figure in the early nineties. The representative from Buffalo in Platt's political conferences was John R. Hazel, a lawyer by profession, who was bound to be influential because of the size of his domain. Shortly after Hazel

[17] New York Tribune, Sept. 9, 1900.
[18] World's Work (1906), XI, 7342.
[19] Fitch, Encyclopedia.
[20] The Elmira Daily Advertiser from 1879 to 1896.
[1] David B. Hill's home was in Elmira.

became a United States district judge he administered the
oath of office to Roosevelt as president of the United States.
Judge Hazel's place in Erie county politics was taken by
William C. Warren, editor and publisher of the *Buffalo
Commercial.* In Syracuse, Francis Hendricks, a manufacturer of photographic supplies and a banker, who had seen
long service as a local administrator and a state legislator,
upheld the policies which were decided upon in the Sunday
councils.[2]   Roosevelt characterised Hendricks as "honest
and competent."[3]   The representative of the organization
in Lockport was Timothy E. Ellsworth, a lawyer, manufacturer, and banker; while in Canandaigua the Platt forces
were marshalled by "Uncle" John Raines, a lawyer and insurance agent.   Both Ellsworth and Raines were Civil War
veterans.   Theodore Roosevelt, in describing the "Platt machine" as he found it when he became governor, no doubt
had some of these men in mind:

   In the country districts especially, there were many places
where his machine included the majority of the best citizens, the leading and substantial citizens, among the inhabitants.   Some of his strongest and most efficient lieutenants
were disinterested men of high character.[4]

   The New York City "brethren" had an advantage over
their country brothers in that they could drop in at the
"Amen Corner" upon week days.   One brother who was
welcome at any time was Benjamin F. Tracy, a native of
Owego and Platt's boyhood friend.   Tracy was elected district attorney of Tioga County the year that Platt was leading the campaign glee club.   Following the Civil War in
which he had risen to the rank of brigadier general, Tracy
took up the practice of law in New York City and Brooklyn.

2 *Who's Who in America,* 1908–9, V, 864.
3 *Op. cit.,* p. 293.
4 *Ibid.,* p. 278.

He defended Henry Ward Beecher in the famous trial, and he served for nearly thirteen months upon the highest court in the state by the appointment of Governor Cornell. When Tracy became President Harrison's secretary of the navy in 1889, he left his law practice to a firm of which Platt's son was a member.[5] It is needless to say that the relations between Platt and Tracy were of the friendliest sort. However, the case of Chauncey M. Depew, who frequented the "Amen Corner" in the late nineties as an intimate of Platt, is not so apparent. Platt and Depew belonged to opposing factions of the Republican party for the greater part of their early careers, but there were "harmony dinners" in the nineties.[6] Depew was known for his legal connections with the Vanderbilts which started in 1866, and, as the railway system attached to that family expanded, Depew's interests and duties also increased. He was president of the New York Central Railroad from 1885 to 1898 when he was made chairman of the board of directors.[7] He was extremely useful in the party councils not only because of his wide business connections [8] but also because he furnished the passes which brought the local leaders from all over the state to the "Sunday school." [9] Another one of Platt's older friends in New York was Edward Lauterbach, attorney in important railway, telephone and maritime cases and a director of the Third Avenue Surface Railroad Company.[10] Lauterbach knew the intricacies of New York City politics. These men

[5] Tracy, Boardman & Platt.
[6] Platt, *op. cit.*, pp. 373, 493.
[7] Depew, *My Memories*, p. 227.
[8] In 1901 Depew was a director in 52 railroad companies, 9 financial institutions, 3 bridge companies, 2 coal companies, 2 terminal companies, the Equitable Life Assurance Co., the Western Union Telegraph Co., The Audit Company, *Directory of the Directors in the City of New York*, 1901.
[9] Statement of Mr. Depew to the writer on September 25, 1922.
[10] Leslie, *op. cit.*

were intimately connected with the economic and social life of the metropolis and their advice therefore carried weight in the party deliberations. Roosevelt, being a native of the city himself, had more chance to know the city "Brethren." He was friendly toward Depew but he was *persona non grata* with Tracy and Lauterbach.

Among Platt's "Young Men" in the great city, two stand out prominently, Timothy L. Woodruff and Lemuel E. Quigg. "Tim" Woodruff, the captain of the Kings County Republican organization, was a man of education [11] and wealth, and like Fassett, Depew and several other Platt councillors, he was in politics because he "liked the game." Woodruff began attending state conventions in 1885, he went to the National Convention of 1888, and in 1897 he appeared upon the state committee. As commissioner of parks in Brooklyn, he acquired great popularity among all classes in spite of his reputation as a member of the "silk stocking district." Because of his interests in grain elevators, manufacturing concerns, and financial institutions in Brooklyn, he was well known in business circles. Platt "recognized" Woodruff as the spokesman for Kings County and put him on the same ticket with Roosevelt. It can hardly be said that Lemuel E. Quigg occupied a position in New York analogous to that of Woodruff in Kings, but Quigg was nevertheless influential with Platt and Roosevelt. Quigg was a newspaper man but not a proprietor of a party organ like Barnes, Fassett, or Warren. From 1885 to 1895 he served as an editorial writer and special correspondent upon the *New York Tribune,* and he was then known as one of Whitelaw Reid's "Boys." In the congressional campaign in 1890 and the presidential campaign of 1892, he had written much of the "literature" of the Republican party.[12] When Platt

[11] A. B., Yale University, 1879.
[12] *New York Tribune,* Jan. 31, 1894.

helped Quigg secure a nomination to Congress, Quigg broke with his former employer and became the editor for a time of the *New York Press,* a Republican paper which was bought by some of Platt's friends.[13] Quigg attracted attention when he won an election to Congress and he was valuable to both Platt and Roosevelt as one of the party's publicity men.

All the members of Platt's "Sunday school," were "influential men." The influence of some depended upon their newspaper, their business, or their professional connections, while others were influential simply because of the size of the vote which they were in the habit of delivering. The sessions of Platt's select "Sunday school," were not always harmonious. There were personal and sectional conflicts which almost broke up some of the meetings. Thus, "Lou" Payn never liked Quigg,[14] and in 1899 Barnes complained to Platt about a "characteristically insolent and insufferable dispatch from Mr. Quigg." [15] The up-state managers in general thought that Quigg was too ardent in serving the interests of his New York constituents. There was a clearer case of the conflict of sectional interests in the "classes" which Platt held upon the liquor question. "Uncle" John Raines, from the heart of an agricultural section of the state, presented the case for high license and state-wide supervision of the liquor traffic. "Brother" Lauterbach realized that such a law would be unpopular with his constituents not only because of their beer-loving propensities but also because the revenue producing sections of the law discriminated against the city in favor of the rural districts. When Platt accepted the views of Raines upon this subject,

[13] New York "Press" investigation, *op. cit.,* pp. 22, 41.
[14] *Ibid.,* p. 454.
[15] *Barnes* v. *Roosevelt,* case on appeal, appellate division, 4th Department (New York Supreme Court), p. 1161. Letter of Barnes to Platt, July 14, 1899.

he had to mollify the chagrin of the metropolitan chieftain as well as he could.[16] Another difference of opinion developed whenever the question of canal improvement came up. Captains Fassett and Dunn, not coming from cities which were on the line of the canal, objected to enormous exped-·itures in the domains of Captains Hazel, Ellsworth, Aldridge, Hendricks, and Barnes. A similar conflict arose over the question of state control of the insane asylums. Under the old system of local control the lunatics were half fed and wretchedly cared for. Some of the up-state leaders objected to state control because it would mean added state taxation in the rural districts and lessened local patronage.[17] The general subject of patronage furnished an everlasting bone of contention for the "Sunday school scholars," and there was bitter strife over the nomination of Roosevelt for governor in 1898. In fact, as Platt's long experience and history shows, internal dissensions among the party managers was the great danger which his organization faced. One of Platt's main functions as a leader was the maintenance of harmony among the "Boys" at all hazards.

A testimonial as to Platt's success in teaching the "Sunday school" and in maintaining order has been given by a high authority. Mr. Elihu Root was not a member of the "Sunday school" as he was often associated with the reform elements of the party, but he knew where the Fifth Avenue Hotel was, and his professional work brought him in touch with some of the scholars. Mr. Root was counsel for the Havemeyers in the Sugar Trust investigation conducted by a committee of the state legislature in 1891,[18] and he was the attorney for the New York newspapers in the Senate inves-

16 Nation, March 18, 1897, LXIV, 194.
17 Statement of Mr. Depew to the writer on September 25, 1922.
18 New York State Legislature, Sen. Doc. No. 79, 1891 (Report of the legislative committe relating to trusts, especially the sugar trust).

SENATOR PLATT AT 49 BROADWAY

(Photograph by Van der Weyde)

tigation of the charges made by the *New York Press* against "Lou" Payn and State Senators Raines, Robertson and Coggeshall. Mr. Root also made some investigations on his own account of the Republican organization in New York County. Mr. Root's distinguished career adds prestige to the words that he uttered before the New York Constitutional Convention of 1915 in defense of the short ballot amendment:

Then Mr. Platt ruled the state; for nigh upon twenty years he ruled it. It was not the governor; it was not the legislature; it was not any elected officers; it was Mr. Platt. And the capitol was not here; it was at 49 Broadway; with Mr. Platt and his lieutenants. It makes no difference what name you give, whether you call it Fenton or Conkling or Cornell or Arthur or Platt, or by the names of the men now living. The ruler of the state during the greater part of the forty years of my acquaintance with the state government has not been any man authorized by the constitution or by the law; and, sir, there is throughout the length and breadth of this state a deep and sullen and long-continued resentment at being governed thus by men not of the people's choosing. The party leader is elected by no one, accountable to no one, bound by no oath of office, removable by no one.[1]

It must be remembered that his speech on the "invisible" government was delivered to prove a point. It would be hard to pick twenty years throughout which it could be said that Platt was a "ruler." He held undisputed sway over the Republican organization in the state of New York from about 1889 to 1901, the twelve-year period in which Roosevelt was making his mark in state affairs.[2] Even in the hey-

[1] Elihu Root, *Addresses on Government and Citizenship* (Cambridge, 1916), p. 202.
[2] In the following chapters it will be necessary to use some material which came out after 1901, but the bulk of the sources are from the period of the nineties.

day of his power during McKinley's presidency, Platt was not a "ruler" in any dictatorial sense. Some of his followers were more determined and forceful than he was. He directed their activity by reconciling their differences. Paradoxical as it may seem, he was a leader because he knew how to follow.

CHAPTER V

NOMINATING ROOSEVELT FOR PUBLIC OFFICE

The hierarchy of party committees was the central framework of the party machinery by means of which Platt "ruled the state." During his long political apprenticeship, Platt had acquired an accurate knowledge of the structure and the functions of these committees and in his "Sunday school" he imparted this learning to his under-officers. It is likely that one of the first lessons that he taught was the importance of the state committee in every branch of the party's work. At any rate, a large proportion of those whom Platt admitted into the inner circle were sufficiently convinced of the importance of this committee to become members of it themselves. Thus, in 1898, Odell, Payn, Barnes, Dunn, Hendricks, Aldridge and Hazel were state committeemen. An impartial observer of the governmental process in the state said, "The members of the state committee were far more powerful factors in determining what should be the policy of the state than any one in the public service of the state." [1] The organization of this committee should be understood before taking up the nominating process itself, as it had more to do with the nomination of Roosevelt for governor and vice-president than any other body.

The Republican state committee consisted of one member from each congressional district, elected by the delegates to the state convention residing in the congressional district

[1] H. E. Deming, "Political Organization in New York, 1882–1904," *New York Conference for Good City Government* (1905), p. 314.

which the state committeeman was to represent.[2] This meant that during Platt's "reign" there were thirty-four state committeemen, fourteen of whom came from New York and Brooklyn. Although the population of congressional district was required by law to be as nearly equal as possible, the party vote varied widely in the several districts. As a result, Committeeman Dunn represented about 30,000 Republican voters whereas several New York committeemen represented around 6,000 Republican voters.[3] The actual selection of the state committeemen was the result of a natural process similar to the process by which Platt was selected general leader. The committeeman was the one to whom the local party workers looked for advice, and usually he was also the man whom Platt "recognized" in the distribution of campaign funds, offices, and patronage.[4] The importance of a committeeman in determining the policy of the party depended upon his personality and the strength of the "organization" behind him. Whatever the policy adopted, it was the duty of each committeeman to carry it out in his particular district. The personnel of the committee varied little during the period of Platt's ascendency, thus showing the tendency among the local leaders to perpetuate themselves in power.[5]

Shortly after the state convention at which they were selected had adjourned, the state committeemen would assemble in the Fifth Avenue Hotel in New York for the purpose of organizing the state committee. Before the meeting Platt would be seen busily talking in the hotel corridors.[6] The

[2] *Ibid.*, and R. H. Fuller, *Government by the People* (New York, 1908), p. 191. Mr. Fuller was Governor Hughes' private secretary.
[3] According to the returns of the congressional elections of 1898.
[4] See below p. 219.
[5] In 1896, ten retired, an unusually large number. *New York Tribune,* Aug. 27, 1896.
[6] *New York Tribune,* May 8, 1898 and Sept. 6, 1900.

first officer selected was the chairman of the committee. In
1894 and 1896 this was Charles W. Hackett, of Utica. In
the latter year Hackett was especially indebted to Platt because he had been seated in the state convention in spite of
the fact that his rivals in Utica had defeated him at the primaries.[7] Long before this Platt had said, "My relations with
Chairman Hackett are of the most cordial nature."[8] Platt
realized that it was necessary for him to use his influence to
select a chairman with whom he could co-operate, because
the chairman often did most of the work of the committee.
In pronouncing his benediction upon "field-marshals who
were faithful," Platt mentions first the state chairmen.[9]
Odell, who succeeded Hackett in 1898, was especially valuable because he thoroughly systematized the work and introduced "business methods."[10] Before Odell became governor in 1901, he and Platt maintained the closest of relations in the management of the party.[11] Following the
election of a chairman, the committee proceeded to elect a
secretary, a treasurer, and a chief clerk. The last mentioned
position, which was held by Reuben L. Fox for many years,
was a salaried post of a highly confidential character. The
committee then proceeded to authorize the chairman to appoint two important committees. The first of these was the
advisory committee, which was made up of men who were
not members of the state committee but whose advice was
likely to be sought in party matters. During the nineties,
when Platt's congressional district was represented by
Colonel Dunn, Platt's official relation to the party was membership on this committee. Other members of the advisory
committee were Chauncey M. Depew, Edward Lauterbach

[7] *New York Tribune*, Aug. 26, 1896 and Sept. 2, 1896.
[8] *Ibid.*, Sept. 8, 1893.
[9] Platt, *op. cit.*, pp. 513, 257.
[10] *New York Tribune*, Sept. 9, 1900.
[11] Platt, *op. cit.*, p. 423.

and Frank Hiscock.[12] The second committee appointed was the so-called executive committee, made up of the eighteen members of the state committee who were regarded as the most active party workers. Odell was the chairman of this committee from 1894 to 1898 when he was succeeded by Barnes who held the office until it was abolished in 1906.[13] The powers of the state committee were often delegated to this smaller body.[14]

While the state committee might reorganize any county committee, the county committees were ordinarily supreme within their own spheres, exercising constantly a wide control over all the other local organizations. Each of Platt's field-marshals in charge of a local division occupied a position with reference to his county committee analogous to Platt's relation to the state committee. In Monroe and Onondaga Counties, State Committeemen Aldridge and Hendricks were members ex officio of their respective county committees.[15] In Albany County, the chairman of the county committee was a faithful and loyal lieutenant of State Committeeman Barnes.[16] This was the usual relation between the local boss or leader and the county chairman although in Chemung County, J. Sloat Fassett, was chairman of the county committee himself for a number of years.[17] No successful field-marshal let his county chairman get out of hand.

The county committees were selected in various ways; in some counties, by assembly districts,[18] in others, by wards

[12] New York Tribune, Sept. 1, 1896.
[13] Barnes v. Roosevelt, loc. cit., testimony of April 30, 1915.
[14] New York Tribune, June 11, 1896.
[15] Rules and Regulations of the Republican Party in the County of Onondaga, 1898; Ibid., in the County of Monroe.
[16] Official New York, III, 62–63.
[17] The Constitution of the Republican Organization of the County of Chemung, addenda, 1901.
[18] Rules and Regulations for the counties of New York, Kings, Cayuga, Onondaga and Monroe.

and towns,[19] or by election precinct districts. The delegates were apportioned in accordance with the number of
Republican votes cast at the last preceding gubernatorial
election in the particular unit used as a basis of representation. Sometimes the selection was made by the party voters
directly in their assembly district, ward, township, or election
district associations. This method was made compulsory in
counties containing cities of the first class by the primary
law of 1898.[20] However, in some of the less populous counties an indirect method was used. The party voters selected
ward and town committeemen who in turn selected one of
their number to serve as a delegate to the county committee.
The actual selection of the county committee, like that of the
state committee, depended upon the dominant clique or boss
and the ability of the ward, town, assembly district, or election district leader to hold his association together.

The other committees of the Republican party in the state
were closely related to the county committee. In populous
urban counties like New York, Kings, Erie, Monroe, and
Albany, the county committee was supreme over and in parts
identical with the judicial, the congressional, the senatorial,
the assembly, and the city committees. Thus, in Monroe
County, the congressional committee was identical with the
general county committee; the city committee was made up
of the general committee, representing the several wards in
the city of Rochester; the two senatorial committees consisted respectively of the members of the general committee
representing the several wards and towns in the respective
senatorial districts of the county; and the four assembly district committees were made up in a similar manner of the
general committeemen from the respective assembly dis-

19 Chemung County.
20 Law 1898, ch. 179, Sec. 9, *Committees and Rules and Regulations
of Parties.*

tricts.[2]   This made nine "different," party committees which
looked to State Committeeman Aldridge for "advice." The
party committees in judicial, congressional, and senatorial
districts which were made up of two or more counties were
usually composed of the general or central committees from
those counties.[3]   By integrating the various committees in
this complicated manner the local leaders were able to con-
solidate and perpetuate their power.

The foundation of all these local committees was the election district or voting precinct leader.   If the precinct captains, even to a slight extent, failed to perform their duties
in relation to the organization of the voters, there was
trouble all along the line of the committee hierarchy.[4]   The
precinct captains in establishing personal and face-to-face
contacts with the voters were performing the foundation
work of the party structure.   There were around 4,600 precinct captains in Platt's political army during the late nineties.[5]   That Platt did not neglect these lesser workers is indicated by the following testimonial from a Republican
paper :

Unlike another diplomatic leader, the late Samuel J. Tilden, Mr. Platt wrote letters.   Hundreds of men in this state
of local importance but unknown beyond their homes have
felt the influence of his master mind expressed in letters
of suggestion and advice that accomplished in the bulk great
things.   There was a subtle flattery in the deferential communication of a powerful leader with the modest local politician in the back town.   Mr. Platt seldom humiliated.   He

[2] *Rules and Regulations of the Republican Party in Monroe County*, 1898.
[3] *Constitution of the Republican Organization in Rensselaer County*, 1901.
[4] See C. A. Beard, *American Government and Politics* (New
York, 1910), pp. 665–67 ; C. E. Merriam, *The American Party System*
(New York, 1922), pp. 68–70.
[5] *Legislative Manual for 1898*.

usually stimulated and developed what was in the man he addressed and his advice was usually taken.[6]

The political conditions in New York County were so peculiar that the organization of the Republican party there deserves special consideration. As Platt himself wrote: "The Democratic majority in New York City is so large, so stolid, made up of elements so difficult to reach and convince, that an occasional victory on the part of Republican and other forces has been found to accomplish little." [7] Roosevelt had also discovered how little the organization could accomplish in the city. The Republican organization in the city never gained a grip upon the enormous municipal patronage and was therefore compelled to look to those who controlled the state and national patronage for political favors. This meant that the president of the New York County Committee had to look to Platt for advice more often than some of the other county leaders and was therefore looked upon as Platt's deputy rather than as a leader in his own right.[8] Although the presidents of this committee in the early nineties were Platt's friends," the election of Edward Lauterbach as president in 1894 gave Platt a more absolute control over the New York County organization than he had exercised before.[9] Nevertheless, it was said that only after a "ruthless and brutal" exercise of power was the committee induced to re-elect Lauterbach in 1896.[10] Platt's absolute control over the Republican organization in the city was continued and strengthened under Lemuel E. Quigg who succeeded Lauterbach as president of the county committee in

[6] *Buffalo Evening News*, March 7, 1910.
[7] Platt, *op. cit.*, pp. 364–65.
[8] Fuller, *op. cit.*, pp. 207–8.
[9] Platt, *op. cit.*, pp. 514, 295.
[10] *New York Tribune*, Jan. 18, 1896: "A howling burlesque, the utter coarseness and brutal horseplay of which had not a single redeeming feature."

1897.[11]   Some of the assembly district leaders who were most active in the affairs of the executive committee of the county committee were state committeemen and federal or state office holders indebted to Platt.[12]   In spite of Platt's claims regarding a stronger and larger Republican organization in the city during the years from 1896 to 1900, there was always a strong anti-machine or anti-Platt minority which gave him considerable trouble, especially in municipal elections.   Although the number of officers elected locally in New York City was never a considerable item in Platt's calculations, the delegates to the state conventions from the thirty-five assembly districts of the city constituted a factor which could not well be neglected, and their selection was accordingly given proper attention.

Since the committee hierarchy was the permanent part of the party structure, Platt watched its make-up with considerable care.   Local factional fights, which usually took the form of a struggle for the control of the county committee, were matters of great interest to him.   His counsel was given freely to committeemen, high and low, and he was always ready to lend a listening ear to their troubles.   His central control over nominations and elections depended upon a strong flexible network of committees.

PRIMARIES

Theoretically the party committees were chosen in accordance with the principles of representative democracy.   The members of the Republican party, organized in assembly district, ward, town or precinct associations, came together at the primary polling places and selected the committeemen who would represent them in party matters.   In actual practice, however, the committeemen exercised sweeping control

11 Platt, *op. cit.*, p. 360.
12 *New York Tribune*, June 15, 1898.
5 *Ibid.*, p. 1887.

over the very associations which nominally chose them. Prior to the passage of the primary law of 1898 which affected only the largest cities in the state, the county committees in every part of the state regulated the qualifications and tests of party membership in town, ward or assembly district associations. The rules and regulations for the conduct of the party primaries were also under their control.[13] Thus, the first step in the nominating process, the setting of a time and place for the holding of a primary to elect delegates to the various nominating conventions, was under the control of the local committee.[14]

Ordinarily there were few objections raised against the way in which the local committeemen perpetuated their power. The indifference of the great body of party voters gave the committeemen a free hand. However, in 1897, John E. Milholland, one of the Anti-Platt leaders, said regarding the conduct of the New York primaries:

The vicious practices no longer possible at the polls are now employed in the caucus and in the nominating convention with an energy unparalleled in the past, although everything undertaken no matter how villainous, is carried on in a manner entirely in keeping with modern methods. The party caucus is today the danger point in American politics. The fountain head of power, it has become the fountain head of corruption.[15]

Mr. Milholland was most familiar with the situation in New York City and he went on to mention party enrollments onehalf fraudulent and caucuses controlled by the worst ele-

[13] Deming, loc. cit., p. 309.

[14] The Law of 1887, chap. 265, applicable to counties containing a town or city of over 200,000, regulated the primaries to a very limited extent and in part recognized the rule making power of the party. See C. E. Merriam, Primary Elections (Chicago, 1908), pp. 22–23.

[15] "The Danger Point in American Politics," Nor. Amer. Rev., CLVIX (January, 1897), 93.

ments of the party which recognized no rule other than that of the mob. A different view was expressed a year later by William Barnes, who said: "I am not one of those who believe that primary elections in the state of New York are largely fraudulent, and from my experience I know that in a very large percentage of instances there are not." [16] This comment upon the primary system of the nineties by one of the members of the organization emphasizes the fact that when things were well in the hands of the leaders there was no need to employ extreme methods to control the primaries. The committeemen simply made up the party rolls from among those who were their supporters. On the other hand, when there was a factional quarrel or when the organization was fighting for its existence, the methods employed were more open to criticism. One instance in point was the "open flagrant proceedings at the Onondaga town caucus on August 14, 1894" where a "herd of Italians, southern negroes and other men" employed by a city contractor were "marched to the polling place" and were beaten off only "after a fierce struggle" in which "the stalwart young Onondaga farmers forced the mob back again and barred the door with an old plow and a crow bar." [17] Another case was described by S. E. North, county judge of Genesee County, before the County Convention at Batavia in August, 1896, in the following words: "I openly declare in the presence of this assemblage that the town caucus of Saturday, August 8, as carried or sought to be carried by the use of money and by indiscriminate treating, was disgraceful and scandalous in the last degree." [18]

The local committee which did not care to use bribery or

[16] *Nat. Conf. on Practical Reform of Primary Elections* (1898), p. 94.
[17] *Syracuse Journal*, July 21, 1896.
[18] *New York Tribune*, March 8, 1898.

violence to control the party primaries, might still master the situation by a skillful use of its power over the procedure of the primaries. The "snap caucus," called by the committee long before the customary time, might take the opposition unawares. Then, too, the committee might take advantage of its power over the temporary organization of the caucus. How this could be done is illustrated by an account of a primary in a town in Tioga County, Platt's home district, which was called to select delegates to the county convention, where delegates to the state convention were to be chosen. According to custom the meeting was opened by a member of the district committee. The rest of the meeting has been described as follows:

This loyal son of the machine nominated R. D. Van Duzer for temporary chairman, immediately upon calling the meeting to order, and proceeded to declare him elected without taking time for the trivial formality of calling for a vote, although other nominations were offered. Mr. Van Duzer, however, was troubled with no qualms as to the method of his election, but took the chair with alacrity and called for nominations for delegates. Senator Johnson then presented the names of the machine candidates, and J. W. Morgan nominated Anti-Platt men. W. L. Watrous, of the Anti-Machine men, demanded a ballot. The chairman not only refused this, but went on to make mincemeat of parliamentary law and common decency by ignoring the Anti-Machine nominees altogether and calling for a vote of acclamation on the first three candidates, those proposed by Senator Johnson. A viva voce vote was taken, and although the motion to elect was opposed by a majority of three to one, the chairman declared the Platt delegates duly elected.

After this ruling, a Platt man at once moved to adjourn. This motion also was opposed by the greater part of the house, but the chairman promptly declared it carried, with the help of Senator Johnson, and brought the meeting to a close 90 seconds after it had been called to order.[19]

[19] *New York Tribune,* July 29, 1896. See also issue of Mar. 8, 1898.

Although the rural districts were not free from complaints about the abuses of the old time open caucus system, the city of New York was the center of the primary reform agitation. One of the disputed points in the city organization was the question of party membership. In 1888, one observer remarked that "membership in the Republican organizations was given or denied capriciously, and that the nominal qualifications became in practice 'acceptability to the assembly leader.' " [20]   In 1893, in the face of a great Republican victory throughout the state, Tammany rolled up a larger vote than ever in New York City. In the light of such treachery and inefficiency, Platt "fully realized the imperative necessity of a reorganization." [1] Mr. Milholland, backed by Whitelaw Reid, started one of the attempts at reform, and he received Platt's support at first. However, another movement, inaugurated by the "heavy respectables" in the party under the leadership of Cornelius N. Bliss and a Committee of Thirty, received the favor of the state committee. According to Bliss, Platt "was only prevented from breaking up the party in this county by the shrewder members of the state committee." [2] In the reorganization which followed, the Committee of Thirty refused to eliminate the old leaders and thereby prepared the way for its own "funeral" and the selection of Lauterbach as the head of the city organization. That conditions were not materially changed was indicated by the circumstances surrounding Lauterbach's re-election to the presidency of the county committee in 1896. The election was held in the middle of January in spite of the protests that it be postponed until after the report of a Committee of Twenty-five under the

[20] A. C. Bernheim, "Political Organizations and Their Nominations in New York City," Pol. Sci. Quart., III, 106.
[1] Platt, op. cit., p. 254.
[2] Statement in New York Tribune, Jan. 28, 1896.

chairmanship of Bliss which was investigating the alleged enrollment frauds.[3] According to the report of this committee, which came out after the election, the Republican enrollment in New York City was from fifteen to forty-five per cent bogus and the names of some Tammany Hall leaders had been placed upon the rolls. Some well known Republicans declared that their names had been stricken off the rolls for no defensible reason.[4] Dr. Parkhurst said: "There is a brazen insolence and a colossal dare-deviltry about these enrollment frauds which is thrilling."[5] Platt placed the responsibility for this enrollment upon the Committee of Thirty,[6] but Lauterbach later defended it partly on the ground that the organization based upon it achieved a great victory that year.[7] The evidence seems to indicate that the delegates to the committee meeting which gave Platt's "friends" the control of the city organization were elected not by primary meetings of the party voters, but by small select clubs, "close corporations" composed largely of "hand picked machine men."[8] Roosevelt was not at this time a prominent champion of primary reform.

The Republican legislature of 1898 seemingly recognized the popular demand for "pure" primaries by passing an elaborate primary law. The skeptics said in advance that the "organizations" knew how they could "beat" the law.[9] Of interest in this connection was the fact that the law was compulsory only in cities having a population of fifty thousand

[3] *New York Tribune*, Jan. 17, 1896. For the report see issues of Jan. 18 and 31, 1896. E. Root, J. H. Choate, Charles S. Smith and Horace Porter were members of this committee.
[4] *National Conference on Primary Elections*, p. 124.
[5] *New York Herald*, Jan. 27, 1896.
[6] *Ibid.*
[7] *National Conference on Primary Elections*, p. 115.
[8] Dallinger, *op. cit.*, p. 109.
[9] *Nation*, March 31, 1898, LXVI, 236.

or more.[10] It was merely optional in cities or villages containing a population between five and fifty thousand,[11] and it did not apply to the rural districts at all. In the debate over the final passage of the bill, Senator Tibbits, of Rensselaer County, said on this point:

> I heartily agree with Senator Ellsworth in his demand for reform of the rural primaries, and I hope the bill be amended so as to give every voter in the state, rural or city, a chance to express his will at the primaries, and to have his vote honestly counted. The same reasons exist for granting rural voters primary reform as there are for granting it to city voters. There is the same fraud, the same bribery, at rural primaries as at city primaries.[12]

Where the law applied, it prescribed the qualifications entitling one to participate in a primary down to the minutest details and its definition of party membership was liberal enough to include all Republican factions.[13] Party rules regarding party membership were supplanted, and the voter was given an opportunity to enroll as a member of one of the statutory parties when he registered to vote. In fact, the entire primary process was placed under the control of the regular election officials. It was supposed that this law would greatly increase the participation of the voters in the primaries. Under the old system primary elections had been held in parts of New York in which less than eight per cent of the Republican voters took part.[14] The new law did not change conditions materially. In 1903, in an assembly district which gave a majority to the mayoralty candidate supported by the Republican party, only nine per cent of the

[10] New York, Buffalo, Rochester, Syracuse, Albany and Troy.

[11] It could be adopted by a rule passed by the county committee or by a referendum vote initiated by the county committee or by a petition signed by one-tenth of the voters.

[12] *New York Tribune*, March 24, 1898.

[13] Fuller, *op. cit.*, p. 44.

[14] Bernheim, *op. cit.*, p. 114.

Republican voters took part in the primary. In the "fashionable Brown-stone district" of New York City, only thirteen per cent of the Republicans availed themselves of the privilege of participating in the primary election.[15] As it was remarked in the *New York Tribune* after the first primary under the new law: "The reformers were allowed to enroll if they wanted to; the machine men were made to."[16] The first county committee selected in accordance with this law re-elected Lemuel E. Quigg as its president.[17]

One of the reasons for the small primary vote in the Republican primaries in New York City was the growth of the non-partisan movement in municipal elections. This movement was given slight encouragement in the law of 1898 which provided for a cumbrous, expensive and complicated method of making nominations to municipal office, unless such nominations were made by organizations that cast at least 10,000 ballots for governor at the last preceding gubernatorial election.[18] In this indirect fashion the law discriminated in favor of the regular Republican and Democrat organizations. The Citizens' Union of New York City did not take part in state elections and consequently did not fulfill the definition of a "political party" as laid down by the law.

The new law not only discouraged independent movements outside of the two regular parties, but it also tended to lessen the danger of factionalism within the party. According to some of Platt's field marshals, the avowed purpose of

[15] H. E. Deming and L. W. Trowbridge, "How the Primary Law Works in New York City," *Proc. of N. Y. Conf. for Good City Govt.* (1905), p. 325.

[16] June 9, 1898.

[17] *Ibid.*, June 15, 1898.

[18] H. E. Deming, "Municipal Nomination Reform," *Annals of the Amer. Acad.*, XXV, 203.

the law was to produce "harmony" in the Republican party [19] and to eliminate the "malcontents" who "posed somewhat successfully as the representatives of the people" and refused to make their contest at the "recognized" time and place on account of alleged primary frauds.[20] Before the law was passed, it had been customary for the party committees to present the party voters with a prearranged list of delegates to vote for at the primary meeting. After the law was passed, the city committees had more power than ever over the making up of "the slate." According to a district committeeman from Buffalo, the law "had a distinctly bad effect in putting obstacles in the way of independent movements within the parties and in discouraging contests."[1] Inasmuch as the party committees and the delegates to the various conventions were all elected upon the same ticket, a man who wanted to make a contest for any one nomination had to obtain the names of the "regular" candidates for the other places on the ticket or put up an entire ticket of his own. Since it was difficult for an individual to follow either of these courses of action, the usual result was that the leaders were left in almost absolute control of the whole ticket. It is significant to note that there were no contests to report at the first state convention which was held after the new law went into effect. "Harmony" reigned supreme.

Platt's contact with the primary elections which continued his committeemen and his delegates in power in the nineties was not very direct. Roosevelt's connection with the primaries in the late nineties was even more indirect. As long as

[19] Timothy L. Woodruff at the hearing on the bill, cited in Senator Tibbits' speech, *New York Tribune,* March 24, 1898.
[20] William Barnes, in the *National Conference for Practical Reform of Primary Elections,* p. 95.
[1] H. A. Bull, "The New York Primary Law," *Mich. Pol. Sci. Asso.* (1905), p. 99.

the structure of the committee hierarchy was unimpaired, both men could watch the primary elections with an air of complacency. The local committees saw that the loyal Republicans were enrolled, that they were furnished with a list of loyal candidates and that they were gotten out to vote for that list upon primary day. A primary election, like a regular election, had many legitimate expenses. Notices and ballots had to be printed; halls had to be hired; and the committee had much clerical work to perform. Platt, through his relations with the state committee, could give financial help to local committees that were confronted with trouble in the primaries.[2]

CONVENTIONS

The precinct captains who were successful in getting out the primary vote looked for their reward to the various committees which supervised the party conventions. The county convention was the most important local assemblage because it formally ratified the decisions and adjustments made by the county committee. The local leader, whose advice was accepted by the county committee, had under his control practically all the important local nominations. This was especially true of the more populous counties of the state where the Republican leader looked forward to the following conventions: city conventions to nominate city officers, county conventions to nominate county officers, assembly district conventions to nominate state assemblymen and to elect delegates to state conventions, senatorial district conventions to nominate state senators, and congressional district conventions to nominate candidates for Congress and to elect delegates to Republican national conventions.[3]

[2] For examples of such interference see *New York Tribune,* Mar. 8, 1898, editorial entitled "Rural Politics."

[3] "The power of the political 'boss' depends upon his ability to

The various party committees exercised autocratic and wide sweeping powers over the conventions held within their respective jurisdictions. The committee which issued a call for a convention also made up the temporary roll of that convention and appointed the temporary officers. Wherever the primaries were close and hotly contested, the faction which had control of the party committee could employ this power to seat delegates arbitrarily in its own behalf. If this device was not sufficient to insure a tractable convention, the methods described in the following account of a New York assembly district convention might be used:

The man who was designated by the county committee to call that convention to order stood upon a narrow platform, with a police captain directly in front of him, called for nominations for temporary chairman, refused every demand for a call of the roll, would not permit a standing vote, but simply called for viva voce vote on the nominations made, and declared that one elected who was favored by the minority of that convention, claiming to base his declaration on his perception of volume of sound. The one so declared elected chairman was immediately inducted into office, the police captain standing in front protecting him in the retention of his place upon the platform, and that man in presiding over that convention never once allowed a call of the roll or a standing vote, but decided everything, even to his declaring the close of the convention, on his perception of volume of sound—recognized no appeal or any objection or protest whatsoever. The real majority of that convention, retaining their places on the floor, were obliged to organize the convention and conduct the proceedings without a platform for the real chairman to occupy.[4]

control the primaries and through that control to fill the offices with men of his own choosing who will be subservient to him." Fuller, *op. cit.*, p. 34. For an example of the great number of conventions within a single county, see *Rules and Regulations of the Republican Party of Monroe County.*

[4] *National Conference on Primary Elections*, p. 126.

Even if a majority of the delegates did organize the convention in their own way, the minority factional leader who had the favor of Platt and the state organization was not without his resources.   He could hold a "rump" convention and appeal to the state committee to recognize the candidates nominated by his convention as "regular." [5]   In matters of party regularity, the state committee usually decided in favor of the party management and its decisions were not generally subject to judicial review.   In fact, the highest court in the state said: "We think that in cases where questions of procedure in conventions or the regularity of committees are involved, which are not regulated by law, but by party usages and custom, the officer called upon to determine such a question should follow the decision of the regularly constituted authorities of the party." [6]   This opinion appeared in the decision of a case in which the Republican secretary of state had agreed with the Republican state committee that a rump congressional convention organized in Westchester County by one of Platt's lieutenants was "regular" and that its nominee was entitled to a place upon the party's ticket to the exclusion of the nominee selected by the anti-Platt faction. [7] As in the primaries, so in the conventions, the party rules and customs helped to conserve the power of the leaders. [8]

The New York Primary Election Law of 1898 endeavored to eliminate the more flagrant abuses of the old convention

[5] *New York Tribune*, Dec. 4, 1897.
[6] *In the matter of Fairchild*, 151 New York, 359.
[7] *New York Tribune*, December 2, 1897.
[8] F. J. Goodnow, *Politics and Administration* (New York, 1900), p. 214, cites another case that arose in Clinton County (48 New York Supp. 407).   While the regular chairman of the county committee was away, a person belonging to the minority faction called the convention to order, and declared the election of a chairman and clerk who was favorable to his faction.   The clerk was directed viva voce to cast a vote for the delegates of the same faction, and the convention was adjourned.   The chairman of the county com-

system that were prevalent in the larger cities of the state. The law contained elaborate provisions regarding the method of apportioning delegates, the election of temporary officers, and the decision of questions as to contested seats. It required that the temporary chairman should be chosen by a roll call and that he bind himself by oath to the faithful performance of his duties. The purpose of this provision was to eliminate such arbitrary proceedings as the one described above. However, the law left many important matters still within the control of the party leaders. The chairman of the committee which issued the call for the convention still had charge of the temporary roll, the temporary chairman still appointed the committee on contested seats, and the convention itself was left as the final authority on questions regarding the seating of delegates. Only certain minor matters could be appealed to the courts.[9] Like other parts of the law, the provisions regulating convention procedure did not apply to the rural districts where some of the old buses were still prevalent.

Platt was interested in the local conventions which were held in various parts of the state inasmuch as he realized that his success depended upon the success of his field-marshals in controlling these conventions, but his main interest was in the state convention which nominated state officers. According to William Barnes, the party leader in the state was the man who, "at the time when state conventions were held, seemed to be the most active operating force in each convention." [10]

mittee then called the committee to order, and it was held by the court that those who remanied in the room constituted the regular convention, and its nominees were given a place upon the party's ticket, while those elected by the other faction were not.

[9] New York Election Law, 1898, chap. 179, sec. 10 and sec. 11.

[10] *Barnes* v. *Roosevelt,* p. 1885. Mr. Barnes' testimony of May 13, 1915.

The call for the state convention was sent out by the state committee several weeks in advance. In the call, the time and places for holding the convention and the number of delegates to which each assembly district was entitled were announced. The conventions for nominating the candidates for the governorship and the other state offices usually met in September in some out of the way town where the danger of a popular uprising stampeding the convention was slight. During the nineties, the state committee seemed to have a special liking for Saratoga Springs, the original convention town of the Republican party in the state.[11] The total number of delegates was usually around seven or eight hundred which meant that on the average there was a delegate to every thousand Republican voters in the state. The delegates were apportioned according to the Republican vote at the last gubernatorial convention, so the convention in form was a representative body. Among the delegates themselves were to be found the most active party workers in the state.

The nomination of a candidate for governor was the most important task performed by the state convention, a task which engaged Platt's attention long before the convention actually met. Thus, Platt started to work for the nomination of Levi P. Morton a year before the State Convention of 1894.[12] In 1900, the nomination of Benjamin B. Odell for governor was part of Platt's program at least seven and one-half months before the convention met,[13] while in 1898 it seems that Platt reached a decision upon Roosevelt's nomination several months before the convention was called to order.[14] In the other state conventions in which Platt was the

[11] G. S. P. Kleeberg, op. cit., p. 18.
[12] New York Sun, Sept. 17, 1894.
[13] New York newspapers, Jan. 15, 1900. The convention met on Sept. 5, 1900.
[14] Albany Evening Journal, September 2, 1898. The convention met on September 28.

"most active operating force," he was unable to reach an early decision regarding he gubernatorial candidate. In 1891, Platt had "sounded out" Andrew D. White regarding the governorship several weeks before the convention met,[15] but when the delegates assembled, it was apparent that J. Sloat Fassett was his choice.[16]   Platt's indecision was even greater in 1896 partly because his own name had been pressed for the nomination. He characterized this convention as "one of the most rousing free-for-all state conventions the party had had since war days."[17]   In this exceptional gathering, he did not decide to support Frank S. Black's candidacy until after the delegates had been in actual session for three days. Since Platt's preliminary choices as announced in the newspapers became the actual choices of the conventions, except in the cases noted, it is apparent that in considering the procedure of state conventions it is important to discuss how "the old man" made up his mind or how circumstances made up his mind for him.

According to the terminology of the professional politicians, the chief qualification of a gubernatorial candidate should be "availability." In the "Sunday school classes" which Platt held in the nineties, this term was the subject of much exigesis. No doubt the first lesson that "Deacon" Platt taught was that "available" meant "available under the circumstances." In 1891 and 1898 this lesson was of great importance. In the other three gubernatorial years, the Republicans were fairly sure of victory. It has already been pointed out that Democratic dissentions made the way easy for Platt and his lieutenants in 1894 and 1896. In 1900 the issues and personalities of the presidential campaign were

[15] *Autobiography of Andrew Dickson White* (New York, 1905), I, 230.
[16] *New York Tribune*, September 7, 1891.
[17] Platt, *op. cit.*, p. 329.

enough like those of 1896 to cause the Republican state leaders to dismiss their misgivings regarding success. It was because 1891 and 1898 were "off-years" that Platt considered men like Andrew D. White and Theodore Roosevelt for the gubernatorial nomination. On the other hand, whatever the circumstances were, certain minimum requirements were laid down. The candidate must have had some experience in public life; he should know enough about the party system to appreciate the function of the "organization ;" and he must have some distinguishing characteristics which would commend him to the electorate. Thus, Fassett had a distinguished record as leader of the state Senate [18] and as national committeeman and collector for the port of New York he had become acquainted with the party machinery whereas Andrew D. White did not "know the boys who did the work." [19] These facts taken together with Fassett's eloquence made him "available" in 1891. Levi P. Morton, before his nomination for governor in 1894, had been a member of Congress, minister to France and vice-president of the United States. Morton was known to the party workers because he had once been a campaign fund collector [20] and among business circles he was known as a successful financier. Frank S. Black, as a member of Congress from "Lou" Payn's district, was close enough to the organization to eradicate the fears of the boys,[1] and while not widely known in 1896 prior to his nomination, he had had some notoriety as a prosecutor of election frauds. Theodore Roosevelt, with his record as state assemblyman, United States civil service commissioner, New York police commis-

[18] New York Tribune, Sept. 10, 1891.
[19] White, op. cit., p. 234. Comments of Professor Jenks of Cornell.
[20] Harper's Weekly, Sept. 15, 1894, XXXVIII, 867.
[1] Platt, op. cit., p. 330.

sioner, assistant secretary of the navy, and Spanish-American War veteran, easily fulfilled the requirements regarding experience in public office and prominence before the public eye. The question remained as to his attitude toward the organization and this he answered by an interview stating that he would not make war on the organization and that he would "consult" Platt.[2] Besides, it was remembered that Roosevelt had always been "regular." In 1900, no one questioned Odell's loyalty to the "organization" or his knowledge about public office. He was commended to the voters as a "successful business man" and a former member of Congress.

It was also important that the qualities enumerated above were possessed by the candidate in moderation. When Platt's name was being considered by the inner council for the gubernatorial nomination, 1896, John Raines had the boldness and frankness to say that "the ticket wouldn't carry his weight."[3] Platt's account of this same meeting ran to the effect that he refused to have his name considered because he feared that his old time Half-Breed enemies would "knife" him in the back.[4] He remembered the fate of Miller in 1888 and that of Hill in 1894, and he had no desire to be "scalped" in that fashion. Another man talked of at this conference was George W. Aldridge, the man who had served the organization well as the dispenser of the canal patronage, but like Platt he was regarded as weak because of his closeness to the "organization." In like manner, Frank S. Black, who was "available" in 1896, was not "available" two years later because his administration had been tinged with partisanship. Since the elimination of Black and the selection of Roosevelt in 1898 illustrate many phases

[2] *New York Herald*, Sept. 18, 1898.
[3] Alexander, *Four Famous New Yorkers*, p. 257.
[4] Platt, *op. cit.*, pp. 329–30.

"WE HAVE DISCOVERED IN MR. ROOSEVELT THE
MISSING LINK."—Joseph H. Choate
(Cartoon by C. G. Bush, *New York World*, Oct. 7, 1898)

of the pre-convention procedure, this event has been selected for special consideration.

"Circumstances" made Theodore Roosevelt an "available" candidate for the Republican nomination for governor in 1898. Platt expressed his views as follows: "I thought at the best we would have a hard time to elect a Republican governor in 1898. Already the canal appropriations were giving us trouble; the frictions between Governor Black and some of the state leaders were a source of anxiety."[5] One of the "frictions" here referred to was touched upon by Quigg in a letter to Roosevelt in which he said: "The Governor's taunt that I am opposed to him because I was 'interested' in legislation which he prevented is dishonest talk."[6] The situation was still further complicated by what Platt called the "ultra-partisan acts of the Blank administration."[7] Although Platt as the general manager of the Republican party in the state had greatly profited by some of these acts, he could not help but noting that the newspapers all over the state, with the exception of a few party organs, had denounced in vehement terms the reappointment of "Lou" Payn as superintendent of insurance.[8] Platt was also having trouble in New York City. Many New York papers accused him of being responsible for the sweeping Tammany victory

[5] *Op. cit.*, p. 364.

[6] *Barnes v. Roosevelt*, p. 2354. Letter dated Sept. 10, 1898.

[7] " 'Starchless' civil service, which put practically every Democratic office-holder out and installed a Republican organization man in his job; the appointment of Louis F. Payn as superintendent of insurance, and the other ultra-partisan acts of the Black administration, while they popularized it with the organization workers, aroused rebellion among the Independents. Black, offering no apologies for running a simon-pure party régime, planned a renomination and secretly nursed a hope that he would land the presidency."—Platt, *op. cit.*, p. 367.

[8] *New York Herald*, Jan. 16, 1897; *Utica Press*, Feb. 3, 1897 (unfavorable). For favorable comment see *Binghamton Republican*, Feb. 4, 1897.

in the first election for the control of Greater New York held the year before. The anti-machine Republicans in the city were loud in calling for Platt's "scalp." [9] Besides, the Republicans had lost the state-wide election of 1897 and had barely retained control over the state legislature. Alton B. Parker, one of Hill's old lieutenants, had been elected chief justice of the Court of Appeals by a plurality of 60,000 over his Republican opponent. All of these events caused Platt "to do a heap of thinking" in 1898. The result of his meditation plus pressure from some of his lieutenants was a decision to "turn down" Black for Roosevelt. The abandonment of a loyal party man like Black for a man of Roosevelt's reputation was an act which required a good deal of flexibility upon the part of Platt.

Roosevelt has stated that it was Quigg who called upon him in August, 1898, at Montauk Point to "sound" him about the governorship.[10] Platt had no fondness for Roosevelt; he had clashed with Roosevelt when the latter was civil service commissioner and he had opposed Roosevelt's policies as police commissioner.[11] However, Platt needed the independent vote in 1898 and Roosevelt was the man most likely to attract that vote. Already several independent movements had begun to use Roosevelt's name in connection with the gubernatorial campaign.[12] Roosevelt did not discourage these movements at first. Quigg was quite well known to Roosevelt personally and after his visit he carried word to Platt that Roosevelt would not

[9] New York World, Nov. 3, 1897; New York Herald, Nov. 4, 1897; New York Tribune, Nov. 4, 1897; IUtica Press, Nov. 3, 1897.

[10] Op. cit., p. 270.

[11] H. Hagedorn, The Boy's Life of Theodore Roosevelt (New York, 1918), p. 176, Letter of Roosevelt written in June, 1896.

[12] J. B. Bishop, Theodore Roosevelt and His Time (New York, 1920), I, 110.

"make war" upon the organization.[13] Quigg afterwards wrote, "The Senator (Platt) has acted, to some extent at least, on my judgment and advice sufficiently to make me feel anxious about the way things turn out hereafter."[14] It has also been asserted that Odell had a large share in bringing about the nomination of Roosevelt.[15] Through a mutual friend Odell communicated with Colonel Roosevelt, while he was in Cuba, advising him that it was his intention to press his candidacy. In conversing with Platt, Odell suggested that Roosevelt was the only man with whom they could win that fall. After two months of hard work, Odell persuaded Platt to waive his prejudice and accept Roosevelt as a candidate. Odell had just been elected chairman of the state committee and he was very anxious to win a victory. According to Roosevelt, Quigg, Odell and Hazel were among the foremost of the leaders who "pestered" Platt, declaring that the sentiment of the Republican voters demanded Roosevelt's nomination and that Governor Black could not be re-elected.[16]

It is impossible to ascertain in any exact manner how much weight the opinion of these leaders carried with Senator Platt. "Outsiders," like the Rev. F. C. Iglehart, claimed that their views influenced the Senator.[17] Pressures were brought to bear upon the aged chieftain from all quarters. On the other hand, it is fairly clear that Platt's choice, once made, did have some influence upon the final choice of the organization. The homage which organization men paid to

[13] Roosevelt, *op. cit.*, p. 271.

[14] *Barnes* v. *Roosevelt*, pp. 2354 ff.   Quigg to Roosevelt, letter of Sept. 10, 1898.

[15] D. S. Alexander, *Four Famous New Yorkers*, pp. 304–305.

[16] *Op. cit.*, p. 270.   Depew, *Memories*, p. 161, claims he convinced Platt.

[17] *Theodore Roosevelt, the Man as I Knew Him* (New York, 1919), p. 131.

Platt's opinion is indicated by the following extract from a letter Quigg wrote to Roosevelt summarizing the views of the local leaders toward Platt:

We are organization men and we will support you as the leader of the organization. We will cast our votes for any ticket that you recommend. If you say "Black," we will be for Black; if you (say) "Roosevelt;" we will be for Roosevelt. We prefer Roosevelt.[18]

It has always been pointed out that State Committeeman Barnes, of Albany, had difficulty in getting along with President Quigg, of the New York County Committee. After Mr. Quigg's visit to Colonel Roosevelt, several of the district leaders of the New York Republican organization came out in favor of Colonel Roosevelt for the gubernatorial nomination. The *Albany Evening Journal* then counselled:

REPUBLICANS BE CALM

Senator Platt is the leader in that organization recognized to be so for many years past. Upon him will rest the responsibility greater than upon the governor. The extent of his influence and the devotion of his large army of political followers should lead him to a calm, wise, dispassionate judgment, which having been reached should be irrevocable.[19]

Eight days after the above editorial was printed, the Senator evidently had made up his mind for the *Albany Evening Journal* then came out with an editorial in which it referred to Roosevelt's nomination as a "foregone conclusion;"[20] The *Binghamton Leader* expressed a similar faith in the "words of the oracle" when it said: "From Montauk to Lake Erie and from the Pennsylvania line to the St. Law-

18 *Loc. cit.*
19 August 25, 1898.
20 "It would not require a Columbus to discover the man whose nomination is earnestly desired almost unanimously by the Republican people of the state."—*Albany Evening Journal*, Sept. 2, 1898.

rence, the 'great' G. O. P. of the state of New York is waiting to hear from the 'old man.' " A counter view was given
by the *Buffalo Evening News* which printed the following
twelve days before the convention met:

There is a good deal of nonsense about the oracle utter-
ance for which the *Leader* thinks Republicans are waiting
with shortened breath. Mr. Platt is not so terrible off the
stage. He is a very efficient listener, and when it comes to
the matter of band wagons, one of which he is supposed to
drive, Mr. Platt is about as alert a jumper for the one that
seems the most likely to lead the procession as the liveliest
of the younger men. His declaration for a candidate for
governor is likely to be a result rather than a cause.[1]

After the decision to nominate Roosevelt for governor
was reached by the inner circle, the party machinery was set
in motion to bring about that result. State Chairman Odell
undertook a systematic canvass of the state with a view
toward ascertaining the sentiment of the Republican leaders
in all parts of the state. He performed this duty in such
business-like fashion that he was able to report two weeks
before the convention met that at least 700 delegates would
vote for Roosevelt.[2] Senator Platt did all in his power to
persuade Black and his supporters to withdraw in order to
produce a harmonious convention.[3] It was reported that Mr.
Aldridge, one of Black's supporters, was offered the privilege of naming a candidate for the state treasureship, but
this "peace offering" was rejected.[4] There was nothing left
for Platt to do but to ride over the opposition ruthlessly.

In spite of Platt's failure to secure complete "harmony"
the Roosevelt canvass moved smoothly until Payn, Lauterbach and some other earnest Black advocates secured "sub-

[1] Sept. 15, 1898. The *News* was a prominent Republican paper.
[2] *New York Herald,* Sept. 18, 1898 and *Troy Times,* Sept. 14, 1898.
[3] *Barnes* v. *Roosevelt,* p. 2354. Quigg's letter to Roosevelt.
[4] *Rochester Democrat & Chronicle,* Sept. 26, 1898.

stantial proof" from the Tammany Democrats that Roosevelt was ineligible as a candidate on account of non-residence in the state of New York. The proof consisted of an affidavit made out by Roosevelt on March 21, 1898, in which he swore off his personal taxes in New York City on the ground that he was a resident of the District of Columbia. According to the state constitution, the governor must have been a resident of the state for five years next preceding his election.[5] Elihu Root and some other great lawyers were called into the meetings of the inner council to propose a way out of this difficulty. At first they could find no solution but finally Odell asked how the question of eligibility could be tested. The reply was that this could be done only by proceedings in *quo warranto* brought by the attorney-general. Odell then suggested that, if Roosevelt should be elected, a Republican attorney-general would also be elected in all probability and he could be counted upon not to bring any such proceeding. Platt said that that was the best law he had heard on the subject and that Roosevelt's nomination should be carried through.[6]

Odell was evidently well acquainted with the methods used in the making up of the "slate" for the minor state offices. The candidates for lieutenant-governor, secretary of state, comptroller, attorney general, and state engineer were chosen in accordance with fairly well formulated principles. The first of these was the axiom of geographical dispersion. No two candidates appearing upon the same state ticket were ever chosen from the same county during the period of Platt's leadership. This meant that the minor candidates upon the state ticket were chosen largely on account of their standing in certain favored local organizations. These organizations could be trusted to name loyal party men. Thus,

[5] Art. IV, Sec. 2.
[6] Statement of Prof. R. C. E. Brown to the author, Sept. 21, 1922.

in 1896 the Kings County Republicans were united upon the candidacy of Timothy L. Woodruff for lieutenant-governor and the Erie County delegates upon the candidacy of William J. Morgan for comptroller. Both of these men were "slated." In selecting candidates an endeavor was also made to recognize certain interest groups, which were not primarily political in character. One or more of the candidates were usually Civil War veterans, prominent in the G. A. R.;[7] some were high up in the masonic orders,[8] while others were known as leaders in their particular religious groups.[9] The requirement of fitness for the particular position to be filled was not allowed to interfere with the proper "making up of a slate" except that the candidate for attorney general must have been a lawyer and the nominee for state engineer, an engineer. There were, however, plenty of good Republican lawyers and engineers.

The pre-convention conferences over which Platt presided also framed the party platforms. In 1898, for example, the platform was drafted by Thurlow Weed Barnes more than a week before the convention and submitted to the "Sunday school" for revision.[10] This platform, like the other platforms of the Republican party in the state, devoted about one half of its planks to national affairs. Upon state affairs it differed from its Democratic contemporary in that it defended the Republican administration, commended the excise law passed by the Republican legislature and praised the

[7] Ira H. Hedges, the candidate for state treasurer in 1891, John Palmer, the candidate for secretary of state in 1893 and William J. Morgan were Civil War veterans.

[8] John W. Vrooman, the candidate for lieutenant-governor in 1891 and Edward A. Bond, the candidate for state engineer in 1898.

[9] J. T. McDonough, the candidate for secretary of state in 1898 was popular with the Catholics. John Palmer was a prominent Episcopalian. A. B. Colvin, the candidate for state treasurer, was a Presbyterian.

[10] *New York Herald,* Sept. 21, 1898.

Metropolitan Election Law.[11] The Republican platform was also somewhat more cautious in its taxation program than the Democratic, a fact which later led to some embarrassment on Platt's part.[12]

The next step in the nominating process, the formal ratification of the "slate" and the platform by the delegates, was not a difficult one if everything had moved smoothly up to this point. The state committeemen, who figured so prominently in the preliminary secret conferences, had absolute control over the makeup of the convention when they chose to exercise their power.[13] The credentials of all the delegates were first submitted to the state committee which made up the temporary roll and thus determined what delegates would have the right to vote prior to and during the temporary organization of the convention. The delegation that was recognized as "regular" by the state committee was thus indirectly given a voice in the final determination of its own "regularity," for it helped select the temporary chairman of the convention who appointed the committee on credentials. Was it any wonder that the program of the state committee was usually unopposed?

The chairman of the state committee called the convention to order within a reasonable time after the hour appointed and asked the secretary to call the temporary roll. The delegate from Tioga usually managed to enter the hall in the midst of this proceeding. Cheers went up immediately from all sides, the band began to play "Hail to the Chief," and the rural delegates crowded around to do homage to the "old man." In 1898 the applause which greeted Platt made that

11 *New York Tribune Almanac for 1899*, "Political State Platforms."

12 It denounced "all attempts to place socialistic taxes upon the fruits of industry and economy." For an account of the tax struggle, see below.

13 Deming and Trowbridge, *loc. cit.*

for the hero of San Juan Hill seem feeble.[14] After the up-roar had subsided and Platt had taken his seat at the head of the Tioga delegation, the calling of the roll was usually continued in a peaceful manner. In 1896, however, Warner Miller insisted upon speaking in spite of the fact that the state committee had refused to recognize him as a "regular" delegate. Confusion reigned supreme until the gentleman from Tioga arose and asked that Miller be given unanimous consent to present his claims. After a burst of applause for this magnanimous act, the tumultuous delegates were hushed and listened in silence.[15] This was a tribute indeed to the will of a single man, but there were more to follow of a less spectacular nature. The state chairman finished his part by announcing the name of the man who had been selected for temporary chairman by the state committee. Other nom-inations might be made, but no delegate ventured to break party custom by exercising this right while Platt was an "ac-tive operating force."

The temporary chairman then made a "key note" speech in which he alluded to the achievements of the grand old party and its prospects in the coming election. "It is with-out doubt the unadulterated fact," wrote a reporter on the *New York Sun* in 1894, "that Quigg captured his audience. In his speech today there were points which pleased mightily this great congregation of Republicans." [16] In 1896 Frank S. Black paved the way for his own nomination for governor by his effective speech as temporary chairman of the conven-tion.[17] In 1898, Sereno E. Payne, the veteran expositor of tariff schedules in the House of Representatives, greatly

[14] *Nation,* Oct. 6, 1898, LXVII, 249. See also *New York Herald,* Mar. 25, 1896; New York *Tribune,* Sept. 28, 1898.
[15] *New York Tribune,* Aug. 26, 1896.
[16] Sept. 19, 1894.
[17] *New York Tribune,* August 26, 1896.

amused the delegates when, as temporary chairman, he un-
ceremoniously passed a typewritten list of committees over
to the clerk to read. His matter-of fact manner in dealing
with the cut-and-dried procedure of the convention "tickled
the fancy" of the delegates.[18] While the committees on credentials, permanent organization, and resolutions, thus appointed, assembled to do their work, the convention took a
recess and the band began to strike up popular tunes again.

The committee on credentials was the first to report. Its
function was to hear the arguments of contestants for seats
in the convention and decide what names should make up
the permanent roll of delegates. In 1894 and in 1896, several contests were heard before this committee. Theoretically, the committee was a judicial body which decided each
case on its merits, but practically it decided as it was directed by the state committee. " 'Pull' and not 'merits,' "
wrote the *Tribune* reporter, "thus decided the cases of Warner Miller and William H. Robertson and the New York
delegates who were deprived of their seats in the convention." [19] Delegate Van Allen, one of Platt's "iron clad"
New York lieutenants, had been commissioned as chairman
of the committee on credentials to perform this task. In his
Autobiography, Platt puts Miller and Robertson in the list
of men who would not "stand when hitched" and who were
therefore "mercilessly" punished.[20] The refusal of the state
convention, which was the highest authority of the party in
the state, to recognize a delegation as "regular" was severe
punishment, for the delegation was thereby deprived of the
local rule making powers and the privilege of recommending
appointments.[1] On the other hand, as in the case of William

[18] *Ibid.,* Sept. 28, 1898.
[19] *Ibid.,* Aug. 26, 1896.
[20] Pp. 504, 507, 508.
[1] Fuller, *op. cit.,* p. 67.

Barnes, Jr., in 1894, "merit and devotion" were rewarded by. a favorable decision on the part of the committee.[2] The convention, of course, was not known to go back upon its committee during Platt's days as organization chief. Although the Primary Law of 1898 produced such "harmony" in the urban counties that there were no contest in the Conventions of 1898 and 1900, still, as Governor Hughes pointed out some years later, there was "no limitation upon the authority of political state conventions and state committees arbitrarily to exclude and expel honestly elected delegates and members."[3]

No great importance was attached to the reports of the other two committees. The committee on permanent organization proposed a list of permanent officers, which, during the period under discussion, was invariably accepted by the convention. The permanent chairman, after he had taken the place of the temporary chairman, was supposed to arouse the delegates with some more convention oratory. The chairman of the committee on resolutions was then called upon to read the party platform, which, as it has been pointed out, was carefully prepared before the committee saw it. Although the task of the chairman of this committee was perfunctory, a strong organization man like Quigg, Raines, or Sereno Payne usually performed it.[4] Like the other work laid out for the convention, the platform was adopted without change.

The chairman next announced that nominations for governor were in order and by some intuitive process he recognized the delegate whom the leaders had chosen to make an elaborate and eulogistic speech placing the candidate of

[2] *New York Sun*, Sept. 17, 1894.
[3] State of New York, *Public Papers of Governor Hughes* (1907), p. 27.
[4] Payne in 1891 and 1894, Quigg in 1896, and Raines in 1900.

their choice before the convention. When Chauncey M. Depew, the delegate so recognized in the Convention of 1898,
reached the name of Theodore Roosevelt, a storm of cheers
and applause burst forth from the "lusty throats" of the delegates. At this same convention Elihu Root "substituted"
for one of the delegates and made his famous speech in support of Roosevelt's candidacy and eligibility.[5] After the
nominating and seconding speeches, the roll of delegates
was called for the first ballot. During the time of Platt's
domination, the first ballot was the last except in the Convention of 1896. It is true that a few Fassett supporters put in
their protest against Morton's candidacy in 1894 and that a
larger number of delegates did the same for Black in 1898
against Roosevelt's candidacy, but in both cases the "organization" candidate was chosen by an overwhelming vote
upon the first roll call.[6] It is interesting to note that these
two cases of "rebellion" did not draw their strength from the
rural districts.[7] In 1900 the first ballot showed that Benjamin B. Odell had the vote of every delegate in the convention. The candidates for the minor state offices were
usually nominated by acclamation as the delegates were tired
out when that part of the program was reached. The delegates then empowered the state committee to fill all vacancies
in the ticket that might arise in the future and the conven-
ion was adjourned.

It is hard to find in the formal proceedings of the state
conventions the concrete workings of representative democracy. The delegates played a purely passive role, like
an audience in a theatre. The main purpose of the conventions seemed to be to arouse enthusiasm among the party

[5] New York Tribune, Sept. 28, 1898; New York Herald, for same
date.
[6] Morton polled 532 out of 732 and Roosevelt 752 out of 990.
[7] New York Tribune, Sept. 19, 1894 and Sept. 28, 1898.

workers. Between the regular sessions the delegates swarmed the hotel lobbies where they exchanged views and gossiped about the program of the leaders. On the other hand, it is not to be supposed that the control of the leaders was as arbitrary as it seemed. The "Sunday school" was in a measure a clearing house for party sentiment. In critical years like 1898, the views of the party voters as pressed upon the precinct captains sifted through the hierarchy of committeemen until they reached the inner council which made up the program of the convention by and with the consent of Senator Platt. The state conventions put a seal upon Platt's work. They enabled him to punish the "insubordinate," to reward the "meritorious," and to place the highest officers in the state under "obligations."

NATIONAL CONVENTIONS

The nominating functions of the state party organization did not end with the work performed by the state convention. According to the apportionment of delegates in the Republican national conventions of the nineties, the state organization was entitled to seventy-two votes in the body which nominated the Republican candidates for president and vicepresident of the United States and which was the highest authority in the party for determining policies and deciding questions of "regularity." These seventy-two delegates comprised about one sixth of the majority necessary to make a choice in the convention. What an opportunity there was here for an astute "boss" who could control these delegates and bargain with their votes in order to secure his desired ends! What a chance for a state leader to demonstrate to his constituents that he could meet equals upon the political tournament ground and outmanoeuver them!

The New York Republican organization of the nineties seemed to have been designed to fit the strategy of national conventions. The state committeemen were selected by congressional districts, the unit for representation in the Republican national conventions. The successful state committeeman controlled the selection of the two delegates from his district in the same way that he controlled other local nominations. Sometimes he had the congressional district convention select himself as one of the delegates. Four-fifths of the state committeemen did this in 1896.[8] At other times, he would simply see that some tried and trusted lieutenants were selected to perform this important party function. Among Platt's field marshals and "Sunday school scholars," Woodruff, Van Allen, "Lem" Quigg, "Ben" Odell, "Lou" Payn, Hendricks, Sereno Payne, "Uncle" John Raines, Aldridge, and Hazel were always familiar figures at the great national Republican assemblages.

The four delegates-at-large from New York to Republican national conventions were selected by a state convention held in March or April at either New York or Albany. In its organization and procedure this state convention was the same as the state nominating conventions which have been described. During the period that his advice was accepted by Republican county leaders, Thomas C. Platt was always chosen as one of the delegates-at-large from New York. This act itself, while it was a compliment to the Tioga chieftain, was not a recognition of his absolute supremacy for the same honor was conferred upon Chauncey M. Depew as many times as it was upon Platt, and in the early nineties the genial Depew was not always happily disposed toward Platt's plans. In 1888, '92 and '96 Warner Miller was also chosen as one of the delegates-at-large, and in 1900 Roosevelt was chosen as a delegate-at-large, showing that the New York Republicans in state convention assembled wanted all shades

[8] *Official Proceedings*, 1896, pp. 70–71, for list of New York delegates. For state committee, see *New York Tribune*, Aug. 27, 1896.

of Republican opinion in the state represented at the national gatherings of their party. In 1896 Platt called the state convention a little earlier than usual, and he received a shock when nearly one-seventh of the delegates in the convention stood up and voted against his very name.[9] Besides selecting the guiding stars for the New York delegation at the national convention city, the preliminary state convention chose the Republican presidential electors for the state and declared its solemn opinion as to national candidates and policies. However, its instructions could only bind the four delegates-at-large.

As in state nominating conventions, the pre-convention conferences were the most important part of the process of selecting delegates-at-large and framing a state platform in presidential years. Mr. Edward G. Riggs, formerly on the staff of the *New York Sun*, has given an account of one of these preliminaries:

"Is Mr. Dana in town?" inquired Mr. Platt.

. . . .

"Say to him, please," continued Mr. Platt, "that we are to have our state convention on March 24, to elect delegates at large to the national convention, and ask him if he will kindly write for me the financial plank we should adopt."

The message was conveyed to Mr. Dana, who promptly took steps to comply with Mr. Platt's request, and Mr. Platt as promptly coincided with Mr. Dana's views, and this was the plank evolved by Mr. Platt, Mr. Dana and Mr. William M. Laffan, the present owner of the *Sun*, and adopted by the Republican State Convention of March 24, 1896, held in the Grand Central Palace, New York City.[10]

The *Commercial and Financial Chronicle*, a New York weekly devoted to the interests indicated in its title, said that

9 *New York Tribune*, March 25, 1896.
10 "Thomas C. Platt" in O. O. Stealey, *Twenty Years in the Press Gallery* (New York, 1906), pp. 392 ff. The Dana here referred to was Charles A. Dana, editor of the *Sun*.

this plank was a "clear and clever method of setting forth the views of the large body of business men of this state."[11] Too much credit, however, should not be given to Thomas C. Platt for the adoption of this sound money declaration because Theodore Roosevelt, Chauncey M. Depew, and Warner Miller also had "sound" reasons for favoring the gold standard.[12]

In 1892 and 1896 Platt and Roosevelt had decided upon different presidential candidates whom they would support long before the national convention was called to order. Because of his "refusal to comply with what were deemed reasonable requests" of Platt and his associates,[13] President Harrison was not "available" for a renomination in 1892, according to Platt's view.[14] Roosevelt, of course, was in favor of Harrison's renomination. Platt picked out James G. Blaine, then secretary of state, as the candidate most likely to defeat Harrison in the convention and schemed to bring about this result. Suffering from similar grievances, Mathew S. Quay, of Pennsylvania, and James S. Clarkson, of Iowa, co-operated with Platt in this plan. Blaine was failing in health and refused to allow his name to be considered, but the Platt-Quay-Clarkson combination persisted in its endeavor.[15] In the early part of 1896, long before the state convention met in March, Platt had shown a bitter and determined opposition to the candidacy of William McKinley.[16]   With such a candidate for the presidency as

[11] March 28, 1896, p. 571.
[12] See *New York Tribune*, June 14, 1896, for Miller's and Depew's views.
[13] Platt, *op. cit.*, p. 210.
[14] *Ibid.*, p. 219.
[15] Cortissoz, *op. cit.*, II, 177, gives an account of the way in which Platt tried to move Blaine to reconsider.
[16] H. Croly, *Marcus Alonzo Hanna* (New York, 1912), pp. 178–79; Alexander, *Four Famous New Yorkers*, p. 251.

Levi P. Morton, whose soundness upon the money question was beyond all shadow of a doubt,[17] Platt objected to the Ohio candidate, an extreme protectionist, whose record upon the financial issue was equivocal, and who, besides, had refused to allow his manager to talk "business." [18] Platt worked with a combination in 1896 that included Quay, Clarkson, and Joseph Manley, of Maine, each of whom planned to put forward a "favorite son" of his own in order to dissipate McKinley's strength.

The first outpost of the "enemy's" lines that the Platt-Quay-Clarkson combination attempted to capture was the national committee. This committee, like the other party committees that have been discussed, had control over the making up of the temporary roll of the convention subject to its call. In 1892 the "combination" occupied a vantage point from which to launch its attack; Clarkson was chairman of the national committee; J. Sloat Fassett, then in Platt's favor, was secretary; Quay was a member of the committee; and a majority of the committeemen seemed inclined toward the candidacy of Blaine. Nevertheless, the Blaine forces were defeated in the initial skirmish by the superior generalship of John C. New, one of the most adroit politicians of Indiana.[19] The national committee did not arbitrarily seat the Blaine delegates, and the backbone of the opposition to the renomination of Harrison was broken. Clarkson's alibi was that "if Ohio had voted with the Blaine

[17] *Op. cit.* p. 398. Morton had grown up with J. P. Morgan in business and finance.

[18] Croly asserts that McKinley refused to consent to any bargain with the "bosses." See also C. S. Olcott, *The Life of William McKinley* (Boston, 1916), I, 300.

[19] *New York Tribune,* June 5, 1892 and E. G. Riggs, "Supreme Moments at National Conventions," *Everybody's Mag.,* XI. 80.

men, on the Alabama contest, Blaine could and would have been nominated, or McKinley might have been." [20]

In 1896, Platt and his fellow "conspirators" did not work under such favorable circumstances; as Platt explained, "Hanna really began his campaign to make McKinley president, immediately after the defeat of Harrison in 1892. He had the South practically solid before some of us awakened." [1] Platt was one of those who had been asleep, and his trusted lieutenant, National Committeeman William A. Sutherland, complained bitterly that he was left without briefs or trustworthy information of any sort to make good cases of contests which the opponents of McKinley raised in the southern states. [2] The national committee refused not only to seat the anti-McKinley southern delegates but also four delegates who belonged to the Platt-Lauterbach organization in New York City. [3] Platt fumed and talked about the justification of a bolt, adding significantly, "The nomination of a candidate does not settle the presidency. Many things may happen between now and next November." [4] In this way, Platt warned Hanna that McKinley, if nominated, would be in danger of losing New York's electoral vote if the New York "organization" was not propitiated. It seemed that Platt's whole campaign of opposition to McKinley was designed to bring Hanna to "terms."

After consulting Quay, [5] Platt next began industriously to button-hole the delegates regarding their stand upon a radical gold resolution. As to who should be given credit for the insertion of the word "gold" in the Republican platform

[20] Platt, op. cit., p. 219, citing Clarkson's memorandum.
[1] Ibid., p. 331.
[2] New York Tribune, June 13, 1896.
[3] Ibid., June 15, 1896.
[4] Ibid., June 13, 1896.
[5] New York Herald, June 13, 1896.

of 1896 was a disputed point at the time of the convention and it has been disputed ever since.[6] Platt's part in the framing of the "gold" plank adopted by the New York Republican State Convention has already been related. What he actually did at St. Louis is not so important as what he made others think he did. Contrary to Mr. Croly's contention,[7] Platt was in St. Louis before Sunday, June 14, 1896; he arrived on Thursday night and announced at once that he "would fight for a gold platform."[8] According to Croly's account, the whole matter was settled, "so far as Mr. McKinley and his friends were concerned, by Friday night."[9] All day Friday, Platt was engaged in an "advocacy of an out-and-out gold plank."[10] How much Platt's championship of the gold standard influenced the conferences over which Hanna presided is doubtful, but it is at least certain that Hanna and his friends were watching closely the sentiment of the delegates upon this question.[11] The New York and New England delegations worked especially hard among the southern delegates in their fight for a resolution embodying the word "gold."[12] Upon organizing, the New York delegation selected Platt as its chairman, and, in making the committee appointments, it chose Edward Lauterbach to serve upon the committee on resolutions. Lauter-

[6] *New York Tribune*, June 18, 1896; *New York Sun*, June 20, 1896; *New York Herald*, June 19, 1896; Peck, *op. cit.*, pp. 486–87 note; Croly, *op. cit.*, pp. 192–204; Platt, *op cit.*, pp. 312–326; H. H. Kohlsaat, *From McKinley to Harding* (New York, 1923), pp. 33.

[7] *Op. cit.*, p. 200.

[8] *New York Herald*, June 12, 1896.

[9] *Op. cit.*, p. 198.

[10] *New York Tribune*, June 13, 1896. The *Tribune* was hostile to Platt at this time.

[11] Croly, *op. cit.*, pp. 198–99 gives a letter of Hanna to A. K. McClure confirming this point.

[12] F. E. Leupp, "The Republican Convention," *Harper's Weekly*, June 27, 1896.

bach was on the sub-committee which had charge of the
final revision of the financial plank and he there acted as a
check if not as a constructive force. These services, at
least, Platt and his friends may be said to have performed.
After the convention, of course, extreme assertions were
made by several parties. The following shows the'devotion
of the *New York Sun* to Platt's reputation at this time:

After all the hero of the St. Louis Convention has been
Thomas Collier Platt, of New York, who forced the wab-
bling McKinleyites into the adoption of an honest money
plank. The St. Louis plank says what anti-free-coinage
declarations mean, and it cannot mean anything other than
what it says. We do not intend by this tribute to Mr.
Platt to rob any other anti-Hannaite of deserved glory for
defeating the Ohio straddle, least of all Hon. Henry Cabot
Lodge, of Massachusetts. But as all important movements
tend to center about some one man, we must recognize Mr.
Platt as the center of the successful fight at St. Louis for
sound money." [13]

While this view was ridiculed by the *New York Tribune*
and other important Republican newspapers, yet it pene-
trated into the interior of the state where Platt's greatest
claim to power lay.[14]   Platt's reputation as a strategist in
Republican national conventions depended upon his success
in making some sort of a pose.   In 1892 he had not been
very fortunate; only thirty-five of New York's seventy-two
delegates had been held in line for Blaine, and Harrison won
upon the first ballot by a margin as great as New York's entire vote.[15]   Although Platt mustered fifty-five votes for
Morton in the Convention of 1896, McKinley's margin was

[13] *New York Sun,* June 19, 1896.
[14] *Syracuse Journal,* Jan. 15, 1897; *Troy Times,* Jan. 15, 1897;
Elmira Advertiser, Jan. 15, 1897; *Binghamton Republican,* Jan. 16,
1897.
[15] *Official Proceedings,* p. 141. Harrison, 535 1/6; Blaine, 182 1/6;
McKinley, 182; Reed, 4; Lincoln, 1.

one and a half times greater than Harrison's four years before.[16] Platt's failure to pick winning presidential candidates on these two occasions subjected him to the criticism of some Republicans. To counteract this bombardment upon the part of his factional opponents, among whom Roosevelt might be numbered, it was attempted through the agency of his organization to magnify his role in the formation of the St. Louis platform; conventions cheered him as the great sound money champion,[17] party committeemen congratulated themselves on their masterful chief,[18] and the organization press throughout the state sang his praises. This was one of the ways in which the morale of the organization was kept up to the proper pitch.

Notwithstanding the importance of the gold plank tradition, the climax of Platt's convention career came when Theodore Roosevelt was nominated for vice-president in 1900. In order to understand the significance of this event some incidents will have to be mentioned here which are explained more at length in later sections of this study. The source of Platt's opposition to Roosevelt's renomination for governor in 1900 has been best summarized by a letter Roosevelt wrote to Senator Lodge, February 3, 1900.

I have found out one reason why Senator Platt wants me nominated for the vice-presidency. The big moneyed men with whom he is in close touch and whose campaign contributions have certainly been no inconsiderable factor in his strength, have been pressing him very strongly to get me put in the vice-presidency, so as to get me out of the state. It was the big insurance companies, possessing enormous wealth, that gave Payn his formidable strength, and they to a man want me out. The great corporations affected

[16] *Official Proceedings,* p. 123. McKinley, 661 1/2; Reed, 84 1/2; Morton, 58; Allison, 35 1/2; Quay, 61 1/2.
[17] *New York Herald,* June 24, 1896.
[18] Platt, *op. cit.,* pp. 319–29, memoranda of Chairman Hackett.

by the franchise tax, have also been at the Senator. In fact, all the moneyed interests that make campaign contributions of large size and feel that they should have favors in return, are extremely anxious to get me out of the state. I find that they have been at Platt for the last two or three months and he has finally begun to yield to them and to take their view.[19]

Platt "sounded" Roosevelt upon the question of a nomination for vice-president in the latter part of 1899; in January, 1900, he told Roosevelt in very strong terms that he ought to take the vice-presidency.[20] The next month Lemuel E. Quigg stated that he thought it was "the plan of Governor Roosevelt's friends from outside states to sweep the convention with such a wave of public feeling as to make it impossible for him to decline."[1] Five days after Quigg's statement appeared, Governor Roosevelt issued a formal statement to the press in which he declared that "under no circumstances" could he, or would he, "accept the nomination for the vice-presidency" and that his "duty" was in New York.[2] A little over two months later, on the eve of the state convention which was to choose delegates at large to the Philadelphia Convention, Roosevelt wrote to a friend; "Again, the big corporations undoubtedly want to beat me. Of course, they will try to beat me on some entirely different issue, and, as they are very able and very unscrupulous, nobody can tell that they won't succeed."[3] Was Roosevelt afraid that the New York State Republican organization would beat him in a fight for a renomination

[19] J. B. Bishop, *Theodore Roosevelt and His Time* (New York, 1920), I, 135-36.
[20] *Ibid.*, p. 134.
[1] *New York Herald*, Feb. 7, 1900.
[2] February 12, 1900 cited in the *American Rev. of Revs.*, XXII, 7-8.
[3] Roosevelt, *op. cit.* (1919 edition), p. 316, letter, April 16, 1900 to Norton Goddard on the political situation.

as governor that fall? The state convention endeavored to quiet him upon this score; both the temporary and the permanent chairmen endorsed his administration and declared that he should have another term, a pronouncement which brought forth many cheers from the delegates.[4] The state convention also elected him as one of the delegates-at-large to the Philadelphia Convention.[5] It is interesting to speculate as to whether Platt foresaw the advantage of having Roosevelt *present* at the national convention.

In his scheme to "shelve" Roosevelt, Platt had the co-operation of Quay as in other affairs of Republican national conventions. Platt valued this co-operation very highly as he pronounced Quay "the ablest politician this country ever produced."[6] At least ten days before the convention met Roosevelt had Platt's promise that he would not be made a candidate by the caucus of the New York delegates,[7] but this promise did not prevent Quay from promoting assiduously the candidacy of the Rough Rider nor did it prevent Platt and his field marshals from using other methods to carry out their plan. Roosevelt was not the choice of McKinley and Hanna for the vice-presidency;[8] Hanna rather favored Cornelius N. Bliss for the position. In order to prevent Hanna from endorsing Bliss's candidacy, Platt made it clear that New York would not present Mr. Bliss's name for vice-president. Bliss withdrew his name.[9] In

---

[4] *New York Tribune*, April 18, 1900.
[5] Croly states that Roosevelt went to the convention primarily for the purpose of preventing his nomination for the vice-presidency, *op. cit.*, p. 310. Was "T. R." unaware of his popularity?
[6] Platt, *op. cit.*, p. 211.
[7] *New York Herald*, June 10, 1900. Platt added, "He would be the strongest candidate who could be named."
[8] Croly, *op. cit.*, p. 310. For John Hay's amusing letter to Henry White on the administration's attitude, June 15, 1900, see W. R. Thayer, *The Life of John Hay* (Boston, 1915), II, 342.
[9] *New York Herald*, June 15 and 16, 1900.

the meantime the Pennsylvania delegation pledged itself to vote for Roosevelt and continued energetically its work among the Southern and Western delegations.[10] One of the New York delegates also went on a "mysterious" mission to the quarters of the Kansas delegation in the Continental Hotel.[11] While it is difficult to determine how much of this was stage play, it must, at least, be admitted that it was clever acting.

One of the chief obstacles to the consummation of the "plot" was the "unalterable opposition of Roosevelt himself to his nomination." While the New York delegates were holding a caucus meeting, Roosevelt had two interviews with Platt, who was confined to his room on account of a broken rib. In the first, Platt insisted that the New York delegation should present Roosevelt's name for the vice-presidency, and the latter declared that there would be "war."[12] However, according to Platt's account, Roosevelt finally said, "I will pledge myself not to formally decline the New York caucus indorsement, but I shall certainly urge the caucus to name another." "And remember I shall pinch you if I see any signs of your getting up and declining," put in Platt's son.[13] Roosevelt went down to the caucus and told a few delegates that he was going to issue a statement to the press announcing his intention to fight for the gubernatorial nomination.[14] Such a step would have eliminated him as a candidate for the vice-presidency. At this juncture, so the Senator claimed, his son Frank Platt "pinched Roosevelt in the leg" and said, "Remember your contract with the Senator, Governor." Roosevelt later

[10] *Ibid.*, June 19, 1900.
[11] *Ibid.*, June 20. 1900.
[12] Croly, *op. cit.*, pp. 312 ft. quoting from Roosevelt's own words.
[13] Platt, *op. cit.*, pp. 387 ff.
[14] Croly, *op. cit.*, p. 313.

Depew   Roosevelt   L. D. Ward   Odell   Platt

THE REPUBLICAN NATIONAL CONVENTON OF 1900

(New York Tribune, June 21, 1900)

ROOSEVELT CAMPAIGNING IN 1898

(Photograph by Van der Weyde)

admitted that Frank Platt did summon him to a second interview with the Senator: "I went up-stairs and Mr. Platt said he had been in great pain and that I must not mind what he had said; that in view of my opposition he would withdraw any idea of nominating me for vice-president and that I would be nominated for governor, and that the delegation downstairs would declare for Lieutenant-Governor Woodruff for vice-president, which it did." [15] At the time Roosevelt told others that he absolutely upset Platt and "stood the New York machine on its head." The next day Roosevelt made no definite statement. Platt had given in at the right moment, and Roosevelt's slouch hat did the rest.[16] McKinley's friends observed the strength of the sentiment among the delegates for Roosevelt, and McKinley himself urged Roosevelt to accept the nomination on the night of June 21, 1900, through the agency of George W. Perkins.[17] Roosevelt was "very much pleased" at McKinley's surrender and capitulated himself.

The task of bringing Hanna into line was more directly under the generalship of Mathew S. Quay and Benjamin Odell. On the second day of the convention, Quay introduced a resolution relating to a rearrangement of the basis

[15] *Barnes* v. *Roosevelt,* Roosevelt testifying at p. 753.

[16] "Rising and advancing to the front row of delegates, where Mr. Roosevelt was seated, Mr. Lauterbach, emphasizing his remarks by gestures almost in Mr. Roosevelt's face, said to him, 'Your very presence at this convention as a delegate-at-large is an allurement to the convention to nominate you. You come here, and moving among the delegates, associating with your old friends from the West, and for that matter in all parts of the country, with the glamor of the Spanish War resting on you, you tempt the delegates to support you and make you the candidate, regardless of what you may say as to your wishes in the matter.' "—Platt, *op. cit.,* pp. 390–91. See also C. S. Olcott, *op. cit.,* II, 269 ff; H. C. Hansbrough, *The Wreck* (New York, 1913), p. 23; *New York Sun,* June 17, 1900; and *American Review of Reviews,* XXII, 19.

[17] Olcott, *op. cit.,* II, 281–82.

of representation in future national conventions so that delegates would be apportioned more nearly in accordance with the number of Republican voters.[18] This resolution created a sensation among the delegates, especially those from the South, who were for the most part federal office-holders and represented a neglible number of Republican voters.[19] This was Quay's method of warming up the negro delegates on the subject of Roosevelt's candidacy; the other delegates were already so hot that it was doubtful whether they could be stopped.[20] Odell then presented to Hanna an account of the difficulties in New York.[1] That night Hanna held a conference with the leaders of the party and the next day his statement "advising" the nomination of Roosevelt by acclamation appeared in the newspapers.[2] The *New York Tribune* interpreted the situation as follows: "The Ohio Senator surrendered, yes, with the best grace he could master, but his prestige as a political manager was rudely shattered in the eye of the convention by his acknowledgment that he had been surprised and outmanoeuvered by Mr. Platt and Mr. Quay." [3]

It may be said that in truth Hanna bowed to public opinion and not to the "bosses" [4] but this does not alter the fact that Platt's prestige was greatly enhanced among certain of his New York constituents by the results of the Philadelphia Convention. Of course, Roosevelt was not "shelved;" he was simply "kicked up-stairs into the vice-presidency." [5] Platt chuckled, the "Sunday school" was hilarious, and the

[18] *Official Proceedings*, pp. 95–102.
[19] *New York Tribune*, June 21, 1900.
[20] Croly, *op. cit.*, pp. 316–17.
[1] *New York World*, June 22, 1900.
[2] *New York Tribune*, June 21, 1900.
[3] *Ibid.*, June 22, 1900.
[4] Croly, *op. cit.*, p. 315.
[5] *Nation*, June 28, 1900; Platt, *op. cit.*, p. 397.

party organs expanded profusely upon the virtues of the Rough Rider. Platt must have mused something like this: no more trouble about campaign contributions in 1900, no more criticism from "past" contributors, no more worries about "reform" appointments and legislation, no more breakfast hours with Roosevelt in which he "had to endure that bull-dog grin." How unfortunate that Platt's peace of mind was to be short-lived! Who could have foreseen the events of 1901?

In the latter part of the year 1900, Platt little dreamed that another year would find his perfectly working party mechanism out of gear in part because of the great convention victory of 1900. The committee hierarchy which he had been instrumental in building up seemed to have the local associations of Republican voters under perfect control. It followed as a matter of course that the delegates selected at the various party primaries were subservient to the few. Nominations for elective offices, whether local, state, or national, came under the general supervision of the man who "advised" the state committee. In like fashion the determination of the party's policies, local, state, and national, came under Platt's direction. There was not a party convention of state or national importance which could escape entirely the influence of the New York Republican State Committee and its chief advisory member.

CHAPTER VI

ELECTING ROOSEVELT GOVERNOR OF NEW YORK

"ROOSEVELT ELECTED GOVERNOR—Rural New York Met Van Wyck's 80,000 at the City Line and Buried it Almost Completely" read the headline in the election issue of the *New York Herald* for November 9th, 1898. This headline clearly indicates the problem which confronted Thomas C. Platt in marshalling the Republican voters of the state. Judge Van Wyck, the Democratic candidate for governor, secured a plurality of 80,000 votes over Roosevelt in New York City, but Roosevelt's plurality in the up-state was sufficient to give him a majority of 17,000 in the state as a whole. An analysis of this vote by the sixty-one counties of the state shows that on the average sixty per cent of the voters in forty of the rural counties cast their ballots for the Republican ticket.[1] The percentage of native stock in the same forty counties ranged from fifty-three in Franklin County to eighty-six in Tioga County, the home county of Senator Platt. From this it may be generalized that the main strength of the Republican party in New York in the nineties lay in the rural districts where the voters were largely native Americans of native parentage. The were two or three rural counties which were exceptions to this rule, and it should also be pointed out that the Republican party polled a considerable vote in the up-state cities like Buffalo, Rochester, Syracuse, and

[1] *New York State Legislative Manual*, 1899.

124

Albany where its strength was about even with that of the Democratic party.

The election of 1898 was not the first election that the Republicans had won on the basis of the rural vote. The alignment of the up-state against New York City in political affairs dated back farther than any one like Platt could remember. There were many counties in the up-state that had gone Republican every year since 1856. There were many Republicans, who like Platt, could boast in 1898 that they had voted for Abraham Lincoln thirty-eight years before. Just as the farmers and the native American city dwellers acquired their Protestant religious faith either through an emotional crisis or a long period of home training, so they acquired their political faith either in the moral fervor of the Civil War or through an extended period of primary group contacts in their home environment. The traditional element in the Republican party of the state of New York was very strong. The sons of the up-state farmers voted as their fathers did, and Platt could count upon a solid array of rural counties no matter how great the urban upheavals might be. A rationalization of the loyalty of the Republicans to their party has been given by Senator Hoar:

The Republican party, whatever its faults, since it came into power in 1860 has been composed in general of what is best in our national life. States like Massachusetts and Vermont, the men of the rural districts in New York, the survivors and children of the men who put down the Rebellion and abolished slavery, saved the Union, and paid the debt and kept the faith, and achieved the manufacturing independence of the country and passed the homestead laws, are on that side, and in general they give and will hereafter give direction to its counsels. On the other hand their antagonist has been, is, and for an indefinite time to come will be controlled by the foreign population and the criminal classes of our great cities, by Tammany Hall, and by the leaders of the solid South.[2]

At the head of his rural army, Platt's great political task was to combat the forces of Democrats recruited from the "foreign" and the "criminal" classes of the great cities. For fifty years Platt had seen the Irish immigrants rally to the support of Tammany Hall. The Irish, being generally Roman Catholic, joined the Democratic party in the forties and fifties because of the strong Protestant character of the Whig party, especially in New York City.[3] Later the Democratic faith of the Irish was strengthened by the Protestant and pro-negro bias of the Republican party. Similarly among the German immigrants, the Catholics, the workingmen, and those who objected to any regulation of the liquor traffic were apt to be Democratic. The new immigration from southeastern Europe gave to the Democratic party and Tammany Hall many Italian recruits.[4] While in the rural areas the Republican orators made the most of the anti-urban anti-foreign sentiment, in the great cities the Republican managers did their best to enlist the support of all racial elements. Among the German Lutherans, especially those of the middle class, they were fairly successful.[5] They also had a measure of success among the Poles and the wealthy Jews. In the southwestern part of the state several Democratic strongholds were changed into Republican communities by the infiltration of foreign-

[2] G. F. Hoar, *Autobiography of Seventy Years* (New York, 1903), I, 200. See also C. H. Betts, *The Naked Truth* (Lyons, 1913), p. 75, "The Republican Party," for a variation of this theme by an editor of a New York country weekly.

[3] M. Ostrogorski, *Democracy and the Organization of Political Parties* (New York, 1902), II, 94.

[4] A. Lipsky, "Political Mind of the Foreign Born," *Pop. Science*, CXXXV, 397–403. (New York City elections of 1912 and 1913).

[5] *Ibid.* See also J. Bryce, *The American Commonwealth* (New York, 1891), II, 34.

ers trained in the school of Pennsylvania Republicanism. While in general the Republican party was made up of native Americans, no political manager could fail to see that this group was a declining element in the state's population. To gain the narrow margin necessary for victory, Platt was therefore ready to welcome recruits of all nationalities.

In getting out the full Republican vote, Platt also had to keep in mind the men whom Senator Hoar said had "achieved the manufacturing independence of the country." A Tammany delegate to the Constitutional Convention of 1894 described this element of the Republican party in the following manner:

To be a Republican in New York City is a fashionable fad, an affectation of the clubs. Your party includes the dude statesmen, the butterflies of politics. In the last apportionment they were put together in the so-called millionaire district, the Twenty-first, otherwise known as the Terrapin or the Brown Stone district.[6]

One of the clubs which the delegate had in mind was the Union League Club of New York, membership in which was conditioned on "absolute and unqualified loyalty to the government of the United States, and unwavering support of its effort for the suppression of the Rebellion." After the Rebellion was crushed its members became interested in other things. John D. Rockefeller found the oil business fascinating, Andrew Carnegie was attracted to the steel industry, the Vanderbilts developed the possibilities of the New York Central Railroad, the Goulds found real estate profitable, James Stillman was building up the National City Bank, and J. P. Morgan extended his interests in many directions. This club not only contained many of the captains of finance and business, but it also had among its supporters some of the leaders of the professional world, edu-

[6] *Record* (unrevised), IV, 1892.

cators like President Seth Low of Columbia University and President Jacob Schurman of Cornell University, and lawyers like Elihu Root, Joseph Choate, and Charles E. Hughes, all friends or acquaintances of Theodore Roosevelt. While the Republicans who belonged to this and the other exclusive clubs were not very numerous, nevertheless they were very influential upon election day. Their views carried weight with the great middle class. It was their presence in the party which led the New York Republicans to call themselves, the "business man's party."

When it is considered that in the state of New York there were Republican farmers and Republican railway magnates, Republican factory workers and Republican factory owners, Republican brewers and Republican temperance men, and Republicans of different racial, religious and social affiliations, it is needless to say that Platt's task upon election day was a difficult one. In a rousing speech in the campaign of 1898, Chauncey M. Depew said: "At the polls the day laborer stands with equal majesty as a citizen and a man with the millionaire or the representative of the corporation."[7] If he had cared to elaborate upon this theme he might have added that at the polls the farmer who wanted low freight rates and a low tax upon real estate stood with equal majesty as a citizen with the railroad director who wanted high freight rates and a low tax upon intangible values and that the city laborer who supposedly wanted low street car fares and better working conditions stood with equal majesty as a citizen with the utility magnate and the real estate millionaire who wanted high street car fares and a minimum of tenement and factory legislation. Platt's problem as a campaign manager was the reconciliation of the differences among the Republican voters

[7] *New York Tribune,* Oct. 26, 1898.

and the fostering of that feeling of solidarity of interest among them which may or may not have had a real basis. Since the voting strength of the Democratic and the Republican parties in the state was about even, the slightest mistake on the part of either side was likely to be fatal. Platt therefore searched cautiously for a personality or a formula which would offend the least number of Republicans and attract the greatest number of independents.

In his task of uniting the conflicting emotions of the different groups within the Republican party, Platt found the organization press most useful. Not only did the party newspaper furnish one of the most effective means of campaigning but at all times when party matters became news, the Republican editors played an important part in determining party preferences. It has already been indicated that many of the members of Platt's "Sunday school" owed their influence to their connections with some of the important Republican newspapers. The circulation of the Republican organs in the state was in a measure an index of the strength of the Republican organization. Loyal Republican voters usually relied upon a party organ for the political news. They found it hard to understand political news which was not presented from their point of view. The weakness of the Republican party in New York City was reflected in the press of that city. Republican editors in the metropolis as well as other Republican workers labored under difficulties. In the early nineties, the most widely read metropolitan daily was the Democratic *New York World* which lost no opportunity to expose and ridicule the weaknesses of the Republican organization. It was also hostile to Roosevelt.[8] By 1900 the *New York*

[8] It had a circulation of 185,000. Statistical material here given is taken from N. W. Ayer & Son, *American Newspaper Annual.* See Heaton, *op. cit.*, chaps. VIII and XII.

Journal, an exponent of William Randolph Hearsts' radicalism, had surpassed even the *World* in circulation and in the vigor of its attacks upon Republicanism and "Plattism." During this same period the Republican metropolitan dailies lost steadily in relative importance.[9]   In the up-state, however, the Republican editors did not encounter such opposition.   In 1890 there were about forty Republican dailies north of the Bronx as compared with the couple dozen maintained by the Democrats.   It is true that some of the up-state Republican dailies had a rather limited circulation, but by 1900 they were clearly predominant over their Democratic rivals both in numbers and in circulation.[10] Even more striking was the predominance of the rural Republican press.   Platt once told the editor of an up-state weekly that he did not "care a rap" about the metropolitan dailies as long as he had the country press with him.[11]   In 1890 there were some 200 Republican country weeklies while in 1900 there were 266.   During the same period of time the Democrats had merely added twenty country weeklies to its 1890 list of 135, and the number of rural periodicals that classed themselves as "independent" remained constant at about the 200 mark.   It is a safe estimate that the combined circulation of the Republican dailies and weeklies in 1900 was at least 660,000 a number equal to the total of the Republican voters who came out for gubernatorial elections in "off" years.[12]   In a close campaign Platt was sure

[9] E. Davis, *History of the New York Times* (New York, 1921), p. 197.

[10] In 1900 the state had 67 Republican dailies, 46 Democratic dailies, and 33 Independent dailies of the general news sort.

[11] Interview with the Hon. C. H. Betts, editor of the *Lyons Republican* on September 27, 1921.

[12] On the average each country weekly had a circulation of about 1,000.   The circulation of the Republican dailies was as follows: 2 had around 100,000; 3 had between 20,000 and 50,000; 11 had

that nearly every Republican voter could be reached by some sort of party organ.

Platt's functions as a campaign manager can be further elucidated by showing his relations with certain typical Republican newspapers. In the early nineties one of the greatest expounders of orthodox Republicanism was the *New York Tribune*, a survival of the old style political newspaper. From the standpoint of the Republican state organization the 80,000 circulation of the daily *Tribune* was probably not as important as the 150,000 circulation of the *Tribune's* weekly edition. Horace Greeley had exerted a tremendous influence over the country weekly, and the farmers kept on subscribing to the *Tribune* under Whitelaw Reid's management more or less as a matter of habit.[13] During President Harrison's administration, Reid did not maintain too critical an attitude toward Platt. In fact, Reid left the French legation in order to bring about "harmony" in New York for the presidential election of 1892. A break came between Reid and Platt in 1894 when the two quarreled over the reorganization of the New York County Committee. After the state committee turned down the Milholland faction in favor of the Committee of Thirty, Reid turned the columns of the *Tribune* against the Platt faction.[14] In a letter to President McKinley written on August 14, 1898, advising against the appointment of Reid as Ambassador to England, Platt paid great tribute to the political power of the proprietor of an important Republican paper. While there may have been some personal animus in this letter, the following portion of it is significant:

between 10,000 and 20,000; 7 had between 5,000 and 10,000; 16 had between 2,500 and 5,000; and 28 had around 1,000 subscribers.

[13] J. M. Lee, *History of American Journalism* (Boston, 1917), p. 404.

[14] Platt, *op. cit.*, pp. 257–58; *New York Tribune*, Dec. 21, 1894.

It is almost literally true, Mr. President, to say that the Republican failures in New York during the last twenty years are to be laid at his door. The *Tribune* has always had a large circulation in New York, and until within the last five years it has exercised very great influence upon public opinion. The utterly selfish and unpatriotic motives that have controlled its policy have at last been discovered to Republicans generally, and its influence now is at the very lowest ebb to which it has ever fallen. If you take the action contemplated your act will operate to revive its destructive power. It is and has been the head and front of opposition to the Republican organization. No organized movement against the party could at any time have been successful except for its dishonest tirades against party leaders throughout the state. It has furnished the Democratic party, every argument that has been efficiently used to the injury of Republican candidates and Republican policies. We have no substantial party majority in the state of New York. When we win, our victory is primarily the result of close, election-district organization. Everything that tends to impair the strength of the organization, to create prejudice against its leaders in the various counties, to create distrust of their motives, to misconstrue their acts, is bound in its tendency to take away from us that very small percentage of Republican votes on which success depends. The prejudicial and disintegrating course of the *Tribune*; its half-hearted support, when it supports at all; its false and ugly criticisms during every session of the legislature; its vicious abuse of individuals prominent in the party; its denunciation of measures judged to be necessary for the party welfare; its magnifying of party mistakes; its diabolical blackguardism of the organization as an organization, have finally rendered the name of Whitelaw Reid so odious to Republicans generally, that his advancement now would be regarded as a personal insult to every loyal member of the party. His course in respect to Governor Black is an interesting and thoroughly significant illustration of his character and conduct. In the first year of the Governor's administration, while he was thought to be entirely dominated by organization influences, Reid abused him like a pickpocket. He couldn't stand up or he couldn't sit down without calling forth the wrath of the *Tribune.* Then, when he did some things which the organization opposed, and refrained from doing some other things which the organization desired, the *Tribune* hugged him to its hysterical bosom; and now, when it fears that the Governor is not "out with" the organization, and fears his renomination may be contemplated, it becomes distant and critical of its late idol and sniffs its doubtful nose. This is the characteristic Reid policy when he is waiting to be "conciliated." It is intended for no other purpose than to inform us that the course of the *Tribune* in the pending campaign depends on whether or not Reid is to get an office.[15]

This letter kept McKinley from appointing Reid to the Court of St. James. Such were Platt's methods of "disciplining" refractory Republican editors.[16] In spite of Platt's prediction, the *Tribune* gave Roosevelt's candidacy active support during the campaign of 1898. Reid could not afford to offend too many of his Republican readers and besides he was one of Roosevelt's personal friends. Perhaps Platt counted upon this when he assumed the risk of the *Tribune's* continued "attacks."

Fortunately for Platt another metropolitan daily came to his aid about the time that he broke with Reid. As late as 1890, the *New York Sun,* edited by Charles A. Dana, had been a bitter critic of Platt and rather friendly to Tammany and Hill, but when Croker and Hill went down to defeat, the *Sun* found it convenient to view Platt and his machinations in a more favorable light. Moreover, the break-up of the Associated Press in the early nineties gave Dana a grudge against Reid. At any rate, the political "stories" in the *Sun,* largely the work of Edward G. Riggs who was inti-

[15] Platt, *op. cit.,* pp. 261–62.

[16] An editor of a Republican up-state weekly informed the writer that he regarded this letter a masterpiece of invective.

mate with Platt and trusted by Dana,[17] contained many
references to the "skillful management of the Republican
organization." [18]   In 1896 it was through Riggs that Platt
requested Dana to frame a financial plank for the Republican State Convention.   At the beginning of the following
year Dana told General Russel A. Alger that he was very
fond of Senator Platt.[19]   As long as Riggs stayed with the
Sun, which was long after Dana's death in 1897, Platt could
count upon his policies and candidates being supported by
this powerful paper which was supposed to be "close to
Wall Street."   Early in 1898 the *Sun* discovered Roosevelt's availability for the gubernatorial nomination.

Another New York paper that Platt relied upon to do
some of his city campaigning was the *New York Press*.
Unlike the *Sun,* the *Press* had always been a Republican
organ.   Platt's main problem, then, was to keep it "in line."
In 1890 its editor, Robert P. Porter, was appointed head
of the United States Census Bureau.   From evidence appearing in Platt's *Autobiography* it is fairly safe to conclude that Platt maintained friendly relations with James
Phillips, Jr., the editor and proprietor of the *Press* from
1891 to 1894.[20]   When Lemuel E. Quigg became the editor
of this paper in 1895, Platt's only fear was that some rash
act would come out of the ultra partisan loyalty of this
impetuous lieutenant.   Quigg's conduct of this paper sometimes furnished a target for the shafts of the *Tribune,* but
Platt at least had the satisfaction of returning part of the

[17] F. M. O'Brien, *The Story of "The Sun"* (New York, 1918),
pp. 375, 344.
[18] For a typical example see the *New York Sun,* Sept. 17, 1894
and January 11, 1897.
[19] W. D. Orcutt, *Burrows of Michigan and the Republican Party*
(New York, 1917), II, 99–102.   Alger's letter to Burrows.
[20] Pp. 266 ff.   Phillips was one of Platt's agents who negotiated
the so-called "bargain with Strong" in 1894.

fire, for Quigg had been trained as an editorial writer and a party platform composer by Whitelaw Reid. After Quigg resigned the editorship of this paper in the latter part of 1896, he still continued to contribute articles presenting the views of the "organization."

There were several other dailies in New York City whose editors belonged to the Republican Editorial Association of the state of New York.[1] The *Brooklyn Times* and the *New York Mail & Express* had smaller circulations than either the *New York Tribune* or the *New York Press* but they could not on that account be neglected by the Republican state committee. Nor did Platt and his city "Brethren" overlook the foreign language newspapers, among which the *Brooklyn Freie Presse* stood out as an influential Republican representative. In one campaign the state committee started a Yiddish paper of its own.[2] While leading an up-hill fight in the great metropolis, the Republican editors did not give up the game.

The problem of keeping the Republican dailies in the upstate loyal to the organization did not present so many difficulties to Platt inasmuch as the more important ones were well "taken care of" by the ablest "scholars" of the "Sunday school." With State Committeeman Warren directing the policies of the Buffalo Commercial, with Committeeman Barnes editing the *Albany Evening Journal*, and with Committeeman Dunn managing the *Binghamton Republican*, there were at least three sections of the state that caused him no considerable worry. His other field marshals may not have been so closely tied up with the local party organs, but they were not upon that account without "influence" with the local editors. When Fassett sold the *Elmira Advertiser* in 1896, he kept a "string" upon its po-

1 *New York Tribune,* Jan. 25, 1895 and Jan. 25, 1900.
2 Interviews.

litical policy.[3] The *Syracuse Journal* was looked upon as
the personal organ of Committeeman Hendricks [4] and early
in 1898 it came out for Roosevelt for governor. The
Rochester Democrat & Chronicle, the most widely circulated paper in central New York, was always amiably disposed toward Committeeman Aldridge. Platt's supervision
over the policies of the up-state Republican dailies did not
need to be of a very rigorous sort. The "faithful" editors
saw that they would be rewarded. Now and then a Republican editor was appointed to an important public office.[5]
Later, as president, Roosevelt appointed some Republican
editors to diplomatic posts. As in the case of the *Albany
Evening Journal,*[6] it went without saying that the party
organ would receive the city, county and state advertising.
It was also likely that the lucrative government printing
contracts would be awarded to the "organization" men.

The country weeklies, Platt found, could stand a little
more active cultivation than their urban contemporaries.
The *New York Tribune* soon discovered after its break
with Platt that the state committee was sending copies of
the *Sun* to its regular subscribers in the interior.[7] The
distribution of boiler-plate "editorials" to the rural press
was another expedient employed by the "organization." [8]
The following letter, printed in the *Tribune* as authentic,
seems to indicate that Platt sometimes made a direct appeal
to the country newspapers for aid promising favors in return:

[3] Interview with T. J. Leyden, formerly on the staff of the *Elmira Advertiser.*
[4] *Syracuse News,* Sept. 15, 1896.
[5] *Nation,* April 18, 1889, XLVIII, 315.
[6] See below, p. 228.
[7] *New York Tribune,* December 12, 1894 and May 9, 1896.
[8] *Ibid.,* January 27, 1898.

UNITED STATES EXPRESS COMPANY,
OFFICE OF THE PRESIDENT,
No. 49 BROADWAY, NEW YORK,
Nov. 26, 1894.

(*Confidential*)

MY DEAR SIR: Herewith I send you a statement of fact, which, as a personal favor to me, I request that you read carefully. If it meets with your approval, I beg that you will make such use of it in your newspaper as seems to you suitable. I do not suggest that you print it in its entirety, for in order to cover the ground fully it has been made rather long, and perhaps too long for your use at one time. My suggestion is that you possess yourself of the salient points in this statement, and use them in editorials of your own writing during the next few weeks. If this request commends itself to your favor, you may be sure that I shall appreciate all you will do in response to it.

Very truly yours,

T. C. PLATT. [9]

(Inclosure)

The inclosure was written in the third person and one of its "statements of fact" ran as follows: "His (Platt's) policies are entirely in line with the interests of the Republican party, and to make war on him just at this time, when every force in the party should be at work to secure a wise and harmonious result to the advantage of the state and the party, is to do what is unfair and generally injurious." [10] The sort of "appreciation" that he would show was not indicated, but other sources have hinted at the way such matters were handled. The printing of the session laws of the state, the insertion of announcements of sales by the sheriff, the publishing of the calendar of the county court, and the printing of election notices were all profitable jobs that a

[9] Dec. 12, 1894. See also Alexander, *Four Famous New Yorkers*, pp. 231–33.

[10] The article insinuated that the *Tribune* was hostile to Platt because it had lost some political advertising to the *Press*.

"loyal" country publisher could count upon.[11]   An editor of
a Republican weekly might also expect to receive the local
postmastership or some other public office.   During a campaign entire issues of local weeklies would be bought up by
the state committee and circulated free among the voters.[12]
The rural editors, taken as a body, were less independent
than the city editors, and therefore more subject to political
control.

In the campaign of 1898 all these various devices were
used to keep the Republican newspapers in line.   Some of
them were not needed.   The reading public of the up-state
regions was largely Republican and would not have tolerated any sheet which did not comment upon the "constructive achievements" of the Republican administration, which
did not print full reports of the speeches of the leading Republican orators, which did not describe the "enthusiasm"
shown at the Republican rallies, and which did not print
"unanswerable" editorials upon the issues of "imperialism,"
"high tariff," "Tammany corruption," "Democratic election
frauds," and "Crokerism."   The *Troy Times,* Governor
Black's tried supporter, was bitterly opposed to the nomination of Roosevelt before the State Convention of 1898
reached its decision, but when Roosevelt secured the nomination in regular fashion, it about faced with astounding
celerity and became one of the Colonel's most ardent supporters.[13]   The campaign arguments printed in Republican
newspapers probably did not convince many Democrats or
Independents of the error of their ways, but in a close campaign like that of 1898 they undoubtedly did arouse the
fighting spirit of the "dyed-in-the-wool" Republicans.

[11] Lee, *op. cit.,* p. 406; *Nation,* August 11, 1898, LXVII, 106; *Albany Argus,* March 30, 1899; G. Myers, " 'Boss' Platt," *National
Review,* XXXVIII (1901), 219.
[12] Interview with Hon. C. H. Betts.
[13] See the issues of Sept. 27 and 28, 1898.

Platt's chief of staff in the campaign of 1898 was "Ben" Odell, chairman of the state committee. The state committee was theoretically the body which determined whether the campaign would be a "speaking," a "silent," a "literature," an "aggressive" or a "defensive" campaign, but in actual practice this decision and the active direction of the campaign devolved upon the chairman.[14] To assist him in his work, Odell could count upon the services of William Barnes, the chairman of the executive committee, who spent most of his time "looking after the expenses and looking after the people who came in from the newspapers and after the advertisements;"[15] the invaluable aid of a treasurer who looked after the collection of funds; and the indispensable help of three paid secretaries, the first remaining always at hand to carry out any command, the second having charge of the literary bureau, and the third looking after the speaking department. In addition he had a sufficient number of clerks, messengers, stenographers, and other office helpers to attend to the routine and clerical work of the campaign. It was the chairman who directed the work of the "organization," the fighting army of committeemen, candidates, officeholders, precinct captains, and party workers.

Immediately after opening headquarters in the Fifth Avenue Hotel, correspondence was begun with the various county committees in order to make sure that the local party workers secured a full registration of all the Republican voters. At this time, Platt's field marshals in the up-state cities also tended to the naturalization of the foreigners who could be counted upon by the Republicans. Odell watched

---

[14] The main facts here given regarding the campaign work of the state committee are taken from an article in the Supplement of the *New York Tribune*, Nov. 13, 1898, "Running a Campaign."

[15] *Barnes* v. *Roosevelt*, pp. 915 ff.

each "advance" during the campaign closely. When a
weakness was discovered in any locality, he sent a man
there under orders for the purpose of finding out the difficulty and bringing about a condition of "harmony."
Toward the end of the campaign all the chairmen of the
Republican county committees were summoned to New
York for a final council of war, after which Odell could
say:

I talked with them one at a time, giving the best information and suggestions I could, and receiving from them any
suggestions of value and information which shows that the
Republicans up the state are doing effective work in the
campaign. We went into many details of the work, such as
registration, methods of getting out the Republican vote
and the steps necessary to prevent fraud and the corrupt
use of money by the Democrats in the election. I am willing to say now without any hesitation, for the first time
since the campaign opened, that we are going to carry the
state and elect the Republican ticket by a safe majority.[16]

Somewhat less effective than the personal house-to-house
canvass by the local party workers but still widely used in
the state was the campaign circular. It had been the custom to send "literature" in large quantities to "influential"
men in every county, but Odell opened the campaign of
1898 by sending matter to voters regardless of their standing in the community and the change was praised by those
who watched the results.[17]   In distributing this material,
the secretary in charge was greatly aided by the official list
of party voters furnished by the enrollment made in accordance with the Primary Law of 1898.   In previous campaigns the committee had been compelled to rely upon lists

[16] *New York Tribune,* Oct. 29, 1898.
[17] *New York Tribune,* November 13, 1898.

obtained from less convenient sources such as registration books, unofficial directories, and the census returns.[18]

Another important feature of the committee's work was that taken care of by the secretary for the speaking department. He had a list of speakers classified according to temperament and nationality; he could furnish "humorous" or "serious" or "allround" ones or those who spoke German or Italian or Polish or "real Irish," as the occasion demanded. All kinds had been lined up and had signified their readiness to work for the cause—for a consideration. In addition there were hundreds who volunteered to serve without pay. In all, the committee had nearly five hundred speakers upon its list [19] and during the last three weeks of the campaign it arranged for more than fifteen hundred meetings.

In spite of the emphasis that was placed upon the speaking department, Odell and Platt were unwilling for a long time to indorse Roosevelt's plan of stumping the state. They remembered too well Fassett's failure to speak his way into the governorship and they seemed to fear that the impetuous Roosevelt would say something "indiscreet." Platt finally gave in to the plan and convinced Odell to do likewise. Strange to say, a Rochester paper of Democratic leanings seemed to share Platt's misgivings, for, when the decision was finally reached, it said, "Roosevelt is soon to be turned loose to stump the state Fassett fashion, with the added accompaniments of a band of Rough Riders, a palatial car donated by the New York Central, and, as other theatrical companies express it, 'an abundance of machinery.' " [20] Upon his trip Roosevelt was accompanied by several other

[18] For Congressman Raines' letter to a census enumerator see below, p. 255.
[19] New York Tribune, October 29, 1898.
[20] Rochester Herald, October 5, 1898.

candidates for office among whom was "Tim" Woodruff
and Chauncey Depew, the latter showing the same mod-
esty and backwardness toward the United States senatorship that Platt had displayed two years before. At the out-
set, Roosevelt and his companions stressed national issues.
The Democrats may have looked with envy upon the "palatial car" which made at least a dozen stops in a day,[1] but
they did not feel obliged to overlook state issues.

With Roosevelt determined to make the campaign one of
the "hoopla" and "hurrah" type, the party workers felt constrained to employ all the many devices known to them
which appealed to the voters' emotions. The local committees arranged for "cart-tail" harangues, torch light
parades, picnics, barbecues, and jollifications. These de-
monstrations were usually held under the auspices of campaign clubs which had been organized for the purpose of
giving recognition to certain racial and economic groups
within the party. Thus, there were business men's, travel-
ling men's, working men's, Colored, Italian, German, Irish
and Polish campaign clubs.[2] These clubs were supplied
with banners, torches, buttons, lithographs, band instru-
ments and other paraphernalia.

In spite of the vigorous onslaughts made in many directions, it seemed as though "General Apathy" was running
the campaign of 1898 until about three weeks before election. Before the "tide changed" the party workers apparently had been unable to stir up any enthusiasm over the
"War," "Sound Money," the "Merchant Marine," the
"Tariff," and the state "Excise Law." The farmers had
been told about the Raines law and its tax saving features,
the working men had heard about the many "labor" laws
passed by the last Republican legislature, and the temperance

[1] *New York Tribune,* October 23, and November 4, 1898.
[2] *Ibid.,* October 23, 24, 26, and 29, 1898.

men had been lectured upon the dangers of Democratic excise administration. None of these appeals aroused any
pronounced response nor did Roosevelt's side-stepping of
the canal issue leave a very favorable impression.[3] The
turning point came shortly after October 2—on which date
Richard Croker committed a grave blunder. The Tammany
"boss" let it be known that Justice Daly had been refused a
renomination to the Supreme Court because he had failed
to make an appointment in his court recommended by the
"organization." Here was a "local" issue of incalculable
value, and Roosevelt, the "spell-binders," the clubs, and the
party papers took up the cry, "An Untrammeled Judiciary."
It was undoubtedly this part of the campaign that Platt had
in mind when he wrote:

> Roosevelt made a dramatic campaign. He fairly pranced
> about the state. He called a spade a "spade," a crook a
> "crook." During the final week of the canvass he made the
> issue Richard Croker, the Tammany boss, who had been so
> excoriated by the Lexow and Mazet committees. The
> Rough Rider romped home on election day with over
> 17,000 plurality.
> I have always maintained that no man besides Roosevelt
> could have accomplished that feat in 1898.[4]

While inaccurate in its details,[5] this account gives an
idea of the new energy this issue and Roosevelt's use of it
gave to the lethargic party members. The *Troy Times*
could say, "There is no denying the fact that Theodore
Roosevelt has grown mightily in the public estimation since
he appeared in person in the campaign."[6] To be sure the
rural voters had been told about the evils of Tammany rule

[3] Alexander, *Four Famous New Yorkers,* p. 318.
[4] *Op. cit.,* p. 373.
[5] The "Mazet" inquiry did not come until 1899.
[6] November 5, 1898. For proof of a "change in the tide" see the
Albany Evening Journal, October 24, 1898; *Nation,* October 27,
1898.

144   BOSS PLATT AND HIS NEW YORK MACHINE

before, but never in so concrete and forceful a fashion.[7] After a careful canvass toward the end of the campaign, Chairman Odell was so confident of the result that he was willing to "place" $20,000 of his own money upon the result. This, indeed, was an inspiring feat for the edification of the lesser workers. At the same time, a final ringing appeal was sent out to all voters couched in proper martial and sportsmanlike terms.[8]

The activities described above cost a considerable sum of money. How much, Platt, himself, said he would not attempt to estimate.[9] Large sums were spent for the support of headquarters, mass meetings, speakers' expenses, advertising, and the distribution of literature. No accounts of such matters were kept by party committees prior to 1906.[10] In 1901, however, a journalist estimated that expenditures for these legitimate purposes made by the anti-Tammany fusionists in Greater New York alone amounted to over $250,000.[11] The method by which Platt obtained the great bulk of the funds for state campaigns from "those abundantly able to give" will be described in a later chapter. The local committees, besides looking to Platt for help, raised what they could by assessments upon candidates and office-holders. Candidates for the higher offices sometimes contributed twice as much as the annual salary of the office for which they were running.[12] Office-holders, on the other hand, were only expected to "donate" a given percentage of

[7] R. Croker, "Tammany Hall and the Democracy," *Nor. Am. Rev.*, CLIV, 229, ridicules this tendency among Republican speakers. For Roosevelt's speeches see *New York Tribune Index*, 1898.
[8] *New York Tribune*, November 4, 1898.
[9] *Op. cit.*, p. 535.
[10] Fuller, *op. cit.*, p. 153.
[11] *Nation*, Nov. 14, 1901, LXXIII, 370.
[12] The salary of the lieutenant-governor was $5,000 a year and in 1896 Woodruff contributed $10,250. See *New York Tribune*, Nov. 14, 1896.

their annual salaries.[13] Although this latter method appears
to be somewhat systematic, it can hardly be said that any
Republican committee in Platt's day used a "budget system." Unexpected "emergencies" prevented such "scientific" procedure. In the dying days of the campaign of
1898, it was felt "necessary" to raise a huge fund to offset
Democratic "corruption." [14] Thomas C. Platt, so the editor
of his *Autobiography* claimed in true newspaper fashion,
was the only man equal to such an emergency and he went
downtown with a list of names headed by J. Pierpont Morgan.[15] Such a "last minute-fund" was distributed among
the "boys" upon "dough day" for the purpose of "getting
out the vote" and "delivering it" upon election day.[16]

"Getting out the vote" in rural New York usually meant
the hiring of teams to "convey electors to the polls," a practice which was permissible under the law. Farmers, so
"hired" usually found their horses exceedingly valuable
upon election day and in some cases were paid for leaving
them in their barns.[17] In the urban districts "workers"
were engaged to "get out the vote," whose chief occupation
seemed to be to stand, or lean near the polling-place a considerable portion of the day and receive $5 a piece for

[13] Fuller, *op. cit.*, p. 148. For an early example of this practice
see Ninth Report of the U. S. Civil Service Commission (1892),
p. 6.·
[14] For a rumor concerning this fund see *Albany Argus*, Nov. 9,
1898.
[15] Pp. 536–39. The story here given in highly colored terms of
"how Platt saved Roosevelt" runs to the effect that a fund of
$60,000 was needed to offset the Democratic canvass, that Roose-
velt was helpless when asked where it could be raised, and that
Odell went to Platt who quickly raised it in Wall Street.
[16] "Dough day" was the Monday before Tuesday of election.
[17] Fuller, *op. cit.*, p. 153–54; J. G. Speed, "Purchase of Votes,"
Harper's Weekly, XLIX, 422–24.

"wearing the badge." [18]   Although there were many teams
and workers that did perform their functions and without
whose help the total vote in state elections would have been
much less, still, as Governor Hill, a practical politician,
wrote to the legislature, much of the money spent for the
avowed purpose of "getting out the vote" was disbursed
under a "thinly-disguised claim," a "transparent excuse for
bribery and corruption" inasmuch as its "real design or
effect is to influence the man whose teams or services are
nominally employed." [19]

In a eulogy upon Platt, Quigg maintained that "money
had become ineffective at elections long before his power
was established." [20]   The secret ballot law and the other
election acts which supposedly accomplished this admirable
result were not, however, without their partisan uses. For
each of the some 4,600 election districts in the state there
were four election inspectors, two poll-clerks, and two bal-
lot-clerks, one half of whom were nominated by the local
Republican committees. This meant that some 18,400 trustworthy Republicans were paid at least $5 each upon election
day to perform functions formerly assumed by the party.[1]
In the city of New York, the Metropolitan Election Law,
or "Force Bill" as it was called by the Democrats, provided
for an additional force of 600 election officials, called
"deputies," one half of whom had to be appointed from lists
furnished by the Republican committees. These "deputies,"
paid in the same manner as other election officials, did not
conduct the work of election, but "supervised and investigated" with a view to preventing and detecting fraud. To
do this important work, these "reliable" party workers were

[18] *Nation,* November 14, 1901.
[19] *Messages from the Governors,* VIII, 674.
[20] *Loc. cit.*
[1] They received the same upon registration day.

given full "police powers" and access to the sacred area within the guard rail. Although "partisan advantage" was the purpose branded by many upon this law,[2] it did lessen certain kinds of election trickery.[3] On the other hand, this and other corrupt practices acts did not wipe out the talk of bribery and corruption. In 1905 one investigator estimated that there were in excess of 170,000 venal voters in the great metropolis, while the corruption of the elaborate in the country districts was "even greater."[4] This same year conditions grew so intolerable in Chemung County that chairmen of the two party committees drew up and signed a formal agreement to limit their election expenses and to refrain from purchasing votes.[5] Voters were "purchased outright" or "paid for their time" or bought by a promise of some future reward. According to one in a position to know, "it was in the year 1890 that the thistle-blow of corruption was first sown."[6] In the case of illiterates, at least, it was possible to know whether the vote had been "delivered."[7] Quigg was, perhaps, a bit pessimistic about the power of money upon election day during the period of Platt's domination.

In fairness to Platt it should be said that he did not bring about these conditions. He and the state committee were waging a continuous battle against "strikers" and "saw dust-

[2] E. D. Durand, "Political and Municipal Legislation," *Ann. Amer. Acad.*, XIII, 217; *Nation*, July 21, 1898.

[3] Fuller, *op. cit., passim*, gives a full account of the New York election law. The Metropolitan act, he asserted, lessened colonization.

[4] Speed, *op. cit.*, pp. 386, 424.

[5] Fuller, *op. cit.*, pp. 141, 178.

[6] *New York Tribune*, Mar. 8, 1898. Judge S. E. North, of Genesee County, speech before County Convention at Batavia in August 1896.

[7] Party workers were permitted to enter the booths and instruct illiterates.

ers" who claimed that they could influence so many votes if they were given a little support.[8] Besides, Platt insisted that his function as a campaign financier was completed when he had handed over the funds to the local committees.[9] In a vast organization, such as the one he headed, it was inevitable that certain mistakes would be made; one man could not keep track of all the details.

What was the net result of the hard and systematic work that Platt and his "close election district organization" put in each year before election day? As in 1897 it might all be spoiled by a rainy day. The bad roads and the primitive methods of transportation in rural New York during the nineties kept many a confirmed Republican farmer from voting upon a rainy day. In 1896 and 1900 the trend of public sentiment in New York was so overwhelmingly Republican that when the returns came in Platt might have said, "Why did I work so hard?" On the other hand, the importance of the state party election machinery should not be slighted. By the aid of the Republican newspapers and the Republican election district organization Platt was able to retain a hold upon the state legislature from 1894 throughout the rest of his political career. It is true that the clauses in the constitution of 1894 which limited the representation of New York City in the state legislature gave him a great advantage over his opponents but in off years he had to fight for a working majority. In a year like 1898 not only the legislature but the governorship hung in the balance. Roosevelt's plurality of some 17,000 votes over his Democratic opponent was a narrow margin of victory, considering that the total vote cast in the gubernatorial election was over 1,300,000. Platt had grounds for boasting that he had "saved Roosevelt." In a state where the

[8] *New York Tribune,* November 13, 1898.
[9] *Op. cit.,* p. 535.

strength of the two major parties was so even, Republican candidates for elective offices, whether national, state, or local, could not afford to neglect the aid of the man who had something to do with the organs of party propaganda, and the mechanics of the election process.[10]

[10] The vote upon candidates for the principal offices from 1888 to 1900 was as follows:

Year	Office	Candidates	Vote		Republican Plurality	Democratic Plurality
1888	President	Harrison	R	650,338	14,373	
		Cleveland	D	635,965		
	Governor	Miller	R	631,293		
		Hill	D	650,464		19,171
1889	Secretary	Gilbert	R	505,894		
	of State	Rice	D	485,367		20,528
1891	Governor	Fassett	R	534,956		
		Flower	D	582,893		47,937
1892	President	Harrison	R	609,350		
		Cleveland	D	654,868		45,518
1893	Secretary	Palmer	R	545,098	24,484	
	of State	Meyer	D	520,614		
1894	Governor	Morton	R	673,818	156,108	
		Hill	D	517,710		
1895	Secretary	Palmer	R	601,205	90,145	
	of State	King	D	511,060		
1896	President	McKinley	R	819,838	268,464	
		Bryan	D	551,369		
	Governor	Black	R	787,516	212,992	
		Porter	D	574,524		
1897	Chief	Wallace	R	493,791		
	Judge	Parker	D	554,680		60,889
1898	Governor	Roosevelt	R	661,715	17,794	
		Van Wyck	D	643,921		
1900	President	McKinley	R	821,992	143,606	
		Bryan	D	678,386		
	Governor	Odell	D	804,859	111,126	
		Stanchfield	R	693,733		

CHAPTER VII

CONTROL OVER LAW MAKING

The control that Thomas C. Platt and his field marshals exercised over the law-making machinery of the state was closely articulated with the control that they exercised over the party nominating and election machinery. No one realized better than Platt how to thwart the plans of a reform governor by means of a "machine" controlled legislature. In his memoirs, Platt said: "I also was influential in securing to the people Republican legislatures continuously, with two exceptions, from 1883 to the present day." [1] This boast could be readily translated into the confession that he could not keep his hands off the Republican primaries whenever nominating conventions were about to meet to nominate candidates for state senators and assemblymen. [2] When it is considered that in thirty-six counties the assembly district was coterminous with the county [3] and that the other sixty-four assemblymen were chosen from districts marked out by the boards of supervisors of the remaining twenty-three counties, it is clear why Platt and the state committee took such care in "recognizing" the proper county chairmen. In other words, the county "boss" who controlled the politics of his county had charge of the selec-

[1] Op. cit., Introduction, p. xx.
[2] New York Tribune, Dec. 4, 1897. Examples of his interference are given.
[3] Fulton and Hamilton Counties were grouped together. They constituted the only exception to the statement made above, which is based on constitution of 1894.

150

tion of one or more assemblymen according to the size of his domain. The nomination of candidates for the state Senate presented a more difficult situation to handle, inasmuch as the senatorial district was not the basis for other Republican activities. However, the state committee could "suggest" a compromise whenever one of the up-state senatorial conventions was deadlocked by the rivalry of county leaders, and, in the ten most populous counties which contained within their boundaries one or more senatorial districts, the delicate task of selecting a man to defeat the Democratic organization candidate was in the hands of men like "Lem" Quigg, "Tim" Woodruff, John Hazel, George Aldridge, Francis Hendricks, William Barnes, and Charles Hackett.[4] The bulk of the Republican legislators came from the rural up-state counties where Republican majorities were large and certain and the Republican "organization" was supreme; the balance came from the "doubtful" counties where an efficient "machine" was necessary to win victories. In either case, the "bosses" were determining factors. As Governor Hughes said of them (the "bosses"), "They control the nomination of the members of the legislature and dictate their votes upon legislative measures. If the latter disobey, they are left at home." [5]

What sort of lawmakers were selected under these conditions? Were they "representative" of their respective communities? How often did a renomination allow them to continue their legislative duties? The legislature of 1899 will be taken to furnish some light upon these questions, inasmuch as this session is representative of the conditions

[4] Thirty of the fifty senatorial districts were in these ten counties. However, in 1899, only nine of the senators from these thirty districts were Republicans. In other words, New York, Kings, and Erie counties were great Democratic strongholds.
[5] C. E. Hughes, *Conditions of Progress in Democratic Government* (New Haven, 1916), p. 103.

in the state in the heyday of Platt's power and influence.

As a whole, the Republican legislators who assembled at the state capitol in 1899 had had considerable political experience. Of the twenty-seven Republican senators, seventeen were old members, some having served three, four and five terms, and five had been advanced from the Assembly; thus, only eighteen per cent had not had previous legislative training.[6] Since the assemblymen were elected every year instead of every two years as in the case of the senators, it could not be expected that the assemblymen would show the same level of legislative experience.   Forty-nine of the eighty-seven Republican assemblymen had seen previous service in the Assembly; only one-third of these veterans were in the legislature before 1898.[7]   However, all of the Republican assemblymen but fifteen had held some public office; ex-members of county boards of supervisors were most numerous, while there was a sprinkling of ex-village trustees and ex-aldermen.[8]   There was scarcely any one in either branch of the legislature who had not been linked up with the organization in some manner, either as a public officer, or as a committeeman,[9] a delegate to one of the party conventions, or a campaign orator.

The age, schooling and pursuit in life of these Republican legislators have been taken as criteria of thir social status in their respective communities.   The senate group was decidedly more of a body of "elder statesmen" than the assembly group; sixty per cent of the senators were over fifty years of age and none were below forty, while one third of the assemblymen were in their thirties and only twenty-two

[6] *The New York Red Book*, 1899, p. 702.
[7] *Ibid.*, p. 724.
[8] Over half of the assemblymen had been supervisors.
[9] Fourteen in the Assembly and four in the Senate had been county committeemen.

had passed the half-century mark. For the most part, these men were in the prime of life. One-third of the senators had received a college training, a second third had not been farther than the common schools, and the last third had been trained in academies. One-fifth of the assemblymen were college graduates, one-third had gone no farther than the public schools, and the remainder had received their training in academics and professional schools. These ratios were better than the general average, but it could not be said that one of these men was a profound student of modern conditions. Over one-half of the senators were lawyers, one-third were engaged in various mercantile pursuits, two were farmers, and one was a physician. Not quite one-third of the assemblymen were lawyers; almost one-half were engaged in businss pursuits, including trading, retailing, banking, manufacturing, insurance and milling; seven were farmers, three were "newspaper men," two were doctors, and one was a labor union official.[10] Considering the support that the rural districts gave the Republican party in the state, it is surprising that there were so few farmers among the Republican legislators. However, many of the "lawyers" and "business men" had been "brought up on the farm" and still kept in close touch with the rural situation. The absence of engineers, mechanics, and educators was noteworthy. On the whole, these men were fairly "representative" of the middle class found in the up-state towns and cities, most of them were members of some Protestant church and all but three were native born Americans. It is difficult to ascertain how many of these men were professional politicians inasmuch as all but two claimed to be engaged in some gainful occupation other than the holding of public office. Some of the lawyers were men

[10] *Ibid., passim.*

without large practice and others were young men from the cities starting out to make their reputations.

The nomination and election of Republican legislators was only the beginning of Platt's work in organizing the legislature. He was sure of a majority because of the constitutional "gerrymander" but what good was a Republican majority if its action could not be controlled upon important measures? Through his "advice" and that of the state committee with reference to the selection of presiding officers, important committees and floor leaders, in both houses, Platt was able to conserve the victories that he achieved upon primary and election days. Inasmuch as it required an absolute majority of the fifty senators and the one hundred and fifty assemblymen to pass a bill,[11] his task was a delicate one whenever there were enough "independent" legislators to make trouble and an "independent" governor to lead them.

One of the key positions to power in the legislature was the speakership of the lower house. It has already been pointed out that as far back as 1885 Platt was influential in choosing this important legislative officer. Nine years later the selection of a speaker became one of his regular annual tasks. In 1895 Payn was active as Platt's agent in securing the nomination of Hamilton Fish for speaker.[12] In 1897 George Aldridge was influential in securing the selection of James M. E. O'Grady as presiding officer of the Assembly.[13] The Republican candidate for speaker was formally chosen by a party caucus at the beginning of a session, but in 1899 Platt asked Roosevelt if he had any committee appointments to suggest before this caucus met. Roosevelt answered, "No," and expressed surprise because he had not

[11] Constitution, 1894, Art. III, Sec. 15.
[12] Nation, Jan. 10, 1895; Harper's Weekly, Jan. 12, 1895.
[13] New York Tribune, January, 1897.

understood that the speaker who made the committee appointments had been agreed upon by the members-elect. "Oh!" responded Platt, with a tolerant smile, "He has not been chosen yet, but of course whoever we choose as speaker will agree beforehand to make the appointments we wish." [14]   The man whom Platt had in mind for the speakership that year was S. Fred Nixon, the man who had seen longer service in the Assembly than any other Republican and concerning whom a *Tribune* reporter prophesied, "As a presiding officer he will be a firm and will transact business with rapidity." [15]   Speaker Nixon was a cool headed man who thoroughly understood his position; he was a man of large frame, with a big voice and the Tammany Hall legislators looked upon him with respect. So sure was Speaker Nixon of his re-election in 1900 that a month before the caucus met which was to nominate him he "appointed" some of the committees by and with the consent of Senator Platt.[16]

The presiding officer of the Senate was the lieutenant-governor who was nominated by the state convention in a manner already described. In 1898 Roosevelt was known as a "reform" candidate for governor, but it could hardly be said that "Tim" Woodruff posed as a "reformer." [17]   The leadership of the Senate was divided between the lieutenant-governor and the president pro tem, the latter being selected by a majority party caucus of the senators at the beginning of a session. The temporary presidency of the Senate was held by Timothy E. Ellsworth from 1896 to 1902 inclusive. It is needless to say that the two "Tims" had little difficulty in co-operating with each other.

[14] Roosevelt, *op. cit.*, p. 284.
[15] *New York Tribune*, Jan. 5, 1899.
[16] *Ibid.*, Dec. 2, 1899, editorial on "the Evolution of a Trust."
[17] C. W. Thompson, *Party Leaders of the Time* (New York, 1906), pp. 412 ff.

After the selection of the presiding officers of the two houses, the appointment of the committees was the next important step in the organization of the legislature. This was invariably an occasion for a meeting of the "Sunday school" at the Fifth Avenue Hotel.[18] Here the leaders of both houses consulted with Senator Platt and prominent members of the state committee as to the selection of the chairmen of the important committees. In the Assembly the important committees were those on ways and means, judiciary, cities, railroads, excise, insurance, taxation and commerce, and at the head of each was placed a strong organization man. There was a tendency for Platt, Odell, and Barnes to slight the reform sentiment of New York even on the Cities Committee [19] and to place their own lieutenants in charge of the committees which had relations with the corporations.[20] In the Senate the crucial committees bore the same names as those mentioned for the Assembly, except that the committee which corresponded to the Assembly Ways and Means Committee was called the Finance Committee. The appointment of these committees was a matter of agreement between the lieutenant-governor and the president pro tem, subject, of course, to the approval of a conference with Platt and his marshals. Inasmuch as both houses depended to a great extent upon their committees to decide what bills should be considered and passed,[1] the determination of the membership of these committees amounted almost to a charting of the work of the session.

There was another centralizing agency in both houses

[18] New York Tribune, Jan. 7, 1899; Jan. 11, 1900.
[19] Nation, Jan. 17, 1895; New York Tribune, Jan. 9, 1896.
[20] New York Tribune, Jan. 11, 1900.
[1] D. L. Colvin, The Bicameral Principle in the New York Legislature (New York, 1913), p. 88. This monograph is an intensive study of the session of 1910 but many of the customs described originated in the nineties.

called a Committee on Rules which in certain important particulars superseded all the other committees. In the lower house, especially, the Rules Committee was an exceedingly powerful body. It was made up of the speaker, the chairman of the Committee on Ways and Means, two other important committee chairmen selected by the speaker, and two minority members, one of whom was the minority leader. The chairman of the Committee on Ways and Means was also looked upon as the floor leader, the party whip, who got the members out and then directed them how to vote. By a rule adopted by the Assembly in 1896 and continued during the period under discussion, this committee of six assumed almost absolute control of the business of the house during the last weeks of a session.[2] The other standing committees were then discharged and the decision of the Rules Committee as to what bills would be considered and what bills would not was the decision of the house, unless otherwise ordered by a two-thirds vote of the members present. This practically meant that in 1899 and for several years afterward, two men, Speaker Nixon and Floor Leader Jotham P. Allds,[3] decided for the most part the fate of legislation toward the close of a session when most of the bills were rushed through the Assembly. The Rules Committee of the upper house was composed of the president pro tempore, his most trusted lieutenant, and the minority leader. Although Temporary President Ellsworth did not possess the same arbitrary powers as the speaker of the Assembly, yet, as floor leader and with the help of "Uncle" John Raines on the Rules Committee,[4] he could direct the work of the Republican senators. Toward the close of a

[2] F. B. Gilbert, "The Legislature" in *Official New York*, III, 26.

[3] Allds was floor leader from 1899 to 1903 when he was advanced to the Senate.

[4] Raines was made president pro tem. in 1903.

session if a bill was not advanced on the calendar by the order of the Senate Rules Committee, it practically had no chance of passage.

What chance had the individual member against a system like this? He could drop his bills in the bill box, but he had no guarantee that they would get any farther than the committee stage. The chairmen of the various committees were governed by no rules; they decided arbitrarily when the meetings would be held, what matters would be considered and what postponements would be made.[5] If by chance or by some clever log rolling the member's bill is reported out of the committee to which it was referred and put on the calendar, the presiding officer and the floor leader are the next persons to be propitiated. There was a tradition about two drawers in the speaker's desk; one was called "grave yard No. 1" out of which a few bills came back to life, the other was called "grave yard No. 2" in which a bill once buried had no chance of resurrection. On the other hand, when the leaders made up their minds, a large number of bills were passed and the avalanche was so great that the individual member was likely to find himself overwhelmed. According to the constitution,[6] each member had the right to show his independence upon the final passage of a bill, but the custom of calling a "short roll" whereby his vote was counted in the affirmative unless he conspicuously arose to protest made him hesitate to exercise this right for fear that his own bills would be jeopardized.

There is not much evidence showing the way in which Platt and his sub-leaders used this power of the party within the legislature. However, the investigation demanded by

[5] For an example of the way in which this power was used, see New York Tribune, April 14, 1899.
[6] Art. III, Sec. 15.

Senator Allds in 1910 to clear himself of certain bribery charges revealed an interesting letter written at the time that Allds was floor leader of the Assembly:

49 BROADWAY, NEW YORK,
APRIL 15, 1901.

Hon. J. P. Allds,
Assembly,
Albany, N. Y.

MY DEAR ALLDS:

I wish to call your attention to the attached letter from Mr. William A. Smyth, the chairman of the Republican county committee of Tioga County, concerning two bills now before the Assembly committee on rules proposing to amend the Highway Law relative to extraordinary repairs of highways and bridges. This legislation will affect very unfavorably the Owego Bridge Co., which is an important interest in Owego, and I suspect that the necessity for this letter of Smyth's arises out of conditions which are exceedingly important. I know that there is a proposition to enlarge the Owego Bridge Co. under this new combination with the American Bridge Co., and I would like very much to aid them in any way that I consistently could. Will you not hold this bill in the committee on rules? Please let me hear from you.

Very truly yours,
T. C. PLATT.[7]

The important thing to note about this letter is that it was written toward the end of the session after the rules committee had taken charge of all the business of the house.[8] Platt realized that it was only necessary to get the co-operation of two men upon this committee in order to smother any bills which he regarded as objectionable. The reasons for his objections to the particular bill mentioned

[7] State of New York, *Senate Documents*, 1910, No. 28, pp. 1244-45. (Proceedings of the Senate in the matter of the Investigation Demanded by Senator Jotham P. Allds).

[8] *Ibid.*, p. 1253.

in the letter will be discussed more at length in another connection. Sufficient details are given to illustrate his method
of influencing legislation. In addition to the letter to the
floor leader given above, Platt also wrote the following to
Speaker Nixon:

APRIL 17, 1901.

Hon. S. Fred Nixon,
Assembly,
Albany, N. Y.
MY DEAR NIXON:
I have written Allds, asking him to endeavor to hold in
the committee on rules Senate bill No. 292, introductory
No. 273, and Assembly bill, No. 491, introductory No. 458,
both of similar purport, namely, amending the Highway
Law relative to extraordinary repairs of highways and
bridges. I have explained to him the reasons for making
this request. I very much want your co-operation in holding these bills in committee. Will you co-operate? Allds
can explain the details.

Yours sincerely,
T. C. PLATT.[9]

Whether these letters were the chief factors in preventing
the passage of the bills referred to will probably never be
definitely determined. However, the fact remains that the
bills were "put to sleep" in the Committee on Rules.[10]   At the
investigation demanded by Senator Allds, corroboration evidence was introduced to the effect that Allds and Nixon received bribes on April 23 from the manager of the bridge
companies for suppressing the very bills that Platt ordered
to be killed,[11] and four-fifths of the senators agreed that
these bribery charges against Allds were sustained. On
the other hand, Allds maintained his innocence to the end,
and his attorneys set up the theory that he held the bills in

[9] *Ibid.*, p. 1251.
[10] *Ibid.*, p. 1253. Allds testifying.
[11] *Ibid.*, pp. 98, 335.

the committee because he had been asked to do so by his party leader. That Platt's correspondence alone would have been insufficient to explain the action taken on the bills seems to be indicated by other testimony that was introduced at the investigation to the effect that for four years after 1901 the bridge companies were able to prevent hostile legislation by making contributions to the Republican campaign funds through the state chairman.[12] After 1901 no money payments were made by the bridge companies to the individual members of the Assembly and yet no measures hostile to the bridge companies were passed. What Chairman Dunn could do certainly was not beyond Senator Platt.

The party leaders outside the legislature were able to convince the legislators to pass certain measures as well as to leave other measures out. An interesting case showing the relations between State Committeeman Aldridge and the legislators from the city of Rochester was brought to light in a fire insurance investigation conducted by the State Superintendent of Insurance in 1910. A bill was introduced in the legislature of 1901 by a Rochester assemblyman which was designed to remove a tax from certain insurance companies. A certain Mr. E. R. Kennedy, an insurance broker of New York City, produced in the investigation a telegram from Committeeman Aldridge, dated February 21, 1901, to the following effect: "I talked with friend over telephone. Friend will take care of the bill when it comes before committee."[13] Another telegram, dated March 20, 1901, said: "Our friends will not permit accident. The bill will pass tomorrow." The bill was passed and Mr. Kennedy regarded Committeeman Aldridge's services of sufficient value to write him a check for one thousand dol-

[12] *Ibid.*, pp. 705 ff.
[13] New York papers, March 20, 1910.

lars,[14] which sum Aldridge said he used for the benefit of
the party in Monroe County.[15]

The fate of the amendments to the Highway Law and the
passage of the insurance bill mentioned above in 1901 did
not attract any public attention at the time. Did not many
other bills fail of passage in that session and what was one
little insurance bill in the great mass of bills that did pass?
There was no reason why the party leaders should parade
such petty achievements which would only be misunderstood
by the ignorant public. In 1915 Committeeman Barnes admitted that he had received many requests in regard to legislation.[16] Persons who wanted their affairs taken care of
with reference to the legislature at Albany soon learned that
the party leaders outside the legislature could handle these
matters in a quiet and efficient fashion.[17]

When considerable public pressure was brought to bear
upon the legislature regarding bills which were featured in
the newspapers, the party leaders found that the simple expedient of a letter, a telegram, or a long distance telephone
call was not sufficient to insure to them control over the situation. It therefore became necessary for Platt to hold a
plenary session of the "Sunday school" to decide what procedure should be followed with reference to measures which
had attracted or were likely to attract widespread public
interest and comment.[18]

The devices that were employed to secure the passage of
the so-called Raines Liquor Tax bill in 1896 illustrate the
methods employed by the party leaders to over-come opposition of various sorts to measures openly favored by the

[14] The check was reproduced in the *Rochester Post Express,* April
8, 1910.
[15] *Rochester Democrat & Chronicle,* March 20, 1910.
[16] *Barnes* v. *Roosevelt,* p. 1998, Barnes testifying on May 14, 1915.
[17] Colvin, *op. cit.,* p. 178.
[18] *Supra.*

"old man." This bill, as introduced by Senator John Raines, provided for higher liquor license fees, abolished the local excise boards and created a state excise commission which was to collect all the liquor taxes and divide the proceeds equally between the local divisions and the state. The brewers' associations, the liquor dealers' associations, the German-American leagues, the chambers of commerce, and other societies in cities like New York, Brooklyn, Buffalo, and Rochester protested violently against the bill. Some of the more independent newspapers looked upon it as one of Platt's patronage schemes,[19] the financing of which would fall most heavily upon the urban communities of the state. It was obvious that considerable pressure would be needed to bring some of the Republican legislators from the large cities into line.

It was decided to push the bill through the Senate first, as this would lessen the responsibility of some of the assemblymen who were voicing the loudest objections. In order to start matters properly, Platt telephoned to Temporary President Ellsworth explaining to him the urgency of the situation.[20] Two days later Platt sent his son, Frank H. Platt, to Albany in order to make sure that the senators went into party caucus regarding the matter.[1] The caucus was held and it labelled the bill a "party measure," after it had made certain amendments by way of concession to those most directly affected. All those who participated in the caucus were expected to support the bill as amended. Senator Raines next dashed off to New York to see if Thomas C. Platt approved of the changes. The Tioga chieftain evidently was pleased, for upon the return of Senator Raines, Senator Higgins, chairman of the Committee on Taxation,

[19] *Harper's Weekly*, March 7, 1896.
[20] *New York Tribune*, February 27, 1896.
[1] *Ibid.*, February 29, 1896.

intimated that immediate action would be taken.[2]   To super-
vise the final process Platt sent State Chairman Hackett,
State Committeeman Parkhurst, and Chairman Lauterbach
of the New York County Committee to Albany.   These
agents saw the bill pass the Senate under a cloture rule and
were also rewarded for their efforts by witnessing the adoption of the bill as passed by the Senate by a caucus of the
Republican assemblymen.[3]   Two days later after a stormy
session in which the doors were locked for seven hours, the
Assembly stamped its approval upon the bill.[4]   A bill passed
in this manner was said to be "jammed through" under the
"gag rule."

There were rumors at the time that a large corruption
fund was being raised by certain brewers to defeat the
Raines bill.[5]   A correspondent upon the *New York Press*
told a story about a fund "big enough to buy all the men in
the Senate who are purchasable." [6]   According to an account cited in Platt's *Autobiography,* the brewers' plan
failed for the following reasons:

But they had reckoned without the "Easy Boss," who
was then in the heyday of his power.   He had set his mind
upon passing the bill—for the good of the party.   Learning
that it was in this jeopardy, he had read the riot act in certain quarters, as coming direct from him, threatening, if the
bill was defeated, a whole lot of criminal prosecutions for
bribery would follow.   It was enough.   The only thing
which could save the bill had happened.   There was a scat-
tering.   The money was sent back to Buffalo, and all those
graft promises were off.[7]

[2] March 3, 1896.
[3] *New York Tribune,* March 11, 1896.
[4] *Ibid.,* March 13, 1896.
[5] *Ibid.,* February 29, 1896.
[6] Cited in *New York Tribune,* February 29, 1896.
[7] P. 472, quoting from account of George L. Carlisle in *New York Times.*

It is singular that a party leader in the final summing up of his life would give credence to such a story regarding his fellow partisans, the legislators whom he helped nominate and elect.

Another one of Platt's favorite measures in 1896 was the Greater New York bill which was passed about the same time and same manner that the Raines bill was pushed through. In the following year impressive opposition developed against the proposed charter for Greater New York,[8] but the bill was hurried through without discussion because the "despot" had said it must pass. One of the members who voted for it said privately, "If it were not for the fact that the 'old man' wants it, I doubt if the charter would get a dozen votes in the legislature outside the Brooklyn and Long Island members."[9] Conditions continued much the same throughout the late nineties and in the early years of the twentieth century. Roosevelt in looking back upon his governorship could write, "It must be remembered that Mr. Platt was to all intents and purposes a large part of, and sometimes a majority of, the legislature."[10] When questioned in the Barnes-Roosevelt libel suit, Roosevelt admitted that the Civil Service Reform bill of 1899 would not have gotten through without Platt's "influence."[11] In 1899 and 1900 Platt's chief agent at Albany when the legislature was in session as well as Roosevelt's constant legislative advisor was State Chairman Odell, whose activities at the

[8] The New York Chamber of Commerce, the Board of Trade, the Clearing House Association, the City Club, the Union League, the Reform Club, and the Real Estate Exchange came out against it.

[9] E. L. Godkin, *Unforeseen Tendencies of Democracy* (Boston, 1898), p. 167, citing a history of the bill by J. B. Bishop.

[10] *Op. cit.,* pp. 286–87.

[11] *Barnes* v. *Roosevelt,* pp. 401, 549.

state capitol were described by the chief Democratic organ
at Albany in the following language:

Mr. Odell is here in a capacity which includes, or super-
sedes, all three departments recognized by the constitution.
He is here as the Personal Representative of the Boss.
Mr. Odell makes the calendars of business in each house.
Mr. Odell makes the reports of committees, decides the fate
of measures, is judge, jury, and executioner at one and the
same time. Has a member, by remiss, neglected to call and
pay his respects to Mr. Odell? Back goes his bill to the
committee, or in the committee stays his bill—as a gentle
reminder which the average legislator is quick enough to
comprehend.[12]

But, it may be urged, these are only isolated cases.
What was the influence of the party leaders upon the work
of a whole session of the legislature? One well known
scholar has made a careful study of this question, taking as
his samples the New York legislatures of 1894 and 1899.[13]
Defining of a party vote of any party as one in which more
than nine-tenths of those of its members who voted were on
the same side of the question, he found that the proportion
of cases where both of the principal parties cast party votes
on opposite sides was about 25 or 30 per cent in the Senate
and 45 or 50 per cent in the Assembly. These figures were so
much larger than those found in examining other state legislatures that he thought New York should be placed "in a
class by itself." [14] On the other hand he discovered that
only about 3 per cent of the bills actually enacted received a
party vote at some stage. Thus, in the session of 1899 only
ten of the 328 public bills enacted and fourteen out of the
268 local bills enacted had party votes in the Assembly at

---

[12] *Albany Argus*, March 23, 1900.
[13] A. L. Lowell, "The Influence of Party upon Legislation in
England and America," *Annual Report of the American Historical
Association for 1901*, I, 319–542.
[14] *Ibid.*, p. 338.

some stage.[15] The second part of this investigation appears to be rather damaging to Platt's reputation, and the conclusion is drawn that the actual influence of party on legislation is small.

An explanation of the untoward conclusion of this statistical analysis may be found along several lines.[16] An examination of the bills enacted shows that the great majority of them were of small importance and the probable result of the long-rolling tendencies of the legislators. Where their own local interests were not affected, there was no reason why the Republican legislators should hold up the local bills of their Democratic colleagues. Furthermore, both parties were not averse to claiming credit for having supported public measures for which there was a genuine public demand and which did not affect party machinery adversely. A "bipartisan" vote upon an important bill might also be interpreted as the result of a "deal" between the Republican and the Democratic "machines." Platt and his marshals always had to contend with a few "independent" Republicans who were very refractory upon certain matters. A little patronage thrown in the way of certain Democratic legislators would be sufficient to offset the negative votes of the "independents."[17] On a proposal like that embodied in the Greater New York bill, where it was said that Platt and Croker had a "community of interest,"[18] why should the two "bosses" oppose each other? Platt and Croker also were reputed to have "combined" upon the passage of the New York police commission bill,[19] which Roosevelt found extremely objectionable.[20] On the other hand, the measures

[15] Ibid., p. 342.
[16] Colvin, op. cit., pp. 161–62.
[17] New York Tribune, January 9, 1896.
[18] Ibid., March 27, 1896; Nation, April 2, 1896.
[19] Harper's Weekly, March 30, 1895.
[20] Op. cit., pp. 170–71.

that were passed by a party vote, such as the liquor bills, the election bills, and the civil service bills, were the few measures that Platt regarded of importance in his work of manufacturing state issues.

An analysis of party votes alone also neglects one of the most persistent and pre-eminent influences of the party upon legislation, and that is the power of the party to smother proposed legislation. In order to make a complete estimate of the law making functions of the Republican organization under Thomas C. Platt it would be necessary to find a record of the "burials" in the speaker's "grave yard No. 2," a chart of the "pigeon-holes" in the various committee rooms, and a copy of the floor leaders' "memo." It is needless to say that these records will never be found.

One reason for the large number of party votes in comparison with actual number of bills passed by party vote in 1899 was the struggle over the creation of a special committee of the Assembly to investigate the public offices and departments of the city of New York. This so-called "Mazet Committee," like its predecessors, the "Fassett" and "Lexow" committees, was the result of a sharp contest between the two "machines" and was therefore the subject of a large number of motions.[1]

Platt was willing to admit that he had been the sponsor for more legislative inquiry committees than any one man in the state.[2] These legislative investigations were called "political smelling schemes"[3] or "strikes for terms" because it was thought that one of Platt's purposes in urging them was to compel Croker to give "specific performance" on some "deal"[4] and incidentally to learn something about

---

[1] A. L. Lowell, op. cit., table on p. 491.
[2] Platt, op. cit., p. 225.
[3] Ibid., p. 228.
[4] Senator Cantor's remarks were to the effect that the resolution was a "political strike," New York Tribune, Jan. 22, 1890.

his enemy's political methods. It is said that the investigation of 1890 under Senator Fassett was ordered because Hugh J. Grant, the Tammany Mayor, refused to make certain appointments in New York City that had been "promised" to Platt in return his support with reference to certain legislation desired by the Tammany organization.[5] Platt was a "power" in 1894 because Tammany was willing to "pay almost any price" if the "Lexow Committee" could be prevented from making a thoroughgoing investigation.[6] As it has already been pointed out, the initiative for this investigation did not come from Platt and the effectiveness of its work depended upon the counsel hired by the Chamber of Commerce. In 1899 Platt personally supervised the creation of the "Mazet Committee" which was "sprung" unexpectedly upon Tammany as a result of a meeting of the "Sunday school" in Albany.[7] In the debate over the resolution one of the Tammany legislators asserted that the real purpose of the appointment of this investigating committee was to establish Lemuel Ely Quigg more firmly as the Republican leader of New York County.[8] Whatever Platt's motives may have been in supporting these investigations, it should be kept in mind that these committees with their wide powers of investigation, their authority to subpoena witnesses and to recommend punishment for contempt, were important agencies in the governing process.

While the influence of the Republican party over the legislative inquiry committees, like its influence over the enactment of laws, was not always of a positive and constructive nature, the party did determine what matters would or would not be investigated. The significance of

[5] New York Herald, March 7, 1910.
[6] Nation, Nov. 15, 1894, LIX, 351.
[7] New York Herald, March 30, 1899.
[8] New York Tribune, March 30, 1899.

this power was pointed out in the minority report of the Tammany members of the "Mazet Committee," which contained the following, somewhat exaggerated, account of this part of the committee's conduct:

But even in this the majority of the committee lack both the courage and candor to point at the typical, though "easy, boss." They may try to mask and conceal him in quite the same subservient manner that they protected him from the subpoena of the committee, and refused our insistent demand that he should be called to the stand as a most unique, necessary and desirable exhibit. The people, however, again and again demanded, in a spirit of fair play, that the boss of our state politics should be questioned as to the source and sanctity of the authority which he admittedly exercises in governmental affairs, as to the character and strength of the recommendations for appointments and nominations which he has dictated, and which he now controls, as to the corporate and other influences operating under guarantee, and the reason therefore (whether political, social or financial), as to his connection with the legislative brokerage concern which undertakes, for a consideration of one kind or another, to insure to the citizen or corporation knowing the ropes the success or defeat of any proposed legislation affecting him or them, or his or their interests just as and when desired, as to his identification with the "family law firm" and his profits therefrom, as to his accumulations by reason of his political connections and political domination, as to whether the signing of the Ramapo Water Bill increased his income, and as to whether the failure of the Astoria Gas Grab had disappointed his financial expectations." [9]

The real test of the subservience of the legislators, however, came in the election of Thomas C. Platt as United States senator in 1897. The issue was unmistakable; the legislators were asked by the party leaders to vote for the

[9] New York State, *Assembly Documents* 1900, No. 27, pp. 3–4. (Final Report of the Special Committee of the Assembly appointed to investigate the public offices and departments of the city of New York.)

man who had shown an interest in their nomination and election, the man who was the personification of the "system," the man who must be reckoned with both within and without the legislature. One of the assemblymen expressed his dilemma as follows:

> I am uncertain what to do. I have various important measures which I desire to introduce in the Assembly, and if I do not vote for Platt, none of them will be allowed to go through. You have no idea of the pressure which has been brought to bear upon me to vote for Platt, and I am not sure that it is the part of wisdom for me to refuse to support him.[10]

Platt very modestly insisted that he was not a candidate, he never had "any affectation about office-seeking and office-holding," he wanted it generally known that the banquet for which the "Boys" were making elaborate preparations was not a "Platt" banquet but a banquet for the winner of the senatorial contest. No one consulted him regarding this matter, but "spontaneously" from all parts of the state voices went up insisting that, unless he should decline positively to be the candidate, nothing could stop his nomination.[11] In the caucus which met to confirm the verdict of all "practical" Republicans, there were no nominating speeches for Platt. Why comment upon the obvious? Why should not this function of the legislature be performed in as quiet and decorous a manner as some of its other "duties?" When it came to the matter of voting, however, Joseph Hodges Choate, the eminent lawyer and orator, received just seven votes, while Platt "had to be content with 142." When the news reached Platt in New York City, he received it calmly and with that subtle touch for the dramatic which he sometimes displayed he asked for the names of

[10] *Rochester Herald*, January 16, 1897; also cited in G. H. Haynes, *The Election of Senators* (New York, 1906), p. 190.
[11] *New York Sun*, January 13, 1897.

the seven men who had voted for Choate and thrust the list into his pocket.[12]

Imagine Platt's feelings upon that occasion. Day and night, through one disaster after another, for sixteen long years he had worked for this "vindication." Who would call him "Me-too" Platt on that night? Even the Mugwumps were saying that he had no rival except Senator Quay, of Pennsylvania.[13] To be sure his old enemy, John Sherman, mindful of the customs controversy of 1877 and the "corrupt bargain" of 1888, was to be secretary of state, but he was to be in the United States Senate where he could safeguard the interests of his organization. With the state legislature so completely under his control was it strange that Platt felt confident in 1898 that he could keep the impetuous Roosevelt from wrecking the organization?

PLATT'S RELATION TO CONGRESS

Although Platt did not return to the United States Senate until March 4, 1897, it cannot be said that he was without influence in Congress during the first two-thirds of the nineties. He was "influential" in Congress for the same reasons that he was a "power" in the state legislature, namely, because he and the state committeemen were interested in the congressional nominating conventions and elections. The state committeemen took special pains with the conventions which nominated candidates for the House of Representatives because the congressional districts were their peculiar domains and they were responsible for all matters affecting the party therein.

As far as its voice in the House of Representatives was concerned, New York's population was a political asset, for in the nineties the state was allotted thirty-four of the 357

[12] *New York Tribune,* January 15, 1897.
[13] *Harper's Weekly,* January 30, 1897.

representatives. By and large, the proportion of Republicans in the New York delegation varied with the proportion of the Republicans in the House as a whole; thus, in the elections of 1890 the number of Republican representatives reached the low water mark of the nineties in the state as well as in the nation.[14] However, for the four consecutive years beginning with 1895 the Republicans of the state wielded an unusual strength in the lower branch of Congress. In the Fifty-fifth Congress there were 202 Republicans and twenty-eight or about one eighth of them were from New York. This meant that in the beginning days of McKinley's first administration, the New York delegation controlled one-fourth of a majority of the Republican caucus in the House of Representatives.

Taken as a body, the members of the New York delegation to the Fifty-fifth Congress were older, more experienced, better educated and more highly versed in the ways of politics than their Republican brethren in the state legislature. More than one-half of this delegation were fifty years of age, seven of them were Civil War veterans, about one-half had received a college education, only five had not gone farther than the common schools, and only five had not been members of at least one previous Congress.[15] Of these twenty-eight legislators, two-fifths were lawyers, over a fourth were business men engaged in such varied lines as the shipping, the contracting, the banking, the glove making, and the electric lighting industries, while the rest were farmers. journalists, or politicians. Among the older members, Sereno E. Payne, a lawyer from the small city of Auburn in middle western New York; James S. Sherman, a lawyer from Utica; James W. Wadsworth, a stock farmer

---

[14] Ten out of the eighty-eight Republican representatives were from New York, in the following Congress fourteen out of 128.
[15] *Congressional Directory*, Fifty-fifth Congress.

from the Genesee Valley; and George W. Ray, from Platt's old congressional district were noteworthy. All of these men had been in Congress throughout the nineties, and Payne had been a member of Congress continuously since 1883. Among the newer members who were later on to be of importance in state politics were: Benjamin B. Odell, Lemuel E. Quigg, William L. Ward, a manufacturer from Westchester County, and De Alva S. Alexander, the noted lawyer and historian from Buffalo.

The most outstanding representative from the state of New York during Platt's period of political management was Sereno E. Payne, who owed his position of prominence to his place upon the Committee on Ways and Means. As a member of this committee, Payne was part of the House "aristocracy," he had helped frame the McKinley Tariff bill of 1890, and he was the most influential member of the House in the framing of the Dingley bill of 1897 next to the chairman of the committee himself.[16] Payne admitted that the Dingley bill was prepared by the Republican members of the committee before the Fifty-fifth Congress met,[17] and when the House refused to concur in the Senate amendments, Payne was appointed as one of the members of the conference committee which drafted the compromise that was finally accepted. Upon the death of Representative Dingley in 1899, Payne was made chairman of the Committee on Ways and Means, a position which carried with it the majority leadership on the floor of the House. From that time on until his retirement in 1913, Payne was a member of the House "machine," a close corporation made up of the speaker, the two majority members of the Committee on Rules, and the floor leader, a group of four which was able to rule the House in despotic fashion by reason of its

16 *New York Tribune,* January 21, 1899.
17 *Ibid.,* June 8, 1900.

power to hold up the local bills of any recalcitrant member.[18]
It has already been pointed out that Payne recognized the
value of "machine" methods in the way in which he ran the
state convention which nominated Roosevelt. In the House
he was not an eloquent talker, but he was "strong on tariff
matters" and he had a "sledge-hammer fashion" of dealing
with Democratic interrupters. It goes without saying that
Payne's power to negative bills was very great; even President Roosevelt could not convince him and his fellow auto-
crats to take up the question of tariff reform.

There were other members of the New York delegation
to the Fifty-fifth Congress who by reason of the committee
positions that they held were not to be ignored by those interested in the work of Congress. No fewer than ten of the
fifty-six committee chairmanships fell to the Empire State.
James W. Wadsworth was chairman of the Committee on
Agriculture, which had control of annual appropriations
amounting to three and one half million dollars and which
considered such important questions as the prohibition of
interstate trade in oleomargarine; James S. Sherman was
chairman of the Committee on Indian Affairs which had
charge of annual appropriations running up to nearly eight
million dollars and all bills proposing to open Indian lands
with their valuable mining rights; and W. B. Hooker was
chairman of the Committee on Rivers and Harbors, which
stood guard over one of the richest of all the "pork barrels."
In fact, all of the members of the New York delegation
were appointed to one or more of the leading and important
committees which had the power of life or death over the
crucial bills brought before Congress.[19] Surely, during

[18] Thompson, *op. cit.*, pp. 157 ff.

[19] Alexander: Judiciary, Reform of Civil Service; Belden: Appropriations; Brewster: Invalid Pensions, Alcoholic Liquor Traffic,
chairman; Chickering: Railways and Canals, chairman, Printing;

the first two years of the McKinley régime when so many
significant measures were being considered, it could hardly
be said that the great state of New York was not well "represented" in the House of Representatives.

It should not be implied that these Republican legislators
were absolutely under the control of the party organization
within and without Congress.   Some of them, like Wadsworth and Ward, were their own political managers to a
certain extent, and others, like Payne, Odell, and Quigg were
in a position to influence the work of the organization itself.   On the other hand, when it came to a matter like a
vote on the Dingley Tariff, there was not one who was present who dared to go against the party decision.[20]   In the
reconciliation of conflicting views, in the distribution of
patronage and campaign funds, Platt and the organization
were centralizing agencies.   Platt, however, could not save
ten of the Republican congressmen from defeat in the election of 1898.

There has been a tendency to disparage Platt's influence
as a legislator in the United States Senate; one Washington
correspondent, for instance, wrote that "Platt of New York
has no more influence on legislation in Washington than the
coruscations of a lightning bug have on the solar system." [1]
This was a journalist's way of saying that when Platt came
into the United States Senate in 1897, he found that body
highly organized with no vacancies in the oligarchy for a

Mahany: Military Affairs, Immigration; Odell: District of Columbia, Accounts, chairman; Quigg: Foreign Affairs, Expenditures of
the Executive Departments, chairman; Ray: Judiciary, Invalid Pensions, chairman; Belford: Elections; Hurley: Naval Affairs; Bennett: Interstate and Foreign Commerce; Gillett: Public Buildings
and Grounds, were among the most important.

[20] *Congressional Record,* Fifty-fifth Congress, First Sess., p. 2750.
[1] Thompson, *op. cit.,* p. 34.

new comer who was declining in health. This same correspondent gave a more tempered view of Platt's legislative activities in a later passage, part of which is reproduced below:

He is simply one of the rank and file. The great leaders of the Senate make up their programmes without him, and he learns of the thing projected when his vote is needed. When a bill comes up he votes with the rest of the rank and file; he offers no amendments and he never speaks. Reporters, seeking to know what is contemplated by the Republican leaders, often go to other senators who are not leaders, thinking that these men may have gleaned something of the leaders' plans. But they never go to Platt.[2]

Another writer said, "Mr. Platt is unique and remarkable for having never, by spoken or written word, declared the shadow of an opinion concerning any of the vital issues of the time."[3]

While true in the main, these estimates err in certain particulars. Platt did make one "leave-to-print-speech" in favor of the retention of the Philippine Islands which appears in the *Congressional Record* as of January 27, 1899. This, however, was the only official expression that he gave of his views while in the United States Senate. Before he took his seat, he outlined his opinions upon national questions at the Albany "senatorial" banquet in his honor. Here he made it known that he did not regard it necessary to enact at once a law for the maintenance of the gold standard, that he thought the enactment of "an intelligent and consistent tariff, based in every schedule upon the principle of preventing the foreign producer of goods that compete with American goods from wholesaling his wares in the American market at prices which compel the American maker of such wares either to go out of business or to reduce the

[2] *Ibid.*, p. 100.
[3] *Puck*, January, 1897.

wages he pays to his labor;" that he favored the principle of arbitration with Great Britain, and that he was opposed to intervention in Cuba.[4]   The striking thing about these views was their remarkable similarity to the expressed policies of the President-elect; it looked as though Platt was trying to show that he was "safe and sane." Many who opposed Platt's methods did not object to the attitude he here expressed.   While in the Senate, Platt was occasionally "interviewed" by reporters upon national questions.   On one particular occasion he declared that he was in favor of expansion for the good of American commerce, that he favored the Nicarauguan Canal proposition, and that the Hague conference idea was, "Beautiful! Impracticable! It never can be." [5]

Platt's vote in the United States Senate was a matter of importance in 1897, for in that year only forty-four of the ninety senators were Republicans.   Thus, the refined sugar amendment, which he had taken a prominent part in advocating in private conferences, passed the Senate by the meagre majority of two.[6]   In 1899 Platt was instrumental in securing as a partner in his senatorial labors, his old "Amen Corner Brother," Chauncey M. Depew, and then there were two votes from the Empire State, which could be counted upon by the leaders as "regular."   Governor Roosevelt did not oppose this arrangement.   With Nelson Aldrich, nominally from Rhode Island but more of a "New Yorker" than Platt, at the helm of Senate, Platt and Depew did not have to worry about working out the deep questions of our national politics.

Like the other senators, Platt was made the chairman of

---

[4] *New York Tribune*, January 27, 1897, also found in Platt, *op. cit.*, pp. 349–54.
[5] *New York Tribune*, May 25, 1899.
[6] *Ibid.*, June 12, 1897.

a committee so that he might have an office and the other
"perquisites" necessary for the transaction of his senatorial
duties other than those performed in the senate chamber.
In the Fifty-fifth Congress, he was chairman of the Committee on Transportation Routes to the Seaboard, a useless
survival of another age, while during the rest of his senatorial career, he was chairman of the Committee on Printing, an innocuous body, which at intervals submitted a resolution providing for the printing so many copies of a document on boll weevils or something of the sort. On the other
hand, Platt was regarded as "safe" enough to be made a
member of some important committees. He served continuously on the committees on census, naval affairs, and
inter-oceanic canals, and in 1899 he was made a member of
the Committee on Finance, the most important committee
in the Senate, as chairman of which Senator Aldrich exe-
cuted his plans for national legislation.[7] Depew did not
fare quite so well as Platt in his committee positions; he was
at first chairman of the transient Committee on Industrial
Expositions and later he was the head of the harmless
Committee on Revision of the Laws of the United States,
and he was a member of the following committees; Forest
Reservations and Protection of Game, Public Health and
National Quarantine, Commerce, Judiciary, and Pacific
Islands and Porto Rico.

Platt's name is not attached to any great public bill but
as to New York matters, he introduced many bills and resolutions which contained in their titles such phrases as "for
relief," "to pension," "for improvements of," "to pay war
claim," etc.[8] He was more active than Depew in seeing that
New York had her fair share of the appropriations.

[7] D. G. Phillips, "The Treason of the Senate," *Cosmop. Mag.*,
1906, XL, 636.
[8] *Cong. Record Index,* Fifty-fifth Cong., First Sess., 1897, p. 200.

The main interest and attention of the Tioga statesman in Washington were concentrated upon the distribution of the federal patronage in New York. Here the time honored rule of "senatorial courtesy" helped him out although no one realized better than he that this rule had limitations. At the beginning of McKinley's administration, he, the Republican congressman from New York, and some members of the "Sunday school" constituted themselves as a sort of a "governing board" or "patronage trust" in order to secure an "equitable" distribution of the federal appointments. It was said that Senator Platt received and answered hundreds of letters daily relative to political jobs, and it was known that he made weekly pilgrimages to New York City in order to hold his solemn councils regarding this subject.[9]   Among other things the "little band" would call at the White House in order to inform the President who was who in New York and as a result of such a conference Platt would usually announce that such and such appointments "would all be made in due season."[10]   Some newspapers were prone to criticize the state leader's silence at Washington; an editorial writer upon the *New York Tribune* ironically replied:

Neglecting duty? Not much. He was up to his ears in work. Working the Committee on Appropriations, working the Executive Mansion, working the departments, working Quigg, working the legislature at Albany, working Van Wyck, working the long-distance telephone, working the *New York Sun*.[11]

The principles, customs, and traditions which governed the organization of the Republican members of Congress were in general the same as those which controlled the or-

9 *New York Tribune,* April 20, 1897.
10 *Ibid.,* September 16, 1897.
11 *New York Tribune,* Jan. 28, 1898.

ganization of the members of the state legislature. The Republican legislator, whether he belonged to the state Assembly, the state, Senate, the United States House of Representatives, or the United States Senate, was primarily a localist, interested in showing his more active constituents that he was taking care of their concerns. In order to make a local record, the individual legislator found it necessary for him to align himself with the dominant clique in his particular law making body. The dominant clique was usually chosen by the rule of seniority, a practice which ordinarily insured the selection of the best localists. Platt was the connecting link between the national and the state law makers and in a sense the best localist of them all. Roosevelt and others found Platt useful when action or non-action on the part of both or either of the two law-making bodies with which he was connected was desired.

CHAPTER VIII.

GOVERNOR ROOSEVELT AND BOSS PLATT

There was no part of the state governmental machinery that caused Thomas C. Platt so much worry and trouble as the governorship. He might control the "hand picked" delegates who assembled every two years at Saratoga to nominate a Republican candidate for this important post, but what good did that control do him when his choice was so limited by the exigencies of election day? The voters were attracted to a gubernatorial candidate who possessed good business ability, firmness, tact, common sense, and above all a strong will. Unfortunately, this sort of a man was not the kind to be easily influenced on certain matters after election day. Furthermore, even when "circumstances permitted" the selection of a person who seemed to be flexible, there was no telling what a seemingly "flexible" person would do once he was elected governor of the greatest state in the union. There were traditions surrounding the New York governorship, which a governor could ill afford to violate. The office had high rank even in the national party system. Had not two governors, Van Buren and Cleveland, been elected to the high office of president of the United States; were not four others, George Clinton, DeWitt Clinton, Seymour and Tilden, unsuccessful candidates for the same office; had not four, George Clinton, Tompkins, Van Buren and Morton, occupied the position of Vice-president; and finally had not ten governors—DeWitt Clinton, Van Buren, Marcy, Wright, Dix, Seward, Fish, Morgan, Fenton, and Hill—been members of the United States Senate? The

182

Republicans gained control of the New York governorship in the middle of the nineties, ten years after Cleveland had been elevated to the presidency largely because he had regarded the governorship as a "public trust." The people at large might forget about the one hundred and fifty inconspicuous legislators at Albany, but the governor was ever before them and they watched with interest, at least many did, the newspaper accounts of his activities, and they held him accountable for the accomplishments and failures of his administration.

Especially with reference to legislation, there was a growing tendency during the period under discussion to place responsibility upon the governor for what was done and what was not done. The constitutional powers of the governor over legislation remained the same: in his annual message, he was required to recommend to the legislature such matters as he thought expedient; in a special or emergency message, he might expedite the process of legislation on certain matters; and by the exercise of his veto power he could practically prevent the enactment of any law that he regarded as undesirable.[1] The actual legislative powers of the governor, however, were expanding, and Platt had to accommodate himself to this development, a task which he did not always find congenial, especially when he had a "safe" margin in the legislature.

In order to understand the relations between Governor Roosevelt and "Boss" Platt in their proper perspective it is necessary to review briefly the attitudes and accomplishments of the two "Platt" governors who preceded Roosevelt.

According to Platt, Levi P. Morton was "the safest governor New York ever had." Business experience had

[1] C. Z. Lincoln, "The Governors of New York," *New York State Hist. Asso.* (1910), IX, 75.

taught him conservatism. He never was influenced by
crazy theorists, but conducted his administration as he did
his great private financial institutions.[2] When Morton
assumed the governorship in 1895, he was over seventy years
of age and he was reported as saying that the arduous duties
at the beginning of his administration were very tiring.[3]
The "man from Wall Street" was amiable, diplomatic, easy
going, and he did his work "without beating of tom-toms or
crash of cymbals." In those days the Governor was wary
of too much newspaper publicity, he kept the reporters at
as much of a distance as possible,[4] and there was little danger of his appealing over the heads of the organization to
the people. In his first annual message, Governor Morton
summed up his views upon matters which were of importance to Platt as follows:

But it is my conviction that the governor should never interfere with the work of the legislature beyond the precise
line which his constitutional duty and obligation warrants.
The veto power, as it is commonly called, is one that should
be exercised with great care and only when the interests of
the state are in question. The chief executive should never
use it as an instrument to aid in impressing or imposing his
will upon the legislature, nor should it be invoked to serve
personal or partisan ends.[5]

Platt's testimonial as to the party loyalty of Governor
Black, the successor to Governor Morton inaugurated in
1897, has already been given in another connection. On
the other hand, Frank S. Black was inclined to put his own
interpretation upon the question as to what were the needs

[2] Platt, *op. cit.*, p. 332.
[3] *New York Tribune*, Nov. 24, 1894.
[4] C. D. Morris, Albany Correspondent of the *New York Evening
Telegram*, "Governors I Have Known," The *Lyons Republican*,
August 3, 1921 (Centennial issue), p. 34.
[5] State of New York, *Messages from the Governors*, edited by
C. Z. Lincoln, IX, 537-38.

GOVERNOR ROOSEVELT

(Negative owned by Roosevelt Memorial Association)

of the organization at any particular time; he was a young man, only forty-three when he started his administration; he was noted for his vigorous and aggressive prosecution of election thugs; and he was a bright, shrewd lawyer capable of comprehending the significance of intricate pieces of legislation.[6] While Governor Black was cold to and fearful of newspaper men and seemed to neglect the value of newspaper publicity,[7] he was an effective speaker of the campaign orator type and he could present his views in forceful language when the occasion demanded. His ideas regarding the proper relation between the executive and legislative branches of the government were not so reassuring to Platt as those of Governor Morton had been:

There should be opportunity for conference and discussion between the executive and members of the legislature. This will afford both a better understanding of measures proposed.

I advise that only such acts be passed as have general application. Cases are rare where the need for local or special legislation exists. A large part of our laws serve no desirable end whatever. They increase the expense, confuse existing law, and are often trivial and uncertain in their character.[8]

So much has been written regarding Theodore Roosevelt in the light of his presidency that it is difficult to get an accurate estimate of Roosevelt as governor in 1899, a man who had had a varied and useful career but who was only forty years of age and whose reputation was yet in the making. An incident which took place at the trial of one

[6] The *Nation*, September 3, 1896, commented upon Black's nomination as follows: "He is a man of undoubted personal integrity, of much force of character, and instead of being a 'dealer' and 'dickerer' with political rascals in his own and other parties, has been a persistent fighter of them."

[7] G. D. Morris, *loc. cit.*

[8] *Messages*, IX, 848.

of Roosevelt's fellow police commissioners in 1896 illustrates the attitude that some of the important members of
the Republican organization had toward this young "reformer" in the nineties. "I say that all these cases were
properly attended to," emphasized General Tracy, the counsel for the commissioner on trial. Mr. Roosevelt shook his
head vigorously as dissenting from this statement. General
Tracy coolly surveyed him for a moment and then remarked,
"I see my friend shakes his head, but there is nothing in
it." [9]   When Roosevelt's name was suggested for governorship, Governor Black who desired a renomination, protested
on the ground that Roosevelt was not fit to be nominated
because he was impulsive and erratic; that his military
record, however it might have attested his personal bravery,
displayed his characteristic rashness and impetuousity and
foolhardiness, and that as governor he would play the devil
with the organization and get the party into all sorts of
tangles and ridiculous positions.[10]   While these two illustrations do not give impartial estimates of Roosevelt's per-
sonalty, they at least give some characteristic views of
Roosevelt common among the organization workers at the
time.[11]

An editorial writer upon the *New York Tribune* gave a
more friendly description of Roosevelt's qualities when he
took up the duties of the governorship, part of which is
given below:

He had youth, abounding health, various talents, experience of public life, a large acquaintance with men and af-

[9] *New York Herald*, June 30, 1896. See Alexander, *Four Famous
New Yorkers*, p. 242.

[10] *Barnes* v. *Roosevelt*, pp. 2354ff.   Quigg's letter to Roosevelt of
September 10, 1898 in which an account of Quigg's conversation
with Governor Black is given.

[11] The same arguments against the nomination of Roosevelt were
given by Platt to the Rev. Iglehart.   See Iglehart, *op. cit.*, p. 131.

fairs, the admiration of the people, the confidence of many who are not his political adherents and a competency which relieves his mind of financial worry.[12]

Governor Roosevelt was not only an able and forceful speaker upon the public platform but he also understood the art of blazonry and knew how to make every newspaper man his publicity agent. One of the first things that he started to do at Albany was to win the friendship of the reporters of the various journals and one of the methods that he used was to furnish them with "lots of copy."[13] Definite hours were set aside by the governor for conferences with the newspaper correspondents, a practice which proved highly useful to all concerned.[14]   In looking back over his career in 1913, Roosevelt stated that more than half of his work as governor "was in the direction of getting needed and important legislation" which he accomplished "only by arousing the people, and riveting their attention on what was done."[15]   Regarding Roosevelt's energy, his powers of concentration, his superior intelligence, and his loyalty to his friends and his own ideals, there is little dispute.   It must have been with some misgivings that Senator Platt looked forward to Roosevelt's term as governor after the election of 1898; he could look for little "peace" from the man who shortly after his inauguration proclaimed the following creed:

I wish to preach, not the doctrine of ignoble ease, but the doctrine of the strenuous life; the life of toil and effort; of labor and strife; to preach that highest form of success which comes, not to the man who desires more easy peace,

[12] January 1, 1899.
[13] G. D. Morris, loc. cit.
[14] W. J. Youngs, Sec. to Gov. Roosevelt, "The Administration of Theodore Roosevelt," *Official New York from Cleveland to Hughes,* I, 169.
[15] *Op. cit.,* p. 282.

but to the man who does not shrink from danger, from hardship or from bitter toil, and who out of these wins the splendid ultimate triumph.[16]

It is difficult to establish just what Platt's influence was with these threè executives but there is no question that Platt was consulted by them with reference to important affairs of the state government. As it has been pointed out, Platt was very particular about being "consulted," because a "consultation" gave him the semblance of power even if it denied its substance. He was a frequent visitor at the office of Governor-elect Morton in the latter days of the year 1894, and when Mr. Morton was asked about the nature of these visits, he replied that he and Mr. Platt "had been warm friends for years" and that "there was no misunderstanding" between them.[17] After Morton was inaugurated, Platt used to make trips to Albany to see him, and upon one occasion, when the governor had been in New York, both of them made the trip together upon a slow train "so as to have time for a nice, long chat." [18] The Governor also used to have "harmony" banquets at the executive mansion to which Mr. and Mrs. Platt were invariably invited.

When Frank S. Black became governor of the state, "Lou" Payn, who had been so very skilful at the state nominating convention, acted as the intermediary between the chief executive of the state and the manager-in-chief of the Republican organization.[19] Although the connection between the two men was not very close, Governor Black said at the "senatorial" banquet in Platt's honor that he was "proud" to number Mr. Platt among his friends. Because

[16] New York State, *Public Papers of Governor Roosevelt,* 1899, p. 293. Speech before the Hamilton Club, Chicago, Ill., April 10, 1899.
[17] *New York Tribune,* Nov. 24, 1894.
[18] *Ibid.,* Jan. 16, 1895.
[19] *Nation,* April 22, 1897.

of the many journeys that his duties in Washington required of him, the aged chief practically discontinued his trips to Albany. The governor showed his independence by failing to visit Platt at the Fifth Avenue Hotel and during 1897 the relations between the two men were often strained. However, the metropolitan newspapers announced one Monday morning in 1898 that Governor Black, Senator Platt, and Chairman Hackett had met in council the previous evening and "had a long talk after dinner about legislative matters at Albany" and that "all three were agreed that the legislature should be out of Albany by the last week of March or the first week in April." [20]

Just as accounts of Theodore Roosevelt's other activities were spread abroad in the newspapers, so his "conferences with the chief," his "breakfasts" with Platt were the subject of comment and discussion on all sides. One reason for comments upon these conferences was their great frequency. While Roosevelt was still governor-elect, the newspapers were heralding the fact that Senator Platt and Chairman Odell had taken breakfast with the Colonel at the home of his sister, Mrs. Robinson.[1] Roosevelt claimed on his part that "a series of breakfasts was always a prelude to some active warfare,"[2] and Senator Platt said of them: "Roosevelt had from the first agreed that he would consult me on all questions of appointments, legislature, or party policy. He religiously fulfilled this pledge, although he frequently did just what he pleased."[3] Mrs. Robinson states that she also was present at these after "breakfast" conferences, much to the discomfiture of the Senator.[4] Platt,

[20] January 31, 1898.
[1] New York Tribune, December 11, 1898.
[2] Op. cit., p. 288.
[3] Op. cit., p. 374.
[4] (Mrs.) C. R. Robinson, My Brother Roosevelt (New York, 1921), p. 81.

however, could do nothing about it as he found it inconvenient to go to Albany except on such rare occasions as Governor Roosevelt's "harmony" banquet.[5] The nature of the Platt-Roosevelt conferences is revealed in part by the following letter:

UNITED STATES SENATE
WASHINGTON, D. C.
FEB. 3, 1900.

Hon. Theo. Roosevelt,
    Executive Chamber,
        Albany, N. Y.
MY DEAR GOVERNOR:
    Your letter of the 31st ultimo came duly to hand and its contents have been carefully considered. It will be agreeable to me to change the date of our breaking bread together, from Saturday the 10th, at luncheon, to breakfast on Monday the 12th.

.   .   .   .

    The question of adopting the policy of the Canal Commission is a very serious one, and I am very much at a loss to decide what is wise and politic. There is no doubt as to what is good business and for the material welfare of the great state of New York, but present expediency must sometimes govern such cases. The farmers in the rural counties are so sensitive on the subject of taxation that we are in grave danger of wasting away our narrow margin of majority. . . .

                                Yours sincerely,
                                    T. C. PLATT.[6]

    The first legislative act of a governor that interested Platt in his capacity as general manager of the Republican organization was the annual message to the legislature, containing such recommendations as he deemed worthy of the consideration of that body. While the governor might in this message dodge his responsibility and submit a general

[5] *New York Herald,* March 29, 1898.
[6] *Barnes* v. *Roosevelt,* pp. 2472–74.

lecture on political principles or public morals, a careful student of the constitutional history of New York thinks that it may fairly be said that "much the larger proportion of executive recommendations as to particular legislation have been adopted and may be found in the statutes of the period."[7]

In Platt's *Autobiography* a long letter, written to Governor Morton on January 3, 1896, is given,[8] which illustrates very clearly some of the precautions that a political manager takes regarding the governor's annual message. The significant portions of this letter, so far as the points at issue are concerned, are given below:

I put it mildly when I say to you that I was disgusted and disheartened when General Tracy handed me yesterday your letter to him of December 31st, relative to Greater New York. When we sought and had the conference with you at General Tracy's house on this question, it was for the purpose of having definitely settled what your position would be on this question. There could have been no misunderstanding on your part as to what was our intention and purpose in that interview with you, because our entire programme was definitely stated and thoroughly explained, and we went away from that conference understanding that you were in full accord and would stand by us to the end. Now, at the very opening of the legislature, as I have expressed it to you before, you "take to the woods" and are leaving us in the lurch. . . . Your message on the subject of Greater New York was, to put it mildly, as weak as dishwater; last year you were quite outspoken. Evidently the raid on you by Mr. Low and Company had its effect. You understand at the interview above referred to that this was what was likely to happen; that the enemies of the measure would do everything in their power to prevent the passage of this bill and would resort to just the arguments that they are using; and would do everything in their power

[7] Lincoln, *op. cit.*, p. 69.
[8] Pp. 307–310.

to intimidate you. This was our reason for calling upon you, so that we might know that you would stand firmly by the programme.

In his annual message for 1895, Governor Morton had said on the subject of Greater New York that "it now becomes the duty of the legislature to take such further steps as are necessary to put the wishes "of the people of the cities involved into effect" and that he suggested "that a commission be at once created, to be composed of the most capable citizens of the various localities interested, and to be charged with the power and the duty of framing a charter and reporting the same to the present legislature, if such a plan can be drafted and submitted before the session closes." [9] In the "dishwater" message of 1896, which was submitted to the legislature on January 1, two days before Platt's letter was written, Governor Morton had merely said: "I recommend that earnest and careful consideration be given to the subject (Greater New York) and that some conclusive action be taken regarding it at your present session." [10] The subsequent history of these recommendations will be discussed in later parts of this chapter; the above quotation is sufficient to show Platt's relations with Morton with reference to the initial stages of legislation.

In Platt's memoirs no letters to Governor Black are given and it is therefore difficult to say how much "instruction," if any, was given to this chief executive in the matter of annual messages to the legislature. The most striking part of Governor Black's first annual message was the part on civil service in which he said that "civil service will work better with less starch," that the system should be ridden of "ideas so delicate as to be worthless in practice," and that greater

[9] *Messages*, IX, 552–53.
[10] *Ibid.*, p. 674.

"discretion" should be given to the appointing officers.[11]   By "civil service" he must have meant the system of choosing civil service employees by competitive examinations, the "reform" which Thomas C. Platt had scored so bitterly twenty years before in a speech before a state convention. Platt had no difficulty in seeing the connection between "starchless" civil service and a "simon pure party régime," so it is probable that he thought he could neglect Governor Black's education somewhat when it came to the matter of recommendations to the legislature.[12]

The way that Governor Roosevelt made up his annual messages cannot be demonstrated in any more striking way than by quoting from a letter of his to Senator Platt:

STATE OF NEW YORK,
EXECUTIVE CHAMBER,
ALBANY, DEC. 19TH, 1899.

Senator T. C. Platt,
   Senate Chamber, Washington, D. C.
MY DEAR SENATOR:

Herewith I send you proof of my message. All the important parts I have had gone over by various experts. Thus the entire canal matter has been laid before General Greene, Supt. Partridge, State Engineer Bond, and Fox and MacFarlane. The part on taxation, franchise tax, public utilities, industrial conditions and trusts has been laid before Stranahan, Elihu Root, President Hadley of Yale and Prof. Jenks of Cornell, as well as in part before Prof. Seligman of Columbia and Judge Cohen, and that lawyer, James A. Dill, of New Jersey. . . . The part about labor I have put before Secretary of State McDonough, Prof. Jenks, and Attorney General Griggs. The agricultural part has been before Assemblyman Witter of Tioga County.
. . .

[11] *Messages,* IX, 749.
[12] The *New York Herald,* Jan. 7, 1897 complained that New York city had been slighted in the message.

I need not say that I want you to make suggestions and criticisms with utmost freedom. . . .
Faithfully yours,
THEODORE ROOSEVELT. [13]

Two of the men mentioned in this letter, the State Engineer and the Secretary of State, it will be remembered were nominated at the same convention which named Roosevelt as a result of that "higgling in the market" process by which minor state officers were selected. Assemblyman Witter, of course, from Platt's home county, was one of the Senator's close friends and lieutenants. It is likely that Governor Roosevelt submitted his message to these men and to Platt also as a matter of courtesy and that after receiving their advice he did as he pleased, but the letter at least shows that Roosevelt regarded Platt as a man well worth flattering.

The annual message of the governor was a constitutional requirement and even a "constitutional executive" could not avoid saying some things of importance in performing this task which were more or less displeasing to the leaders of the legislature. This was a condition which the organization workers had to accept with as much equanimity as possible. Thus, Governor Morton's remarks upon the subject of civil service [14] and Governor Black's comments on the advantages of biennial sessions [15] were not welcome to all the law makers. On the other hand, when it came to the transmission of special messages, the governor might upon his own volition place the legislature in a most embarrassing position. The necessity of the immediate passage of some "obnoxious" measure which had been "put to sleep" in the

[13] *Barnes* v. *Roosevelt*, p. 2463.
[14] *Messages*, IX, 560. Morton was friendly to the question of civil service reform.
[15] *Messages*, IX, 753–54. This recommendation has repeatedly been made but the legislature refused to act.

committee might be certified or a special session might be called to consider some "dangerous" subject. Attention would then be focused upon the legislators, a condition of affairs which they did not always find comfortable. It therefore seems to the writer that Platt's influence and that of the organization over the governor's power to send special messages to the legislature must be judged as much from the point of view of what was not done as well as from the standpoint of what was done.

Governor Morton sent special messages to the legislature on such subjects as the dedication of Chickamauga Military Park, the advisability of celebrating the capital city centennial, the reorganization of the New York criminal courts and police, and the need for economy in appropriations.[16] The last two matters were of great importance, but the proposals were not "revolutionary." Governor Morton also certified for immediate passage such bills as the Regulation of the Civil Service bill, the Election Law, and the Supplemental Supply bill. Although there was some opposition in the legislature to the first of these bills, it can hardly be said that Platt regarded any of them as "unsafe." While Governor Morton filed a memorandum with his approval of the bill regulating horse racing, there was no ringing message on the subject like the one with which Governor Hughes startled the lawmakers some thirteen years later.

Governor Black likewise did not make any rousing appeals to the voters over the heads of their representatives at Albany. It is true that he asked for power to appoint a commission to investigate the canal improvement but this was largely to please his own appointees.[17] It also is true that he certified for immediate passage the Metropolitan

[16] State of New York, *Public Papers of Governor Morton*, 1895–96, *passim*.
[17] *Messages*, IX, 849–51.

Elections bill, the bill to regulate primary elections, and the
military appropriation bill, but these measures were accept-
able to the organization in their final form.[18]   In justice to
Governor Black, however, it should be noted that some contemporaries regarded the primary reform law which he
sponsored as "bitterly distasteful to the Platt machine." [19]

It remained for Governor Roosevelt to shock the "organization" by his use of the special message to secure the
passage of the Franchise Tax bill.   In his annual message
for 1899, his remarks upon the subject of taxation had been
general enough to cause the organization leaders no alarm.
Toward the end of January Senator Ford introduced a bill
authorizing the taxation of franchises of street railway, gas,
electric light, and telephone companies as real property.[20]
This bill was not revolutionary because the utility companies
had been subject to such taxation prior to a judicial decision
in 1892.   Hearings were held upon the bill and toward the
end of March the Governor showed his interest in the subject by telling the newspaper correspondents that he thought
franchises should be taxed.[1]   On March 27, he sent a
special message to the legislature in which he said that the
farmers, the market gardeners, and the mechanics and
tradesmen having small holdings, were paying an improper
and excessive portion of the general taxes and that one
thing was certain, that the franchises should in some form
yield a money return to the government, especially franchises bestowed upon gas companies, street railroads and
the like.[2]   This message did not have an immediate effect

[18] See *New York Tribune,* Feb. 2, 1898, for Platt-Black conference on the primary reform bill.
[19] *Nation,* April 7, 1898.
[20] *New York Tribune,* Jan 26, 1899, for discussion of bill by
Sen. Ford.
[1] *Ibid.,* March 22, 1899.
[2] *Messages,* X, 35–36.

upon the Ford bill because it contained an indirect suggestion that such a measure should be referred to an investigating committee, a sort of committee which might take a year or so for its work.[3]

Governor Roosevelt, however, did not let the matter drop at this point. His announcement to the newspaper correspondents that he thought the Ford bill should be passed at once was sufficient to persuade the Senate to take action upon it.[4] In the Assembly the bill ran into all sorts of obstacles. The Committee on Taxation and Retrenchment to which it had been referred refused even to hold hearings upon the matter.[5] These dilatory tactics continued so long that the time came when the Rules Committee assumed its absolute sway over all bills and then it was thought that the measure was "safely put to sleep." In spite of the protests of the organization leaders, Roosevelt would not let it "rest in peace," and he kept talking to the newspaper men about its desirability.[6] Finally on the eve of the day set for adjournment he sent a special emergency message to the Assembly which should have had the effect of taking the bill out of the Committee on Rules. Roosevelt's account of what happened after this runs as follows:

The machine leaders were bitterly angry, and the Speaker actually tore up the message without reading it to the Assembly. That night they were busy trying to arrange some device for the defeat of the bill—which was not difficult, as the session was about to close. At seven the next morning I was informed of what had occurred. At eight I was in the capitol at the executive chamber, and sent in another special message, which opened as follows: "I learn that the emergency message which I sent last evening to the

[3] *New York Tribune*, March 29, 1898.
[4] *Ibid.*, April 12, 1899.
[5] *Ibid.*, April 14, 1899.
[6] *Ibid.*, April 15, 1899.

Assembly on behalf of the Franchise Tax Bill has not been read. I therefore send hereby another message on the subject. I need not impress upon the Assembly the need of passing this bill at once." I sent this message to the Assembly by my secretary, . . . with the intimation that if this were not promptly read I should come up in person and read it." [7]

When this second emergency message was read there was a great flutter in the Assembly. The assemblymen who had read the morning papers commenting upon the "shameful conduct of the Assembly leaders" of the night before, probably thought of their rural constituents and their attitude upon this question. Floor Leader Allds reported the bill from the Rules Committee and an irresistible tide of public opinion carried it through.[8]

The organization leaders were stunned but not beaten. They thought they saw visions of disappearing campaign funds, but these visions were not yet reality. On May 6 Platt wrote a long letter to the Governor which ran in part as follows:

Please take the time to read this letter through carefully. . . . But the Ford bill shot into the heart of the business community out of a clear sky, worked by Tammany Hall for political and individual plunder is a bad thing and I sincerely believe that you will make the mistake of your life if you allow the bill to become a law. With a political experience that runs back nearly half a century I do not hesitate to predict that the signing of this bill, with the tremendous power it conveys to the Tammany assessors, will give New York to the Democratic party in 1900.

I hope that you will not consider that I am making anything in the nature of a personal request. The subject is too serious for anything of that kind. I am asking and ad-

[7] *Op. cit.*, p. 302.
[8] *New York Tribune,* April 29, 1899.

vising in the public interest and for reasons that I have here set forth.[9]

Governor Roosevelt thanked the Senator for the "frankness, courtesy and delicacy" with which he wrote, but his keen sense of this made "it more unpleasant to have to disagree" with him.[10]   After the corporation lawyers had been given a hearing, the Governor admitted that the assessment feature was "wrong," but he insisted upon the bill with this feature rather than no bill at all.   A compromise was reached when the Governor agreed to reconvene the legislature for the purpose of considering certain amendments to the bill which would remedy this defect.[11]   A few changes were made and the fight against the bill, based principally upon these very changes, was then carried into the courts.[12] But the "damage" had been done by the emergency message, as Platt admitted in the following words, written before the extra session was called: "But at the last moment, and to my very great surprise, you did a thing which has caused the business community of New York to wonder how far the notions of Populism, as laid down in Kansas and Nebraska, have taken hold upon the Republican party of the state of New York." [13]

Governor Roosevelt sent many other special messages to the legislature, but none of them were so striking as the one which has been discussed and even Platt was willing to admit that his other messages had "created a good opinion throughout the state."   These other messages touched on

[9] *Barnes* v. *Roosevelt,* pp. 2368 ff.
[10] *Barnes* v. *Roosevelt,* p. 2375, Roosevelt to Platt, May 8, 1899.
[11] "It is easy to say that the Governor has called the extra session to get himself out of a scrape, and the people who want him to be in a scrape are quick to say it.   As a matter of fact the extra session was called at the suggestion of the franchise-holders."— *New York Tribune,* May 23, 1899.
[12] *Messages,* X, 71.
[13] Roosevelt, *op. cit.,* p. 300.

such subjects as civil service reform, rapid transit for New York City, the regulation of tenement houses, and the Public Health Law. On the last three of these matters, Platt gave his "grudging and querulous assent."

The third great constitutional power that the governor possessed over legislation was the veto power. After a bill was passed it had to be submitted to the governor for his approval before it could become a law, except that if he held a bill ten days before the legislature adjourned without any action, it might become a law without his signature.[14] If a bill failed to meet his approval he could of course veto it within the ten-day period or use the veto as a threat to secure certain amendments. A direct veto was overridden by a two-thirds vote of the legislature only on rare occasions. The situation was different, however, during the thirty-day period allowed to the governor for the consideration of bills after the adjournment of the legislature, for at this time the governor's veto was absolute whether it was of the explicit or the "omnibus" variety, bills not signed during this period being deemed in the latter category. Since the governor could veto specific items in an appropriation bill, his "omnibus" veto was a very powerful weapon. It could be used to embarrass legislators who were overzealous in caring for the local interests of their constituents.

Governor Morton did sign some "organization measures," and this fact was interpreted by some as "proof that he was in close alliance with Platt."[15] Among such measures might be classified the bill for a "bi-partisan police board" for West Troy which was designed to secure to the two "machines" a "voice" in the distribution of the local police

[14] Constitution, Art. IV, Sec. 9.
[15] *Nation*, April 30, 1896, LXII, 336.

patronage,[16] a bill for the relief of Tioga County which aimed to recompense Platt's county for certain expenses in connection with a railroad strike,[17] a bill relative to guarantors and sureties which permitted such foreign corporations as the Fidelity and Deposit Company of Maryland, in which one of Platt's sons was interested, to do business in the state,[18] a bill to regulate race track gambling which left out the penalties, a bill to amend the Insurance Law which sanctioned discriminations against foreign insurance companies,[19] the Raines Liquor Tax bill, and the bill relative to the creation of Greater New York. Perhaps the fact that these bills were signed was one of the things that led Platt to call Governor Morton, the "safest governor that New York ever had." It should not be supposed that all of these bills were signed without a struggle; for instance, Governor Morton could not help but pay some attention to the determined opposition to the Greater New York bill which developed alarming proportions. Additional portions of Platt's letter to Governor Morton, dated January 3, 1896, will show what tactics the wily chief employed to meet this contingency:

I say to you that this whole business utterly discourages and demoralizes me; and it makes me wonder *what would be the result if you succeeded in becoming president of the United States* and had to meet such issues as are involved in the questions of the present hour, for instance, the Venezuelan question and the Bond question. . . . And if you are to persist in the policy which you have outlined in your letter, we might as well quit right where we are and not introduce any resolution or bill for Greater New York; but I

[16] D. Wilcox, "Party Government in Cities of New York," *Political Science Quarterly*, XIV, 687.
[17] *Messages*, IX, 593ff.
[18] See below p. 247.
[19] See below p. 278.

assure you that you will be the greater sufferer from such a cowardly policy. *In such case I will not feel like taking off my coat and doing the work I contemplated in the presidential matter.* I might as well be frank with you now. If matters of legislation are to be run on the issue of the presidential candidacy, it will be impossible for us to accomplish anything upon any questions which involve sharp differences of opinion, however strongly the balance may be in favor of the course which the organization is recommending.[20]

The editor of Platt's *Autobiography* called this letter the "clincher" to Morton which, it was believed, "induced" the Governor to attach his signature to the bill. If this was so, it had a long time to work, because the bill was not finally signed until May 11, 1899. Governor Morton was not tractable upon all matters. Platt had a favorite bill which aimed to give the governor direct power over the New York City police, but this bill was so offensive to Morton that he said he would not sign it until it was so amended as to give Mayor Strong the power to appoint the commission to reorganize the force. Platt saw that he had to retreat and the changes were made in the bill.[1] Governor Morton likewise showed a stubborn independence in his treatment of thirty-day bills, an "interference and opposition" which Platt called "executive back-fire on our friends in the legislature."[2] Among these "humiliations and sad experiences" were the governor's vetoes of some of Senator Lexow's bills referring to New York City and numerous other measures of a local or "pork barrel" nature.[3]

That Senator Platt had "influence" with the next governor was surmised from the fact that Governor Black

[20] *Op. cit.*, pp. 308–9.

[1] *Nation, February 7*, 1895, LX, 101.

[2] Platt, *op. cit.*, pp. 307, 309.

[3] *Ibid.*, and *Public Papers of Governor Morton*, 1895, *passim*.

signed the Greater New York charter bill, the work of the commission created by the law passed during Governor Morton's administration. At any rate, in recognition of the interest which the Senator had shown in the passage of the bill, the Governor sent him the pen with which he had signed it.[4] With reference to the civil service bill, the primary elections measure and the metropolitan elections bill, there was no need for such courtesy because the governor himself had been one of the initiating forces.

Governor Black's "executive back-fire" was probably more constant and "saddening" than Governor Morton's had been. At the beginning of the session for 1898 he openly declared that he would not give his approval to any measures amending the Greater New York charter except such as might be found essential to its actual working and that he would not sanction "deals" of any kind.[5] He told the Senator personally that he would veto any anti-caricaturist bill,[6] and his threat was sufficient to prevent the passage of any such measure just as it had thrown out the metropolitan police bill the year before.[7] The anti-cartoonist, or "press gag" bill, was the only "personal favor" that Platt was supposed to have asked of the legislature and the police bill was strenuously sponsored by Messrs. Quigg, Gibbs, and Lauterbach, but the Governor "riddled" both. During his régime the "organization" also fared badly in the matter of thirty-day bills: he refused to sign bills invading the rights of various up-state cities;[8] he vetoed the New York City school salary bill by which the municipal authorities sought to evade their responsibility; he kept from the statute books

[4] *Nation*, May 13, 1897.   See Alexander, *Four Famous New Yorkers*, p. 292.
[5] *Nation*, April 7, 1898, LXVI, 256.
[6] *New York Tribune*, February 1, 1898.
[7] *Ibid.*, May 18, 1897.
[8] *Ibid.*, Jan. 8, 1898.

the Burns Insurance bill which sought to increase the inequitable burden of policy holders; and he failed to approve some dangerous amendments to the Railroad Law.[9] It was because of his vetoes, he claimed, that certain of Platt's lieutenants opposed his renomination for governor in 1898.[10]

The organization leaders did not need to be told that Governor Roosevelt would not be subservient when his approval for certain bills was desired. In 1898 the margin of the Republican organization in the legislature was so narrow that it could not ruthlessly control the law-making process. Because of Governor Roosevelt's decided stand upon the franchise tax question, the leaders of the organization were constrained from pushing any of their "favorite" measures.[11] When the Governor disapproved of certain provisions in a measure, he would request that it be recalled from him and amendments made. Although no "conspicuously bad" laws were passed during this session, the omnibus veto kept 105 bills from the statute books, most of which were of a local or special character.[12] During the next session of the legislature, the Governor was more politic, and instead of trying to force the party leaders to accept his views by peremptory methods, he arranged the program with them in a spirit of concession. A friendly interpreter said that "this course was doubtless by him considered wise, in view of the approaching election of a president and a governor." [13] In spite of the "harmonious" character of the session and its negative achievements, the omnibus veto fell upon 169 measures.[14] The legislators were tending more and more to shift the responsibility for legislation to the

[9] *Ibid.*, May 5, 1898.
[10] *Barnes* v. *Roosevelt*, pp. 2354 ff, Quigg to Roosevelt.
[11] *New York Tribune*, April 29, 1899.
[12] *Messages*, X, 48–64.
[13] *New York Tribune*, April 7, 1900.
[14] *Messages*, X, 150–79.

governor and to say among themselves, "Let us put it up to the governor." On the other hand it cannot be said that Governor Roosevelt's use of the veto power was any more spectacular than that of his predecessors.

APPOINTMENTS

Another feature of the governor's work that attracted widespread attention was his use of the appointing power. While many administrative officers were made elective by the constitution and others were given statutory terms longer than that of the governor, still many appointments were made by the governor, and this task often involved the delicate responsibility of selecting high judicial, military and administrative officers, and also important local officers, especially to fill vacancies.

Platt was said to have "influence" with that governor who appointed prominent members of the "organization" to some of the high positions in his gift. When Mr. Morton became governor, he found that the "Republican organization" had pledged the office of superintendent of public works to State Committeeman Aldridge. This office, which had extensive control over the canal patronage and other public works, was the most important at the governor's disposal, at least from Platt's point of view. Aldridge's name was pressed by many active politicians who lived in Rochester and by some who lived in New York. Among the latter was Chauncey M. Depew.[15] Attention has already been called to the fact that as mayor of Rochester, Aldridge acquired the reputation of being a "spoilsman of the Platt type." [16] It was thought that he would use the canal patronage to build up a "machine" to control caucuses,[17] and so

[15] *New York Tribune*, January 3, 1895.
[16] See above p. 62.
[17] *New York Tribune*, November 24, 1894.

when Governor Morton, among the first acts of his administration, sent in the name of this "unfit candidate," the reformers shook their heads and the "Boys" shouted for joy. The senators, of course, Republicans and Democrats alike, did not hesitate to confirm such an appointment.

Among the other appointments which Governor Morton made, several called forth adverse comment. One of these was his choice of a "practical" politician for the office of civil service commissioner, to replace an incumbent who was satisfying the reform element. Another was his appointment to the state inspectorship of gas meters of a person whose recommendations were afterward shown to be false and misleading.[18]   Still another was his appointment of Lyman as state excise commissioner, a new state officer of great "political" importance whose powers grew out of the Raines Liquor Tax Law.[19]   The crowning use of his power for "the good of the organization" was his elevation of "Jake" Worth, the "boss" of Brooklyn, to the Kings County clerkship, a position which entailed large fees.[20]

In the matter of appointments, Governor Black soon dispelled all doubts as to his loyalty to the "organization." Superintendent Aldridge, who had gained great "popularity" along the line of the canal,[1] was reappointed to his old position, and thus a graceful courtesy was accorded to one of the leading candidates at the Saratoga Convention who had come so near to success. "Boss" Worth was reappointed to his "$40,000 County Clerkship," [2] and State Committeeman Dunn, from Platt's congressional district, was selected as one of the railroad commissioners. The "brav-

[18] *New York Tribune,* January 12, 1896.
[19] *Nation,* April 30, 1896.
[20] *Ibid.* Nov. 5, 1896.
[1] *Utica Press,* January 8, 1897.
[2] *New York Tribune,* April 12, 1897.

est" act of the Governor, however, was his appointment of "Lou" Payn as superintendent of insurance, "Lou" Payn, the life-long friend of Platt, the self-confessed lobbyist, whom Elihu Root had called but two years before "a stench in the nostrils of the people of the state of New York," was to deal with some of the largest and most powerful corporations in the state. The Democratic and "Mugwump" press went into spasms.[3] Even some of the senators who usually voted "regular" were constrained to "bolt" this appointment. It was thought for a while that Governor Black was trying to set up an organization of his own and to become "boss" in Platt's place.[4]

After Roosevelt's election in 1898, every one knew that "things would be different." Platt said that "Governor Roosevelt started in whirlwind fashion to clean house at Albany."[5] Only now and then was the Senator able to impede the process. The Daly-Cohen controversy affords an interesting example of one of the methods that he employed. A Democratic justice of the Supreme Court, Judge Morgan J. O'Brien, talked of resigning his office in order to become the head of the firm of Tracy, Boardman and Platt (the so-called Platt family law firm). Roosevelt wanted to appoint Judge Daly, a Democrat whose independence of Croker had furnished the Republicans with an "issue" in the previous campaign, but Platt favored the appointment of Cohen, a Republican. When Roosevelt indicated that he would not be moved, Justice O'Brien changed his mind about resigning.[6] The inference was that Platt had informed Croker of the Governor-elect's decision and the Tammany chief had used his influence to keep Judge

[3] *Binghamton Republican,* February 4, 1897.
[4] *New York Tribune,* April 12, 1897, "Black, Not Platt, the Boss."
[5] *Op. cit.,* p. 374.
[6] *New York Tribune,* December 11, 1898.

O'Brien upon the bench.[7] Discipline was a matter of importance to both organizations and this was what the politicians called a "move." When asked whether he had inspired it, Platt winked wickedly and smiled. Governor Roosevelt used one of his favorite similes to the effect that he was playing the game on the table and not under it.

The first real clash between Platt and the Governor-elect came over the appointment of a superintendent of public works whose office Roosevelt regarded as by far the most important under his care. During the last weeks of Governor Black's administration, Superintendent Aldridge had asked that he be suspended while certain charges against him were being investigated. The canal scandals furnished one of the reasons why Platt consented to have Roosevelt run for governor, and the appointment of Aldridge's successor was therefore watched with great interest. Rumors were current around the Fifth Avenue Hotel that Francis J. Hendricks, of Syracuse, an organization man with a highly respectable reputation, had been "slated" for the position.[8] At a Platt-Roosevelt-Woodruff conference, the Senator informed the Governor-elect that he had a most admirable man for the place as he had just received a telegram from Hendricks saying that he would accept the position. Roosevelt saw that this was a test case and replied that he was sorry but he could not appoint Hendricks whom he liked or any other man who was chosen for him, and that he must choose for himself. He then presented the names of four men for the place. Platt soon saw that Roosevelt was determined, so he consented to the selection of one

[7] J. L. Steffens, "Governor Roosevelt." *McClure's Mag.*, XIII, 63.

[8] *New York Tribune*, December 29, 1898.

THE GLAD HAND

Wait Till the Light is Turned Out and the Air Will Be Full of
Eye-Glasses and Pointed Whiskers.

(From *The Verdict,* April 16, 1900. Original owned by Roosevelt Memorial
Association)

of these four, Colonel Partridge, of Brooklyn, a relative of "Tim" Woodruff.[9]

After the appointment of Partridge as superintendent of public works, Roosevelt thought that he had established his relations with Platt on pretty nearly the right basis. The Senator, however, did not show his full hand as manager of the organization until over a year later when the spectacular struggle over the appointment of a successor to "Lou" Payn, superintendent of insurance, was staged. There was a story that Roosevelt had made a pre-election pledge to Quigg, to deliver "Lou" Payn's political head on a charger.[10] This certainly was not part of Platt's program, for Platt sent an ultimatum to the Governor that Payn must be reappointed when his term expired in February, 1900, or else there would be a fight.[11] The announcement from the executive chamber that Payn would have to go was answered by a flood of petitions from the insurance companies asking for his retention. Roosevelt still persisted in his determination. Platt then began to show his real weapon; Payn could not be ousted because the assent of the Senate was necessary to appoint any successor and the incumbent continued in office until his successor was appointed. As to Platt's control of the Senate on this matter, Roosevelt testified later as follows:

"After full investigation I became convinced in my own mind that the organization controlled the majority of the

[9] Roosevelt, *op. cit.*, p. 285. W. J. Youngs, *Administration of Theodore Roosevelt as Governor* (Manuscript in Roosevelt Memorial Association Library).

[10] *Albany Argus*, January 15, 1900. In his *Autobiography* Platt said, "He threw Superintendent of Insurance Louis F. Payn out of his job so quickly as to send that official to me with a cry: 'I warned you that fellow would soon have you dangling at his chariot wheel.'" Platt was evidently under the false impression that this occurred at the start of Roosevelt's administration.

[11] Roosevelt, *op. cit.*, p. 291.

Senate, and that if I wished to discuss questions of appointment that were apt to come to an issue between me and the Senate, it was advisable for me to go to where the real power was, to talk with Mr. Platt, and not to talk with men who I had become convinced in my own mind would merely carry out the bidding of Mr. Platt, therefore that I must consult with him if I wished to get affirmative action." [12]

There can be no doubt that Platt was consulted upon the question of the appointment of a superintendent of insurance.[13] The Governor found out that Platt's arrangement with the organization Democrats was "iron-clad" on such matters, and that a great majority of the Democratic senators would vote with the Republican organization upon this question.[14] Roosevelt next decided to send in the name of Francis J. Hendricks for the position. Platt had desired to put Hendricks in one high administrative position, surely he could not object to Hendricks being placed in another position of about equal importance. Besides Hendricks was an ex-senator and very popular with his old friends in the state Senate. That body certainly could not refuse to endorse him. An offer was sent immediately to the gentleman from Syracuse. Imagine the Governor's surprise when that gentleman declined the nomination! Here was another example of what the politicians called a "move." [15]

Roosevelt had one weapon left. He remembered that Platt had said the retention of Payn was demanded by certain big-monied men of both parties, whose contributions to the organization in the past had been very heavy and who possessed such influence upon newspapers in the business

[12] *Barnes* v. *Roosevelt*, p. 690.
[13] Platt, *op. cit.*, p. 375; Roosevelt, *loc. cit.*
[14] *Barnes* v. *Roosevelt*, answer to complaint and p. 1308; J. B. Bishop, *op. cit.*, I, 130, letter of Roosevelt analyzing votes in the Senate.
[15] J. L. Steffens, "Governor Roosevelt as an Experiment," *McClure's Magazine*, XV (1900), 110.

world that it was not safe to antagonize them.[16] About this time, a petition to the state superintendent of banks was published alleging that certain directors of the State Trust Company had lent enormous sums of money to themselves and others on several varieties of unsatisfactory security. Among these loans of doubtful legality, was one to Louis F. Payn for $435,000.[17] This disclosure gave the Governor the whip hand. It appeared that if charges were brought against Payn, many others higher up would be involved. Platt was now frantic lest he would not be consulted in the making of the final choice.[18] Francis Hendricks, who had thrice declined the office, sent a telegram to Roosevelt that "he would accept the office if the 'Republican organization' would support the nomination." This support was promised by the "Republican organization." [19] For some reason, legal proceedings were not brought against the directors of the State Trust Company, and that institution with all its records went out of existence a few months later when a law was passed permitting its merger with the Morton Trust Company.[20] Francis Hendricks was established in the office of state superintendent of insurance until after the insurance investigation of 1905. Roosevelt later pictured this incident as one of his great victories, but at the time it was looked upon as an organization victory.[1]

[16] *Barnes* v. *Roosevelt,* answer.
[17] *New York Tribune,* January 14, 1900.
[18] *Ibid.,* January 19, 1900.
[19] *Ibid.,* January 27, 1900. See also the *Nation,* February 1, 1900; Steffens, *loc. cit.*
[20] B. J. Hendrick, "Great American Fortunes and Their Making," *McClure's Mag.,* XXX, 324. Roosevelt told the newspaper men that he regarded the company as solvent (*New York Tribune,* January 30, 1900), but the results of his investigation were never published.
[1] The writer was informed by D. S. Alexander that Roosevelt was drawing the "long bow" in his account of this affair. Roosevelt, *op. cit.,* pp. 293–94, and Alexander, *Four Famous New Yorkers,* p. 331.

With reference to the other appointments which he made, Roosevelt admitted that in almost all cases, although in not all, he consulted with Platt even though he was obliged to disregard his advice in some cases, especially where candidates for judicial positions were being considered.[2] The following letter reveals the way in which Platt handled such matters:

MARCH 31, 1899.

Hon. Theo. Roosevelt,
    Executive Chamber, Albany, N. Y.
MY DEAR GOVERNOR:
    I am in receipt of yours of March 30th. Gelshenen is a first-class man in every respect and I should think would be as acceptable as anybody, as a Democratic appointee. I think it would be well moreover, to please Grady.
    I find that I have been mistaken with reference to Leopold Stirn. He has no connection whatever with Stirn Brothers family, and is not a relative. Different family entirely. He is a downtown jeweler of wealth and reputation. He was very generous last fall, and therefore Quigg is anxious that he should receive the appointment. So you will excuse me if I change off my mind. . . .
                                        Yours sincerely,
                                            T. C. PLATT[3]

To this letter Roosevelt replied on April 1st as follows: "All right I will appoint Stirn and Gelshenen. Grady does not know the last named." [4] When he was questioned with reference to this letter, Roosevelt replied that there were times when he relied entirely upon the knowledge and suggestion of Mr. Platt and that the appointment of Gelshenen was made partly as a matter of pleasing Grady, the leader of the organization Democrats in the legislature.[5] Another

[2] *Barnes* v. *Roosevelt*, p. 771.
[3] *Ibid.*, exhibit 50 (17).
[4] *Ibid.*
[5] *Ibid.*, p. 542.

letter, written a little later that same year, illustrates perhaps more clearly the usual manner in which Platt made recommendations for appointments:

AUGUST 11, 1899.

Hon. Theo. Roosevelt,
  Oyster Bay, New York.
MY DEAR GOVERNOR:
  Our friends in Delaware County have settled upon a nominee for county judge and surrogate, in place of Sewell, whom you recently made Supreme Court Judge, in the person of John P. Grant of Stamford, N. Y., an old time Republican. As you will see, he is indorsed by the organization and by the whole Bar of the County. It is a good appointment, and I think the sooner it is disposed of the better.

Yours truly,
T. C. PLATT.[6]

In answer to this letter the Governor's secretary sent a telegram to Platt on August 24 announcing that Grant had been appointed. Roosevelt later explained that he did not know anything about the man appointed personally but that he had relied upon the judgment of Judge Sewell who gave him first hand information and then obtained recommendations from the members of the bar.[7] The letter reveals, the narrow range of choice exercised by both Platt and Roosevelt.[8] It was Roosevelt's custom to eliminate all those except the ones highly recommended and to send this

[6] *Barnes v. Roosevelt,* p. 2447.
[7] *Ibid.,* p. 771.
[8] In regard to the appointment of a new surrogate for New York City, Roosevelt wrote to Platt, under date of Feb. 10, 1899, as follows: "I have not the slightest purpose beyond getting a thoroughly good man who will do the work well, who is a Republican, but who is also a man thoroughly satisfactory to the bar and to the people." J. B. Bishop, *op. cit.,* I, 118.

list of the leaders of the organization for them to make the final choice.[9]

From the evidence adduced above, scanty as it may seem, it may safely be concluded that Platt was "consulted" with reference to the great majority of appointments that were made in the state service. Often the recommendation came in the form of an impersonal request from the "organization" and the governor may not have been conscious of Platt's influence, but the system was centralized.

GENERAL EXECUTIVE DUTIES

The New York State Constitution of 1894 declared that "the executive power shall be vested in a governor," but, paradoxical as it may seem, subsequent provisions of the document went on to deprive him of a large part of that power. As Governor Hughes remarked in his inaugural address in 1909, after two years experience in office: "While the governor represents the highest executive power in the state, there is frequently observed a popular misapprehension as to its scope. There is a wide domain over which he has no control, or slight control." [10] He went on to point out that there were several elective state officers not accountable to the governor, who exercised within their prescribed spheres most important executive powers. In discussing the statutory boards and officers he said: "The terms of officers are generally longer than the governor's term. And in their creation the legislature, with few exceptions, has reserved the final administrative control to the Senate in making the heads of departments, to whose appointment the Senate's consent in necessary, removable only by it."

[9] Youngs, *op. cit.*, p. 4.
[10] State of New York, *Public Papers of Governor Hughes* (1909), p. 8.

While Thomas C. Platt cannot be given the credit for devising this intricate and chaotic system of administrative organization, it is nevertheless true that he found this system operated in a way very much to his advantage. Thus, a governor like Roosevelt might cause a good deal of irritation in the organization by an independent use of his legislative and appointing powers, but there was little danger that he would overturn the entire administrative system, built up as it had been over the course of a number of years by various organization men planted in well nigh impregnable positions. The controlling consideration in the legislature in prescribing methods of appointment and removal, runs one very keen analysis of the governor's executive functions in New York, was not "to make the government responsible directly to public opinion or to make anyone responsible for leadership, for fidelity, or for efficiency and economy in carrying on the business of the state," but rather the dominant motives were "to prevent responsible leadership, to diffuse authority and to set one officer up against another so that no agent could have any power to do harm." [11]

The powers of removal that the governor did possess were carefully hedged about by many restrictions and were not sufficient to enable him to really direct the course of his administration. For example, he might suspend the treasurer for violation of his duty but he could not remove him; he might remove the superintendent of public works but he must report the cause of such removal to the legislature; he might remove the superintendent of prisons but this could only be "for cause" and after a hearing in which the ac-

[11] New York Bureau of Municipal Research, *The Constitution and Government of the State of New York, An Appraisal* (1915), p. 37. See also New York Executive Chamber, *Report of the Reconstruction Commission on Retrenchment and Reorganization in the State Government*, 1919, chap. I.

cused had a chance to make his defense; and finally, he might remove some of the important statutory officers but only with the consent of the Senate. The evidence which the writer has been able to find with reference to Platt's influence over the exercise of the governor's power of removal has been entirely of a negative character. During the six years of Platt's most successful management of the Republican party in New York which have been chosen as a basis for illustration in this chapter, there was only one actual removal by the governor of a high state administrative officer. In addition to the removal of a state lunacy commissioner by Governor Roosevelt, there were several removals by the governors of local officers, but otherwise the records on this subject are a blank.[12] It is clear that Platt did not need to do very much "consulting" about the use of this power. On the other hand, it is probable that when it was used even in connection with local officers, his advice was asked.[13]

In the performance of certain of his executive functions the governor did enjoy a fair amount of freedom. Within the limits of the law, the governor could lay down such regulations regarding the civil service as he deemed fit. Governor Morton exercised this power in such a way as to "cause deep pain" to Superintendent of Public Works Aldridge,[14] and he thereby won the commendation of the civil service reformers.[15] Governor Black carried out his ideas as to the proper nature of civil service examinations by establishing a set of "starchless rules." After the Civil Service Law of 1899 had been passed, the organization could do

[12] At least as shown by an examination of the public papers of Governors Morton, Black, and Roosevelt.
[13] New York Herald, June 9, 1900.
[14] Nation, February 7, 1895, LX, 101.
[15] Ibid., Dec. 17, 1896.

nothing to prevent Governor Roosevelt from supplanting the "starchless rules" by a set more rigid than had yet been established in any state. In the granting of pardons and commutations, the governor was also comparatively free from any interference on the part of the organization. It is interesting to note, however, that requests for executive clemency usually came from the local party organization, the trial judge or the district attorney, and in some cases from men like, Chauncey M. Depew, George W. Dunn, J. Sloat Fassett, or Cornelius Van Cott.[16]

Toward the close of the nineteenth century the governor came to be looked upon more and more as the official head and spokesman for the party in the state. The people came to look to him for the carrying out of the party's legislative program as well as for the driving force in administration. When the leaders of the organization decided upon a program of action, they expected to get the governor's co-operation in the work of its fulfillment. Governor Morton allowed his name to be used in the game that Platt and his lieutenants played in the Republican National Convention of 1896. Governor Black came to New York City in 1897 and made a speech in the interests of a factional fight that Platt and the "organization" were waging there.[17] Governor Roosevelt likewise showed an interest in New York City politics [18] and in the State Convention of 1900 he was called upon to make a eulogistic speech in behalf of the new candidate of the organization which had striven so hard to "shelve him in the vice-presidency." [19]

Platt's position as head of the "invisible" government of

[16] These names appeared in the public papers of Governors Morton and Roosevelt in the explanations of why certain pardons and commutations were granted.
[17] *New York Tribune,* October 21, 1897.
[18] *Ibid.,* June 29, 1900.
[19] *Ibid.,* September 6, 1900.

the state depended in large part upon his maintaining satisfactory relations with the governor who stood at the head of the visible government. When Governor Roosevelt wrote special messages upon touchy topics, when he vetoed the organization measures, when he refused to make appointments recommended by the organization, and when he insisted upon publicity for all phases of public administration, he threatened the place of the political manager who operated behind the scenes. Yet Platt held his place through this trying governorship. Platt made himself useful to Roosevelt. His contacts with the Republican organization enabled him to advise the governors about the probable effect of a message to the legislature, about the political consequences of certain appointments, about the practicability of certain administrative schemes. A governor in the state of New York in the late nineties who failed to heed or to listen to Platt's advice might be warned as to his fate before the next Republican convention, but ordinarily the over-burdened chief executive of the great industrial state of New York welcomed political information of the type which Platt was interested in gathering.

CHAPTER IX

THE DISTRIBUTION OF THE SPOILS

To Platt the distribution of the spoils of public office was a serious business. At times he seemed to be more concerned with the "equitable" allotment of the political patronage than he was with his own private affairs. Roosevelt viewed the spoils system with an air of amused tolerance, especially as it concerned appointments. As civil service commissioner, Roosevelt fought the spoilsman hard, but as governor of New York and later as president of the United States he did not try strenuously to "wreck the organization" by drying up the sources of its power as he might have done. Roosevelt concerned himself with large matters which attracted public attention, while Platt was concerned with the minute details of the system of party rewards and punishments.

LOCAL PATRONAGE

It is difficult to ascertain just what Platt's part was in the distribution of local rewards to the petty politicians. It is even more difficult to determine Roosevelt's relation to the patronage system. The centralization of control over the party machinery through the hierarchy of party committees made it necessary for the local leaders to "consult" those higher up when they desired favors from the state and national governments, but in local matters they were usually allowed a free hand. As long as a local leader carried his district, the state committee did not pry too closely into his affairs. On the other hand, local elections as well as state and national elections were run by the same organization, and it was one of the duties of the state leaders to see that each unit of the state organization was in proper working order. When the necessities of discipline demanded it, the state leaders could and did deprive refractory local leaders of their control over their local organizations.[1]

In each one of the sixty-one counties of the state there were at least seven elective officers, i. e., a judge, a treasurer, a sheriff, a clerk, a district attorney, a superintendent of the poor, and one or more coroners. Anyone desiring to hold one of these offices outside of New York City was practically compelled to seek it at the hands of the local Republican party manager. In 1899, for instance, between forty-six and fifty of the fifty-seven up-state counties were Republican.[2] In other words, one of the functions of the Republican party in New York was the nomination and election of over three hundred county officers. In addition the party had charge of the election of town officers in about eight hundred towns.[3] Since there were at least sixteen elective officers in each town, i. e., a supervisor, a clerk, four justices of the peace, three assessors, two school directors, two overseers of the poor, two or more constables, and a superintendent of highways, there must have been about thirteen thousand town officers in the Republican state organization. Then, too, there were about three hundred and seventy Republican villages, each with an elective president, treasurer, collector, police justice, and from two to eight trustees, containing in the aggregate over three thousand elective positions for the local Republican organizations to fill.

[1] Platt, *op. cit.*, pp. 504ff.

[2] *New York Red Book* (1899), p. 756. In 46 counties both the sheriff and clerk were Republicans.

[3] *Legislative Manual*, 1900, the election returns for 1899 show that about 800 out of the 930 towns were Republican.

It is not too much to say that the elective county, town, and village officers laid the basis for the Republican state organization which Platt directed during the nineties. However his fortunes might fluctuate in state wide and national politics, he could count on a solid phalanx of rural office holders year after year.[4] The disbursements which these local officers controlled were of no mean proportions. In 1910 the State Comptroller estimated that the counties outside of New York City expended each fiscal year over $30,000,000, while the incorporated villages expended around $7,000,000 annually.[5] These expenditures were directed for the most part by Republican officials and a large part of them went for personal services. The salaries of elective county officers ranged from $500 to $10,000 a year,[6] and those paid upon a fee basis sometimes received as much as $20,000 a year.[7] In a populous county like Monroe County, which contained two hundred thousand people, there were over three hundred and fifty county employees whose annual payroll amounted to over $300,000 a year.[8] State Committeeman Aldridge had trouble with his city but he never lost his county during the period under discussion.

[4] *Official New York from Cleveland to Hughes, passim.* Lists of county officers with their political affiliations are given for the years 1883–1911.

[5] *Report of the Comptroller on Municipal Accounts,* 1910, p. 13. Only part of these disbursements were controlled by Republican officials.

[6] *Ibid.,* 1908, p. 14. The figures are based upon the fragmentary reports of local officers submitted for 1907.

[7] Westchester County Research Bureau, "Organization of Westchester County" in New York State Constitutional Convention Commission, *County Government in New York,* 1915, p. 114.

[8] New York Bureau of Municipal Research, "Government of Monroe County" in New York State Const. Conv. Com., *City and County Government* (1915), p. 7. These figures are too high for the period under discussion but an examination of 1908 report of the Comptroller shows that the error is not enormous.

In another county, with a population of fifty thousand, there were about one hundred employees whose services cost about $140,000 a year.[9] The money spent for salaries and wages in the towns and villages probably ranged from $100 to $20,000 a year.[10] Inasmuch as the merit system was not applied to the civil service of any town or county during the nineties, it is likely that the selection of these employees was based largely upon political considerations. One of the signs of the disintegration of the old régime was the extension of the civil service rules to Erie County in 1900 and to four other up-state counties in 1905.[11]

Another sign of a changing era was the passage of a law in 1905 providing for the examination of county and village finances by the state comptroller. Hitherto the administration of county affairs had attracted little attention. Unfortunately for the Republicans, the enforcement of this law came into the hands of a Democratic comptroller due to the untoward election of 1906. The first report that he made upon municipal accounts must have startled many of the country politicians and have caused much grief among the "henchmen" of State Committeeman Dunn. A portion of this report reads as follows:

The County of Broome was first selected for examination and investigation in that county disclosed an astounding condition of affairs. It was found that the moneys of the county were being disbursed absolutely contrary to law; that county funds were regularly loaned to private individuals and county officials and that there was unmistakable evidence of defalcations aggregating many thousand dollars. During the process of investigation the clerk of the board

9 *Ibid.*, "The Government of Nassau County." This should be taken with the same qualifications.
10 *Ibid.*, *passim*. The disbursements for personal services in several towns and villages are given.
11 R. W. Belcher, "Merit System and County Civil Service," *Annals of the Amer. Acad.*, XLVII, 101.

of supervisors was indicted upon eight counts, charging forgery and larceny; charges were preferred against the county treasurer, who resigned two days prior to the date set for the hearing before the governor; the county treasurer was arrested upon information obtained from one of the examiners and has since been twice indicted for misappropriation of public funds; the superintendent of the poor placed his resignation in the Comptroller's hands when his accounts became subject of the Comptroller's investigation, and made a written confession of serious irregularities in his office." [12]

One of the Broome County officials indicted as a result of this investigation was found guilty upon trial and sentenced to a term in prison. The sum of $30,000 was recovered by a suit upon the bonds of the former county treasurer.[12] The examination of other counties revealed conditions that were equally amazing and the excuses offered by the county officials showed that county financing had been in a deplorable state for some time back. In Nassau County the disclosure of a shortage of about $45,000 resulted in the suicide of one of the persons involved and the subsequent punishment of the other. In each of the twelve counties examined during the first two years that the law was enforced, irregularities of some sort were discovered. Among the most common were: overcharges by county sheriffs for the board and transportation of prisoners, illegal retention of fees by sheriffs, treasurers and clerks, payment of personal and family expenses out of the county funds by sheriffs and superintendents of the poor; excessive charges for mileage and wages by supervisors; and illegal retention of funds by town tax collectors. In one county it was found that jurors' certificates had been issued to dead men and the

[12] *Annual Report of the Comptroller,* "Municipal Accounts," 1908, p. xxxvii.
[13] *Report of the Comptroller on Municipal Accounts,* 1909. The facts in this paragraph are taken from this report.

money due on such certificates drawn from the county treasury. In Onondaga County it was brought to light that the duties of the county treasurer had been "farmed out" to the State Bank of Syracuse. In the village of Watkins it was shown that a certain village officer was engaged in a private banking business and that he sometimes got his public and private duties confused. The next state comptroller, who was a Republican, placed the blame for these and other irregularities upon the tendency among local officials to follow precedents rather than the law.

An investigation made of the general affairs of the county of Albany in 1911 illustrates other possible ways in which county offices were used for partisan and factional purposes.[14] It is true that this inquiry came many years after the zenith of Platt's power, but it was found here as in other counties that there was a strong disposition among the county officers to follow "precedents." Republicans had been elected to county offices in Albany by and with the consent of Committeeman Barnes as far back as 1894 so it is not too much to imagine from what was reported in 1911 how things were managed in the late nineties. In 1908 the Comptroller found that the affairs of Albany had become a tangled mass because of special acts of the legislature, that several county officials had illegally retained certain fees, and that a unique and costly job of indexing had been maintained in the county clerk's office since 1893.[15] In addition to abuses of the sort mentioned, the Democratic legislators in charge of the investigation of Albany in 1911 thought they saw in this county a "settled policy to keep the civil judicial system under the influence of Republican leaders" by

[14] New York State Legislature, *Report of the Special Committee Appointed to Investigate the City and County of Albany*, transmitted to the Legislature, March 29, 1912.
[15] *Ibid.*, p. 72.

selecting the trial jurors according to their political affiliations and they also claimed to have discovered a "sinister
use of indictments for political purposes" in the district
attorney's office. At the end of the year 1907 when the district attorney's office changed hands, 465 indictments were
dismissed in one day and the holder of the office in 1911
was of the opinion that it was his duty to pigeon-hole indictments in order to keep the defendant under control.[16]
The conclusions of this investigation perhaps explain the
absence of any crusades against crime in Albany such as
occurred in New York City in the late nineties.

So far nothing has been said about the forty-one cities of
the up-state, varying in size in 1900 from Oneida with a
population of 6,364 to Buffalo with a population of 352,382.
The fact that the Republican and Democratic parties were
fairly evenly divided in most of these cities makes it necessary to discuss the party spoils system found in them apart
from the strongly Republican rural municipalities. At a
time when Platt's power was most complete, an exact student of municipal affairs pointed out the nature of party
government in the cities of New York.[17] After commenting
upon the great increase in the number of acts creating bi-
partisan boards for the administration of the police, fire,
public works, and other departments of the cities in the
state, he said, "Indeed, the clear purpose of these acts has
so commonly been a division of spoils between political parties, that even lawmakers themselves have in a number of
cases been constrained to adopt frankly the word 'bi-partisan,' with whatever stigma of selfishness that word may be
burdened." [18]

[16] *Ibid.*, pp. 81ff.
[17] D. F. Wilcox, "Party Government in Cities of New York State,"
Political Science Quarterly, XIV (1899), 681ff.
[18] *Ibid.*, p. 692.

One of the cities in which the bi-partisan system flourished during Platt's time was the city of Albany, which was located in the bailiwick of William Barnes, Jr. This able pupil of Platt converted what had been a Democratic stronghold into dependable Republican territory. Some of the methods which he used in accomplishing this feat were disclosed by the special investigation of 1911, to which reference has already been made.

The majority of the "Bayne" Committee, as the body which made the inquiry of 1911 was called, claimed that it had discovered the reasons why the mayor whom it found in office was willing to "take quite largely, pretty largely" the advice of Committeeman Barnes and to act strenuously upon that advice.[19] This mayor, before his election in 1909, had been for many years chairman of the county committee of his party, a position which he held when Roosevelt was governor. In addition to this mayor's political activities, it appeared that he had been busy along many other lines. He was a director of the gas company which supplied the city gas and electricity, he was a director and large stock holder in a coal company which sold coal to public institutions, and he was a director and stockholder in a banking concern which received deposits from the city.[20] The Republican member of this committee was convinced that the dual position of the mayor evinced a "decided lack of propriety" and that the average bank balances carried certainly seemed excessive for a city the size of Albany and might indicate that the profit of the institutions carrying these balances was considered rather than the interest of the tax payer.[1] He also thought that the mayor was in a large measure responsible for the shortcomings of the appointive officers of the

[19] P. 120.
[20] Ibid., p. 29.
[1] Ibid., p. 128.

city and that his removal should be recommended to the governor.

Viewed from another standpoint the "short comings" of the subordinate city officials were reasons for their loyalty to the organization which Barnes had built up. In 1908 the State Comptroller's examiner had discovered that scarcely any attention was paid by the city officials to the statute requiring a contract for supplies, the price of which would exceed $500, to be let to the lowest bidder.[2] One of the most flagrant violations of the law discovered by the investigating committee was the failure to suppress vice, gambling, and drunkenness. The minority member said that "the condition in the district in which vice is segregated could hardly be worse" and that the commissioner of public safety "should be summarily removed for neglect of duty."[3] The majority members claimed that vice in Albany was under the "protection" of Republican politicians who levied tribute upon the unfortunates in the segregated district by compelling all those who were engaged in running disorderly houses to make purchases from certain favored real estate dealers, liquor dealers, furniture dealers, bondsmen, plumbers, painters and others.[4] All those who were connected with the traffic of the underworld in Albany whether directly or indirectly were expected, it seems, to turn out for their share of the work to be performed upon election day. There were protests against this system, but the reformers soon grew tired and discouraged. How could they get ac-

2 *Op. cit.,* p. 27.

3 *Op. cit.,* p. 128.

4 *Ibid.,* p. 111. On page 35 the report reads: "There is in the lower part of the city of Albany a notorious section known as 'The Gut.' This part of the city, in the Fourth Ward, is devoted to prostitution openly carried on, without molestation on the part of the police or other officials of the city whose duty it is to suppress such violations of the law."

tion from the district attorney's office? If they did stir up some trouble, how could they then prevent the city officials from raising their assessments or harassing them in some other way?

The bi-partisan character of the Barnes régime in Albany is revealed by a "graft" disclosure in which Barnes himself was named. The way in which the Republican leader and practical owner of the *Albany Evening Journal* co-operated with the firm which published the leading Democratic paper of the city is shown by the following quotation from the report of the "Bayne Committee:" [5]

We shall not repeat in detail the uncontradicted facts brought out before us to the effect that the contract for printing the proceedings of the Common Council of the city of Albany was the result of a scheme whereby the successful bidder was assured of getting additional work in violation of the law, and fixed his bid lower than any outside printer could do the work for, that the work was padded to an incredible extent merely to increase the cost of the job and the value of the contract thus obtained, that Mr. Barnes' concern, the Journal Company, without having any plant to do the work with, nevertheless got, in violation of the law, orders for duplicate copies of the work done by the public bidder, and farmed these orders to that bidder who paid Mr. Barnes' concern 25% on the job, that on the work obtained at public bidding the successful bidder paid Mr. Barnes' concern 15%, that these payments were made to Mr. Barnes' company because, to use the language of a witness who knew the facts, "Mr. Barnes dictated where the printing goes and the *Argus* gives up to the *Journal* in order to obtain the printing." [6]

It should be kept in mind that the investigation cited above covered but one up-state city and was the work of

[5] *New York Evening Post*, September 19, 1910. An article by W. T. A. (W. T. Arnt) on conditions in Albany.
[6] *Op. cit.*, p. 119.

what the politicians would call a "political smelling committee." Furthermore, it should be remembered that "politics" probably played a larger part in the life of the Capital City than in the other up-state cities. In the middle eighties Theodore Roosevelt commented upon the temptations which confronted the legislators at Albany.[7] Moreover, Platt's other field marshals may not have been able to build up such thorough going "organizations." [8]

The outlook for Republican "Stalwarts" in New York City was always discouraging, at least in Platt's time. It seemed as though the more the city departments expanded and multiplied and the higher the city budget mounted, the more firmly entrenched became the Tammany Democracy on the one hand and the more influential became the "independent" reformers on the other. Since Platt was never able to "rule" the great metropolis, he was compelled to resort to "deals" with the Tammany leaders in order to keep his own regulars "satisfied." [9] His "influence" at Albany was his principal stock in "trading with the enemy."

As far back as the days of the notorious Tweed, the idea of a "bi-partisan" police board had gained a foothold in New York City. Since the police "graft" was the most lucrative and the most coveted of all forms of "spoils" in the great city, the development of this idea in that department can be taken as typical of conditions in general. Abram S. Hewitt, mayor of New York in 1887 and 1888, described in the following words the police situation as he found it: "The police were managed by four men, who divided up the patronage into four parts. Two of them were Democrats, two of them were Republicans, and each one

---

[7] *Century Mag.*, XII (1885), 820.
[8] This was the opinion of W. T. A., *op. cit.*
[9] Heaton, *op. cit.*, pp. 108–9.

had his portion." [10]   At the "Lexow" investigation no direct evidence was given to establish the complicity of the police commissioners in the general extortion, but John McClave, the Republican commissioner resigned after a searching and pointed examination.[11]

The year 1894, it will be remembered, was a time of storm and stress for the Tammany organization.   Out of the calamities of the enemy, Platt was able to wring two "places" on the police board.[12]   As he naively put it, "Early in 1894 the term of Commissioner Charles F. McLean, . . . (who was a Democrat), expired.   Mayor Gilroy asked me to recommend a Republican to succeed him." [13]   The other "place" was created by McClave's resignation.   The next year Platt sought to conserve these "places" by the enactment of a law which provided that not more than two of the four commissioners should "belong to the same political party" or "be of the same political opinion on state and national issues."[14]   Unfortunately, Mayor Strong violated his "trust" and used the newly enacted power of removal law to "lop off the heads" of the Platt place holders to make room for Theodore Roosevelt and Fred D. Grant as commissioners.[15]   Nothing could have been more fatal to Platt's intrigues than Roosevelt's fearless and rigid enforcement of the law.   Platt's anger was shown by his attempt to pass a law vesting the work of reorganizing the New York police

[10] E. P. Wheeler, *Sixty Years of American Life* (New York, 1917), p. 336, citing Mr. Hewitt's speech of November 1900.

[11] See report for May 21, 1894, also *New York Tribune,* May 22, 1894, and July 17, 1894.   McClave resigned upon the latter date.

[12] *Nation,* November 15, 1894, LIX, 351.

[13] *Op. cit.,* p. 268.

[14] Wilcox, *loc. cit.,* p. 688.

[15] Platt, *op. cit.,* pp. 272ff.   At the time, Mayor Strong denied the existence of any "bargain;" *New York Tribune,* Dec. 1894.

department in the governor.[16]   He had to console himself,
however, with efforts to neutralize Roosevelt's influence.
This was done by bringing "pressure" upon Grant to deadlock the board and by persuading the governor not to remove the Democratic commissioner who was doing his best
to perpetuate the old system.[17]   Mayor Van Wyck, whose
election is described below, might have been expected to do
better, but his interpretation of the words, "the same political party," was more distasteful than Mayor Strong's had
been and in despair Platt abandoned bi-partisan police board
idea.   No wonder that he was pessimistic about New York
City politics!

Contemporary observers seemed to believe that signs of a
Platt-Croker alliance were most apparent around election
time.   Since the defeat of Tammany was likely only when
all anti-Tammany elements were united, whenever the Republicans refused to join with the fusionists and ran a third
ticket of their own, it was said that "Platt had made a bargain with Croker."   This was the case in 1886 when Roosevelt ran against Hewitt and George for mayor and in 1888
when the Republicans ran Erhardt for mayor against
Hewitt, independent Democrat, and Hugh J. Grant, the
Tammany candidate.[18]   In 1892 when the fortunes of the
Republican party were at a low ebb, it later came out that
Platt had "knifed" the Republican ticket in New York City,
supposedly to avoid being found outside the "breast-
works." [19]   In 1894 he actually did co-operate with the other

[16] Governor Morton's refusal to countenance this has been described above.

[17] J. B. Bishop, op. cit., I, 62–64 and Roosevelt, op. cit., pp. 170–72.

[18] M. P. Breen, Thirty Years of New York Politics Up to Date
(New York, 1899), p. 828.

[19] New York Tribune, October 30, 1897.   The affidavit of a dis-
gruntled Republican, who ran a paper devoted to the liquor interests, claims that Platt directed the policy of the paper as follows:

anti-Tammany elements, but immediately after the election he regretted it.[20] It remained for his true "colors" to be displayed in the famous mayoralty campaign of 1897, the first under the newly created Greater New York charter with its "magnificent possibilities." Early in the campaign, Platt issued a statement to the press to the effect that he surest way to save the new city from Tammany misrule was by a union of all the anti-Tammany elements under the leadership of the Republican party.[1] The Citizens' Union, a permanent municipal-reform party, issued a platform which held that "good city government cannot be secured through the agency of existing parties organized upon national and state issues," and that "it can be secured through the united action of citizens earnestly determined that the city shall be governed solely with reference to the welfare of the city and its citizens." [2]   Seth Low, the well-to-do president of Columbia University, twice Republican mayor of Brooklyn, contended to run upon this platform. He was backed by such Republicans as Theodore Roosevelt, Elihu Root, Joseph H. Choate, and Nicholas Murray Butler, but the Republican party refused to endorse him and placed in the field a third candidate of its own choosing, Benjamin F. Tracy, the law partner of Platt's son. The result was a sweeping victory for the Tammany Hall Democracy, although the combined vote of Low and Tracy considerably exceeded that of the Tammany candidate, Van Wyck.[3]   An up-state Republican newspaper commented upon the debacle as follows:

"Now I tell you that I don't think Einstein (the Republican candidate) is in it. You better support the Tammany ticket."
[20] *New York Tribune*, Dec. 15, 1894.
[1] *Ibid.*, May 8, 1897.
[2] Wheeler, *op. cit.*, p. 359.
[3] The vote stood: Van Wyck, 233, 997; Low, 151, 540; Tracy, 101, 540; George, 21, 693.

It is due solely to the selfishness of Thomas C. Platt that Van Wyck, the representative of Tammany Hall, is to occupy the office of mayor in Greater New York during the next four years. Thousands of Republicans desired that their party should endorse the nomination of Seth Low but because Platt could exact no promises or pledges, the machine was manipulated to prevent such endorsement being made.[4]

Edward Lauterbach had made a frank confession that he and his Platt associates would rather see a Tammany man elected mayor than have a non-partisan succeed in getting office. Platt, himself, afterward admitted that "for the doctrine of non-partisanship in local elections" he had "the sincerest and the profoundest contempt" and that "the success of such attempt would have a demoralizing effect on party organization." It was thought at the time that another phase of "costly" bargain between the two "machines" was the desire of both to retain the campaign "contributions" of the public utility corporations which were directed by men who evidently preferred to pay for "protection" rather than to take a chance with a man like Low.[5] In a closing address Low had said that he stood for the principle that for every franchise or privilege granted to a corporation or an individual the city should receive full and fair compensation.[6] One of the admirers of Platt maintained that Low was ambitious for the presidency and the whole "citizens" movement was a "covert scheme to discredit the Republican organization."[7] Such movements should be nipped in the bud. As James Bryce pointed out:

[4] *Utica Press,* November 5, 1897. The *Press* was an "independent" Republican newspaper.
[5] *Nation,* October 7, 1897, LXV, 269. See also Breen, *op. cit.,* pp. 832-36. Breen holds that Platt was hoodwinked by one of his deputies who was close to the traction companies.
[6] *New York Herald,* November 1, 1897.
[7] *Albany Evening Journal,* November 5, 1897.

To win without the help of the Republican machine would deal a heavy blow at city machines everywhere, for it would enable an example to be set in the greatest city of the Union of a municipal government relieved from all obligations to find places or contracts for its party friends, free to think of nothing but securing the best men for its service and making the best bargains for its taxpayers, free to study the interests of the people and the people alone.[8]

With every machine leader in the up-state watching him, what could Platt do?

Before his rural constituents Platt liked to pose as the only possible "redeemer of the wicked city."[9] From the brief survey that has been made of his career in New York City politics, it can hardly be said that he tried very hard to carry out that pose in practice. He tried to block the efforts of Roosevelt at reform in the police department. The fact that Colonel Waring gave the citizens of New York clean streets for the first time in many years meant nothing to him except that "no organization leader could get a place from him (Waring) during his entire administration."[10] When the Tammany organization failed to "come through" with its part in a deal, he "struck for terms" by ordering a legislative investigation.[11] These feeble efforts, however, made little impression either upon the power of feudalistic Tammany or upon the growing strength of the reformers.

STATE PATRONAGE

One of the most obvious interpretations of Platt's pop-

8 "The Mayoralty Election in New York," *Contemp. Rev.* LXXII, 759.

9 See above p. 84.

10 *Op. cit.,* p. 293.

11 In answer to the criticisms, Platt wrote, "New York City is still a part of New York State, and just as much interested in a continuance of the wise and successful administration of state affairs as any other part of the state." *Autobiography,* p. 364.

ularity as a state convention manager was the fact that he had at his command the distribution of the enormous patronage of the Empire State. When this interpretation is qualified by the consideration that he only remained in "substantial control" of the state executive departments for about six years, there are no doubt a good many elements of truth in it. In the first year of Governor Morton's administration the total expenditures for the ordinary expenses of the government exclusive of debt fund transactions amounted to about $10,500,000 and in the last year of Governor Roosevelt's term these expenditures came to about $15,700,000. The peak of "extravagance" during the Platt era was reached in 1898 under Governor Black when $16,-700,000 was spent by the state government for its ordinary expenses.[10] Including debt fund transactions, of which payments from the canal fund were the most important, the total expenditures of the state government reached the unprecedented figure of $30,900,000 in that year.[13] Considering the $150,000,000 budget of Greater New York City for the same year,[14] it is clear why Platt felt himself cramped as compared with Croker. Besides, Platt had to contend with "independent" executives.

The term "ordinary expenses of the government," as used above, included such items as the salaries and wages paid for personal services, office expenses, construction of public works and the maintenance of public institutions. Thus, the expenses of the governor and the other elective administrative officers came to about $400,000 annually dur-

[12] D. C. Sowers, *The Financial History of New York State from 1789 to 1912* (New York, 1914), Appendix, pp. 320-21, "Classified Expenditures."

[13] *Ibid.*

[14] New York City, *Annual Report of the Comptroller*, 1898, p. 95.

ing the six years under discussion:[15] the legislature spent on
the average $1,200,000 a year to keep itself going and well
supplied with printing and legal services; it cost over $800,-
000 annually to keep the state prisons in proper order, and
about $1,000,000 to maintain the state militia. The most
considerable item of state expenditure was that for curative
purposes, for state asylums, hospitals and reformatories,
which reached a maximum point of $7,000,000 in 1897 al-
though the services performed in that year were not as extensive as those rendered in 1900 for $6,500,000.[16] In 1897
the regulative functions of the state also seemed unduly
costly, in view of subsequent developments, and the canal
expenditures became an open "scandal." The gradual in-
creases in the expenditures for educational, for agricultural
and health purposes throughout the period is accounted for
by the fact that the newer social and economic activities of
the government were increasing in a corresponding measure.[17]

How much of these disbursements was available for distribution among the "Boys?" The *New York Tribune*
pointed out one very important limitation in the following
terms:

Light-weight politicians have talked about the state
patronage which Mr. Platt will have to pass out to his
friends, but what is that around here? What does it
amount to altogether? Just about $4,000,000. This in-
cludes the governor's salary, the salaries of the judiciary,
members and employees of the legislature, heads of departments, clerical help, commissioners, superintendents and all
persons employed by the commonwealth. A large part of

[15] Traveling, office, legal expenses and salaries. The salaries
ranged from $5,000 to $10,000.

[16] *Nation*, Aug. 14, 1902 for an interpretation of the "cost of
state government" and Sowers, *op. cit.*, for the figures.

[17] See above p. 200.

it is useless for partisan purposes on account of the Civil Service Law. . . . Not only this, but look where the state patronage is distributed. Most of it is at Albany, 150 miles from New York and Brooklyn and of little practical use. The greater part of the canal patronage goes to Republican counties up the state and will be swallowed up so quickly as to be out of sight in a few weeks.[18]

It is obvious that this was written from the standpoint of a"machine politician" in New York City, but nevertheless the comments are of general significance, after certain qualifications have been made. In 1895 there were fifty-four hundred persons, not counting laborers, in the employ of the state. Of these, one third were in the class chosen by competitive examination, six per cent were unclassified or exempt from examination and the remainder were in the non-competitive or "pass examination" class.[19] The roster of state employees in 1900, the last year of Roosevelt's administration, included eight thousand persons, of whom slightly more than one third were in the competitive class, sixteen per cent not subject to any examination and the remainder in the non-competitive class.[20] In other words, in the former year 340, and in the latter year 1300, of the "choicest" positions in the state service were not subject to the merit system at all, while the great bulk of the persons seeking state jobs had to pass merely a non competitive examination.

The fact that one third of the state employees were protected by the competitive system did, however, cause Platt and his lieutenants considerable trouble. Platt no doubt regretted the indifferent attitude he had taken while the

[18] January 14, 1895.
[19] *Thirteenth Report of New York Civil Service Commission* (1895), *passim.*
[20] *Eighteenth Report of the State Civil Service Commission,* 1900, *passim.*

delegates to the Constitutional Convention of 1894 were incorporating the principles of the merit system into the fundamental law of the state. At any rate his henchmen, like Assemblyman Nixon of Chautauqua and Assemblyman Howe of Tioga, were among the most vigorous opponents of any bill which carried out the constitutional mandate and it is significant that no such bill was passed in 1895.[1] Governor Morton's appointment of a "practical" politician as civil service commissioner has already been commented upon. Platt also "stood by" while Governor Black gave his approval to the bill "to place the civil service of the state at the mercy of machine politics," a bill which Republican newspapers regarded as "a perversion of Republican principles and a betrayal of reform."[2] It is true that he favored the White bill which repealed the "Black Law" and put some "starch" back in the service, but this he probably did to please Roosevelt and to inconvenience Tammany, rather than from a fundamental change of heart.[3]

The actual administration of the Civil Service Law can best be studied by following the history of the department of public works which during these years happened to be subjected to several investigations, official and unofficial. The New York Civil Service Reform Association found that of the 1500 men employed by Superintendent Aldridge to carry out the $9,000,000 canal improvement, only 200 were held subject to classification, that the total number of competitive appointments made during two years was only thirty-eight, and that persons had been appointed to clerical positions under title of mechanical class in order to secure

---

[1] *Good Government*, September 15, 1895, XIV, 208.

[2] *Ibid.*, June 15, 1897, XVI, 76; "The Press on Governor Black's Memorandum."

[3] This is the writer's interpretation. By the time Roosevelt became governor, most of the political workers had been "placed." Civil service rules might have helped to keep them in.

their exemption from examination.[4] At first Superintendent Aldridge openly defied the rules promulgated by the governor including his department, and he made fifty-one appointments without reference to the Civil Service Commission but he was checked in this move by the highest court of the state which held that the merit principle of the constitution was operative without action on the part of the legislature.[5] A typical example of the sort of thing that was done with the canal fund is given in the following quotation from the report of an investigating commission appointed by Governor Black in 1898:

On January 1, 1898 on account of a change in the administration of the city government of Rochester, many employees lost their places; of these ten or fifteen were appointed inspectors on the canal work without civil service examination. The evidence shows that it must have been known at the time of their appointment that some of these temporary appointees were not competent to properly discharge the duties of inspectors, and it follows that the money paid for their services was not properly expended.[6]

It was also shown by this same commission that great gangs of inspectors were employed in the season of open navigation when there was comparatively little use for them. There is little wonder that Aldridge was so popular with the "Boys" at the State Convention of 1896! Yet Roosevelt thought the evidence against Aldridge insufficient to warrant a prosecution.

But the canal improvement was not the only branch of the state service that furnished "places" for the expectant party workers. As a member of the reorganized Capitol

[4] *Good Government,* September 15, 1896, XV, 103.
[5] *People ex rel. McClelland* v. *Roberts, Comptroller,* 13 Misc. Rep. 448, 91 Hun, 104.
[6] *Report of the Commission Appointed by the Governor pursuant to Chapter 15 of the Laws of 1898,* p. 34.

Commission, Aldridge was instrumental in turning out some skilled workmen in order to make room for some "good Platt men." [7] Commissioner Lyman, of the Excise Department created by the Raines liquor law of 1896, refused at first to appoint some of his special "confidential" agents on the basis of competitive examinations, but, like Aldridge, he was blocked by the courts in his efforts to reward the "faithful." [8] There was some hope left, however, for the "Black Law" and its accompanying rules provided that the written examinations should only count one-half in the final rating and that "experience, character, tact, and even muscle" should be considered by the appointing officer. Under this new administration of the merit system, Superintendent of Insurance Payn and Superintendent of Public Works Aldridge were given leeway for their "operations," [9] and, as Platt expressed it, there was " 'starchless' civil service, which put practically every Democratic office-holder out and installed a Republican organization man in his job." [10] It was not to be expected that even a reform governor like Roosevelt would remove many of these Republicans.

It should not be supposed from the two decisions of the New York courts cited above, which involved the interpretation of the merit principle embodied in the state constitution, that the judges were entirely impervious to the sorts of pressures that were brought to bear upon other state officers. To be sure they were fortified by longer terms [11] and by

[7] *Good Government*, August 15, 1895, XIV, 197.

[8] *People ex rel. Sweet .v Lyman*, 157 N. Y. 368 (1898). Over half of the "confidential" appointees who did finally take the "pass examination" failed. See the *Nation*, May 28, 1896.

[9] *Good Government*, July 15, 1897, XVI, 82–83.

[10] Alexander, *Four Famous New Yorkers*, p. 288–89.

[11] County judges were elected for six years, supreme court justices and judges on the Court of Appeals for fourteen years, Constitution, Article VI.

traditions of independence, but they were nominated and elected by the same party machinery which had charge of the selection of the other state officers. Roosevelt discovered this when, as a legislator, he tried to bring about the impeachment of a judge. Although Platt was clever enough not to antagonize the sentiment of the legal profession in the brazen way that Hill and Croker did,[12] there were many "good Republicans" who found their way to the bench. Platt mentions with pride in his *Autobiography* some of the "able jurists" that were "elevated by the organization" of which he was "leader." [13] His letter to Governor Roosevelt regarding the appointment of an "old time Republican" to a vacancy in a county judgeship has already been given. A delegate to the Constitutional Convention of 1915, a "plain country lawyer," said that he had found the judges "human," that he had seen them "jack up their salaries by intense persistent application to the legislature" and apply for private secretaryships which were filled with their "relatives." [14] As to the decisions of the judges, the "organization" could expect little. By one decision, Platt, himself had been ousted from the office of New York quarantine commissioner.[15] On the other hand, Roosevelt found the New York courts impervious to some social reforms. He bitterly resented a decision which annulled a favorite tenement house law of his.[16] In 1897 when the Court of Appeals, the highest court in the state, held that the machinery for conducting civil service examinations was entirely de-

[12] The Maynard incident in 1893 and the Daly incident in 1898.
[13] Pp. 511-12.
[14] *Record* (unrevised), III, 2523.
[15] *People* v. *Platt,* 3 New York Supp. 367.
[16] *In the Matter of the Application of Peter Jacobs,* 98 New York, 98.

pendent for its existence upon laws passed by the legislature,[17] other reformers had their complaints:

> In achieving this triumph, the enemies of civil service re-
> form have had to get an apparently partisan construction of
> the constitution unsupported by the weight of judicial au-
> thority. Judges Haight, Bartlett, Martin and Vann, all
> Republicans, have overruled Judges Gray, Andrews and
> O'Brien, and all the Judges of the Appellate Division, as
> well as the trial judge, on a point so simple that a child can
> understand it; when the constitution says that no man shall
> shall be appointed to office except by competition, if compe-
> tition is "practicable," the courts, and not the legislature, or
> the governor, or the mayors are to decide whether it is prac-
> tical in view of the duties which the office has to perform.[18]

In other words, the reformers thought that this decision
made the constitutional mandate upon the merit system a
pious recommendation which could be safely ignored by
passing such an act as the "Black Law" taking the "starch"
out of the civil service. The legal theories of this same
tribunal regarding the determination of party "regularity"
also fitted in with the exigencies of Platt's position as a
political manager, for in a famous case it held that such
matters were determined finally and conclusively by the
highest authorities in the party.[19] Finally, it is well established that the "organization" profited from the way in
which the judges regulated the appointment and work of
certain official referees.[20]

Offices were not the only "plums" which could be plucked
from the patronage tree furnished by the state government.

[17] *Chittenden* v. *Wurster,* 152 New York, 345 (1897).

[18] *The Nation,* April 29, 1897.

[19] *In the matter of Fairchild,* 151 New York, 359, cited and explained in F. Goodnow, *Politics and Administration* (New York,
1900), pp. 210ff.

[20] For the principal abuses, see Sowers, *op. cit.,* pp. 252–54, "Courts
and Trust Funds."

The report of Governor Black's commission to investigate the canal improvement, which has been cited above, contained a reference to "the traditions and habits of the canal contractors" as a "power for evil which required continual watchfulness to oppose."[1] According to the report, where some of the resident engineers were "watchful," they were "snubbed and overruled" by the state engineer. Improper classification of the material excavated was the chief abuse the commission found in the work done by the contractors. For instance, on the middle division, a "very large proportion of the material returned as rock," which was paid for at the rate of $1.25 per cubic yard, was "earth under the specifications" and should have received but 24 cents per cubic yard.[2] The commission concluded that in this and in other ways "not less than $1,000,000 had been "improperly expended."[3] But what was the "political" significance of this manipulation of accounts in favor of certain contractors? The following extract from the report of the committee will help to explain:

In investigating the subject of mucking we discovered a clearly deliberate abuse of the canal work for political purposes. On two contracts in and near the city of Rochester the contractors were induced to accept and put upon their force men who came to them with "tickets" from officeholders in the city of Rochester. . . . The work which they did was to a great extent unnecessary.[4]

It was the report of this commission that Platt had in mind when he said, "Already the canal appropriations were giving us trouble." In his campaign speeches Roosevelt said that if any wrong had been done, those responsible for

[1] *Op. cit.,* p. 9.
[2] *Ibid.,* p. 83.
[3] *Ibid.,* p. 137. The report of this commission is analyzed in the *Nation,* August 11, 1898, LXVII, 106.
[4] *Op. cit.,* p. 54.

it would be prosecuted, but the counsel he appointed for that purpose as governor decided not to institute criminal proceedings because the officials involved were within the "wide discretionary" powers granted to them by a law passed in 1896.[5] Little wonder that Aldridge gained the reputation for being a "shrewd politician."

The contracts for state printing were let to publishing houses in Albany and New York, which, according to some observers, had propensities not unlike those of the canal contractors. At any rate the "Bayne Committee" charged that Mr. Barnes' company "had obtained unlawfully from the state the sum of $13,504 . . . on the pretext of furnishing work which his concern had not done."[6] That there were difficulties in the printing game is indicated by the following bitter complaint of Barnes to Platt, dated July 14, 1899: "For six years men assumed to be friendly to you have systematically prevented me from getting anything in the printing line in Albany."[7] That some of these difficulties must have been absolved some five months later is suggested by a letter Barnes wrote to Roosevelt, which is given below:

THE JOURNAL COMPANY, PUBLISHERS
WILLIAM BARNES, JR. PRESIDENT
Albany, New York,
December 22, 1899.

DEAR GOVERNOR:

It is rumored that you contemplate in your message advising the establishing of a state printing house.

I write you this because I presume that your message will be a matter discussed between you and our friends tomor-

---

[5] *Report* (Counsel appointed by the governor to prosecute certain state officers for alleged criminal practices in carrying out the canal improvements under chapters 79 of Laws 1895 and 794, Laws of 1896).

[6] *Op. cit.*, p. 119.

[7] *Barnes* v. *Roosevelt*, p. 1161.

[11] Roosevelt, *op. cit.*, p. 291.

row. It is not my desire to intrude my personal matters
upon you, but I wish merely to state the fact that the estab-
lishment of a state printing house here would be a serious
if not fatal blow to me financially.

Very truly yours,

WILLIAM BARNES, JR.[8]

It appeared in the "Bayne Committee" report of 1911 and
in the Barnes-Roosevelt libel suit of 1915 that Barnes had
owned for some time a large block of stock in the J. B.
Lyon Company which had extensive business relations with
the state. It was probably the operations of this company
as well as those of his own that he had in mind when he
wrote about the "fatal blow." His letter did not deter
Roosevelt from advocating a state printing house in his message, but the legislature did not act upon that recommendation.[9]

Certain of the legislators, whose expenses ran beyond the
$1,500 annual salary and other usual perquisites of a New
York law maker, were able to make both ends meet in various and sundry ways. Jotham P. Allds, one of the "faithful," the Assembly floor leader while Roosevelt was governor, furnishes as good an example as can be had. When
this solon was handed a thick envelope by the agent of the
bridge companies in 1901, it is reputed that he said, "Guess
it's all right, Conger, it feels good." [10] Allds was a member of the Assembly Committee on Public Lands and Fores-
try in the year 1896 and he learned so much upon this committee that the next year he was hired as an attorney for
the State Forest Commission at a stipend of about $3,000.[11]
Thus in the course of several years he received from the

[8] *Ibid.*, p. 335.
[9] *Messages*, X, 123.
[10] The "Allds" Investigation, p. 335.
[11] *Ibid.*, p. 1327.

state in attorney's fees about $16,000 in addition to his regular salary as legislator. He also accepted a retainer of $6,000 from the Argus Company "for no apparent reason unless it was for promoting a bill for the Argus Company against the state." [12] Speaker Nixon's name was also involved in the Allds investigation. It was said that he extorted as much from the bridge companies as Allds did in 1901. This and other evidence seemed to reveal the existence of a legislative cabal which made money by blackmailing the corporations.[13]

Legislative business of a decorous nature, was handled by the law firm of Tracy, Boardman and Platt, the first mentioned name standing for none other than Benjamin F. Tracy and the last for Frank H. Platt, one of Platt's sons who showed great interest in politics. The counsel for the "Fassett" investigating committee was this "well known" law firm. When General Tracy became secretary of the navy, he transferred all his legal business to this firm, which thus became heir among other things to the Ramapo matter. The Ramapo scheme was called a "plot of water-right and water-option owners to exploit" New York City through a "water system half public-owned and half privately controlled," and it caused a great uproar when it was later sponsored by Tammany Hall.[14] Before Tammany Hall had become "interested," General Tracy had cabled to Governor Morton asking him to sign the bill which gave this corporation its powers.[15] That consent was given. The "family law firm" was not so fortunate in another matter, namely, the Astoria gas "scandal," for the bill which was designed

[12] *Lyons Republican*, April 1, 1910.
[13] *Report*, pp. 676, 681. See below, p. 311.
[14] Heaton, *op. cit.*, p. 167.
[15] *Assembly Doc.* 1900, No. 26, p. 4660. (Report of the special committee to investigate the public offices and departments of the city of New York). The so-called "Mazet" committee.

to confer certain privileges upon this corporation failed to pass the Senate.[16]   However, the services of the firm were of some value, for later on in the same year that this bill failed it took charge of the land patent forwarded by Governor Roosevelt which conveyed to the Astoria Company certain lands under water at the usual rate.[17]   When Richard Croker was hard pressed on the witness stand by the counsel of the "Mazet" committee of 1899, he blurted out the following:

The gentleman who put you here to examine us, go and examine his firm. They are at the bottom of all the corruption in the city; there is more corruption in that firm than any where else. They are retained by mostly all the corporations in this city. You go and examine their firm; now, be fair, bring their books here.[18]

Platt had another son, who as vice-president of the Fidelity and Deposit Company of Maryland, was interested in the bonding business. It also appeared that Charles Raines, a son of "Uncle" John Raines, was also deeply interested in the same company.[19] The connection is perhaps clear when it is remembered that the Raines Liquor Tax Law required that the liquor dealers should bond themselves for the strict observance of the law. The above mentioned surety company did a "roaring business" in furnishing the bonds required by the State Excise Department.[20] The comptroller of New York City required two sureties on each city contract, and here, in co-operation with the "Croker" Surety and Bond Company, the "Platt" company found an excel-

[16] New York Tribune, March 26, 1899.
[17] New York Tribune, December 27 and 28, 1890. No aspersions on Roosevelt are here intended.
[18] Report, I, 451.
[19] Nation, April 9, 1896.
[20] Ibid., May 7, 1896.

lent field for its operation.[1]   Last but not least, was the
"roaring business" which the Fidelity and Deposit Company did in the supplying of bonds required of the canal
contractors.[2]

While Governor Roosevelt was writing books and making
campaign speeches in the west, Senator Platt remained in
New York working night and day with the buried wires
which connected him with the local leaders.   A diligent
political manager could pick up some crumbs even under a
reform governor.

FEDERAL PATRONAGE

Because of the location of the largest post office and the
largest custom house of the country in New York City, the
federal patronage played a large part in the politics of the
state during the latter half of the nineteenth century.   Since
the Republican party was almost in continuous control of
the government at Washingtoon during that time, the "federal crowd" constituted one of the controlling factors in
Republican state conventions.   The civil servants of the
United States government who held their legal residences in
the state of New York made up a considerable political
army.   At the end of President Harrison's administration
there were over eight thousand post office employees alone
to say nothing of the two thousand custom-house workers [3]
and the some six hundred employees of other branches of
the Treasury Department.   The Brooklyn Navy Yard provided jobs for at least sixteen thousand men.[4]   All told
there must have been over fifteen thousand New Yorkers

[1] Mazet Committee, *Report*, I, 537.
[2] Canal Commission, *Report*, Appendix.
[3] *Ninth Report of the United States Civil Service Commission*,
1891–92, "Civil List," pp 291–92.
[4] United States Civil Service Commission, *The Executive Civil
Service of the United States*, 1896, p. 334.

holding positions under the federal government, a considerable portion of whom had grateful feelings toward the chief dispenser of political favors in the Empire State.

As in the state civil service so in the federal civil service, the merit system made many offices useless for partisan purposes. It was one of the ironies of fate that in 1889 when Platt began to distribute some of the federal patronage through Senator Hiscock, Theodore Roosevelt was made civil service commissioner. Roosevelt began at once to make a searching investigation of the New York Custom-house and some of the New York post offices.[5] This action was a bitter reminder to Platt of former humiliations connected with the New York Custom-house. On the other hand, some of the most sought for and the most responsible positions in the federal offices in New York were "unclassified" or excepted from the rules requiring competitive entrance examinations. It was these posts that the "independent journalist" had in mind when he wrote to President Harrison; "On the Republican side the president, in cordial alliance with 'Tom Platt' is making arrangements to turn over all the federal offices and patronage to the 'Boys' for the purpose of building up a Republican machine which shall carry everything before it."[6] Platt was a difficult man to please: he later called Harrison a "pouter pigeon" and the "White House Iceberg" on the ground that as president he "either forgot or ignored the men most responsible for his victory."[7] The personnel of Republican state conventions in the early nineties, however, furnished proof that neither Harrison's inaction nor Roosevelt's ac-

[5] Bishop, *Theodore Roosevelt and His Time*, I, 46–47.

[6] *Nation*, April 11, 1889, p. 295. See also Alexander, *Four Famous New Yorkers*, p. 180.

[7] *Op. cit.*, pp. 210, 215, 252.

tion eliminated the influence of the federal office holders upon state politics.

In 1897 Platt did not have to contend with Roosevelt as civil service commissioner nor did he have to invoke the aid of the rule of "senatorial courtesy" through another. He found McKinley the "most tender-hearted man" in politics, who, as president, invariably when an office was to be filled requested that he, as chief of the organization and United States senator, submit his choice. That choice, so Platt testifies, became the president's except in rare cases.[8] Of this situation the reform journalist made the following complaint: "The president, by allying himself with Platt and his rotten machine at this time, has done all that he could to prevent the success of honest government for this city." [9] During McKinley's administration, Platt built up an organization which continued to be a factor in state politics during Roosevelt's two administrations as president of the United States.

Outside of the selection of the cabinet officers, the president's appointments to the diplomatic service probably attracted the most attention. During the period of Platt's leadership both the diplomatic and consular services were beyond the pale of the Civil Service Law. It is likely that on this account Platt did not regret his support of Blaine in 1884 when Blaine, as secretary of state in 1889, was besieged by New York politicians who wanted to "see the world." New York was fairly well represented in the foreign service during Harrison's administration. Whitelaw Reid, the owner and editor of the *New York Tribune,* was appointed minister to France,[10] Andrew D. White,

[8] *Ibid.,* p. 398.

[9] July 8, 1897, LXV, 22.

[10] Reid's able biographer (Cortissoz, *op. cit.,* II, 121–25) claims that Reid did not seek public preferment.

minister to Russia,[11] "Fred." D. Grant,[12] minister to Austria, to say nothing of appointments to posts of lesser importance. While Platt may not have been the "determining" force in any one of these appointments, it is significant that he himself was offered the Spanish mission in 1890 which he declined ostensibly because of "numerous business engagements" but in reality, as he later claimed, because he suspected that Harrison was trying to "get him out of the country." [13] Under McKinley, New York certainly did not fare worse as far as the important embassies were concerned; with Choate in London, Porter in Paris, White in Germany, and Woodford in Madrid, few could complain that New York was under represented abroad. It is true that Senator Platt consented to Choate's appointment only because he hated the suggestion of Reid's appointment,[14] but Woodford can be regarded as a "stalwart." [15]

The Post Office Department was the center attraction for a state party manager because it furnished "rewards," large in the aggregate and widely distributed. While the main body of the postal employees came under the civil service rules, the thirty-five hundred or so postmasterships in New York were "exempt" during the time that Platt was most actively concerned in their distribution. Under Harrison, Platt had a "voice" in the selection of postmasters through Senator Hiscock and the New York congressmen. He probably did not complain when President Harrison held up the extension of the civil service rules to the railway mail

[11] Appointed in 1892.

[12] One of Platt's close friends (the son of U. S. Grant).

[13] Op. cit., pp. 208–9. The letters showing the offer and its rejection are given.

[14] T. G. Strong, Joseph H. Choate (New York. 1917), p. 81. Report of conversation with Choate.

[15] He presided over state conventions.

service,[16] nor is it likely that he objected to the displacement of the efficient H. G. Pearson by the "faithful" Van Cott in the New York City postmastership.[17] Postmaster General Wanamaker, whose appointment was "suggested" by M. S. Quay, together with First Assistant Postmaster General Clarkson, Platt's friend from Indiana, were able to find quite a few "places" for "worthy" Republicans.[18] At least three-fifths of the presidential postmasterships were "rotated" in the proper direction. These changes were beyond the scope of Civil Service Commissioner Roosevelt's power. McKinley's postmaster general was another "man from Pennsylvania," so it is not impossible to suppose that he played his part, especially when he was aided by the President's "liberal" order of April 29, 1899.[19] Under this latter régime, Van Cott was restored to his old place in New York City, and Platt, as United States senator, was able to keep a somewhat stricter system of accounting.

The Treasury Department was next in importance from the standpoint of New York "organization" Republicans. This was one of the reasons why Platt, himself, had sought to be the head of this department in 1889. The New York Custom-house contained some of the richest "plums" in the state and the collectors of internal revenue were exempt until the middle of the nineties when President Cleveland put them under the rules. Although the displacement of Silas Burt from his position at the head of the New York Custom-house alienated the reformers, Collector Erhardt, his successor proved "unacceptable" to the organization. One

[16] C. R. Fish, *Civil Service and Patronage* (New York, 1905), p. 223.
[17] *Nation*, May 23, 1889. See also W. D. Foulke, *Fighting the Spoilsmen* (New York, 1919), p. 51.
[18] Foulke, *op. cit.*, p. 60.
[19] *House Documents*, Fifty-fifth Congress, First Session, No. 1, p. xxxii.

of the reason's for Erhardt's failure to please Platt and the organization is revealed in the following explanation he gave for his resignation in 1891 :

I have resigned because the collector has been reduced to a position where he is no longer an independent officer with authority commensurate with his responsibility. . . . The recent policy of the Treasury Department has been to control the details of the customs administration at the port of New York from Washington, at the dictation of a private individual having no official responsibility. The collector is practically deprived of power and control, while he is left subject to all responsibility. The office is no longer independent, and I am. Therefore we have separated.[20]

The "private individual" was, of course, Thomas C. Platt and among the "details" was the removal or resignation of some three hundred and seventy-five employees who were for the most part Democrats.[1] This was another change which Roosevelt was powerless to prevent. J. Sloat Fassett was then made collector of the port of New York, and he held the position until he was nominated for governor two months later when Francis Hendricks' name was sent in and confirmed for the position.[2] Judging from his actions, President McKinley did not neglect the interests of the Manager-Senator in the New York offices of the Treasury Department, for George R. Bidwell, a "man who represented nothing but the machine which Platt had built up,"[3] was appointed collector and the total number of excepted places was increased.[4]

The work of acting as an employment agent for a politi-

[20] Foulke, op. cit., p. 291.
[1] Seventh Report of the Civil Service Commission, 1889–1890, p. 10. See also the Nation, August 6, 1891.
[2] Nation, September 24, 1891, LIII, 226.
[3] Ibid., July 8, 1897 ; Platt, op. cit., p. 398.
[4] Eighteenth Report of the Civil Service Commission, 1900–1901, p. 564.

cal party was not always pleasant, and it was probably the
irksomeness of this task that led Benjamin F. Tracy, secretary of the navy under President Harrison, to adopt a registration system for the employees of the navy yards.[5]   It is
surprising that such a step was taken by one so close to
Platt, but responsibility sobers some party men and General Tracy had other things to consider besides the "good of
the organization."   John D. Long, McKinley's secretary
of the navy, presented another problem which possibly
caused Platt some embarrassment.   Theodore Roosevelt's
name was presented by Senator Lodge and others for the
position of first assistant secretary of the navy, and Platt
was asked to approve the selection.   Roosevelt, the man
who had caused him so much trouble as civil service commissioner and police commissioner, could he ever get rid
of this "disturbing element"?   After listening to "Jack"
Astor's plea, Platt reasoned that Roosevelt was "not essentially harmful" and could "probably do less harm to the organization as assistant secretary of the navy than in any
other office that could be named."   The desired consent of
the Republican Senator from New York was given.[6]

In 1890 and 1900 the Department of the Interior became
a matter of prime importance to Thomas C. Platt, for in
those years a federal census was taken, and the vast army
of workers which was required to do this work was not
then under the civil service rules.   In 1890 Platt's expectations with reference to the Census Office as a source of
"gifts" began to rise when Robert P. Porter, editor of the

[5] Fish, op. cit., p. 224.
[6] For Lodge's part in this appointment, see Bishop, op. cit., I,
70-72.   In an addenda to Platt's Autobiography, (pages 539-41), a
most interesting account of the way Platt "got Roosevelt a Federal
Job" which the latter "needed to make both ends meet."   "Jack"
Astor acted as Roosevelt's spokesman and the significant thing to
Platt was that McKinley had asked that he (the Senator) be "consulted."

New York Press, a "stalwart" Republican organ, was appointed as superintendent of the census.[7] The following circular, sent to the district leaders by C. H. Murray, the supervisor for New York City, shows how appointments were made to this important service:

Dear Sir: You will please forward to this office a list of the applicants that the Republican organization of your district desires to have named as census enumerators. This list must be sent here on or before April 1st.[8]

Grave scandals developed in the taking of this census, especially in New York City. The National Civil Service Reform League made an investigation of the enumeration of the population of that Democratic stronghold and concluded that the work was open to the suspicion of partisan considerations chief of which was the apparent intention of reducing the representation of New York City in Congress[9] Another way in which the census enumerators were instructed to do political work is illustrated by the following letter written by Congressman John Raines in ignorance as he claimed of the law imposing secrecy:

My Dear Sir: As it is quite likely that you will in a few days be appointed enumerator for your district, I write you this in the strictest confidence. I would like very much that you should take the trouble, before you make your report to the supervisor of the census, and after you have taken all the names in your district, to copy in a small book the name and post office address of every voter on the list. After you have done so, I wish you to send the book to me at Canandaigua. I ask you to do this as a personal favor and to make no mention of the matter to anyone. What I want is a full list of all the voters in your enumeration dis-

---

[7] *Nation,* May 23, 1889.
[8] Foulke, *op. cit.,* p. 66.
[9] *Ibid.,* p. 68.

trict. Will you please treat this matter as strictly confidential?[10]

Although fairly accurate, the Twelfth Census was not altogether free from the sort of influences that had rendered the Eleventh Census uncertain. President McKinley appointed Governor Merriam, of Minnesota, director, largely for political reasons, and Merriam considered for appointments only those who had been recommended to him by congressmen.[11]

The federal judiciary also did not escape from the pressures which the Republican state organization brought to bear upon the other branches of the federal government. When President McKinley appointed Asa W. Tenney United States circuit judge of the Eastern District of New York, the *Nation* made the following comment: "Mr. Tenney is a working politician of the 'Wheelhorse' type, whose chief claim to the position is a lifetime of 'loyal devotion to the party.'"[12]   Much wider opposition was encountered when State Committeeman John R. Hazel, of Buffalo, was recommended for a position upon the federal bench. A Republican paper, like the *New York Tribune,* noted with alarm "Mr. Hazel's own patent lack of judicial qualities" and denounced the appointment as a "perversion" of a federal judgeship to the use of a "Senatorial Patronage Trust" of which Platt and Depew were the most conspicuous beneficiaries.[13]   Since the federal judges held their offices for life, there were not many of them to appoint during the period of Platt's leadership, but those who were on the bench could serve their party organization in many ways, among which was the appointment of prominent Republi-

10 *Ibid.,* p. 66, note.
11 *Ibid.,* pp. 76–77.
12 July 8, 1897, LXV, 22.
13 May 29 and June 4, 1900.

cans to "fat" receiverships. For example, State Committeeman Dunn was made receiver for the Binghamton
General Electric Company in 1893 and two years later he
was made receiver for the Merchants' Bank of Binghamton.[14] Of course it cannot be charged that the Judge made
these appointments because of Colonel Dunn's political importance, nor can it be charged Judge Wallace that he appointed Thomas C. Platt as receiver for the New York and
New England Railroad at the request of the law firm of
Tracy, Boardman and Platt because it was "good politics." [15] It only appeared that Republicans received their
fair share of such desirable positions.

There were many other expenditures of the federal government, a portion of which were distributed in accordance
with the principle, "To the victors belong the spoils." The
list would include such items as disbursements for veterans,
pensions, payment to river and harbor contractors, costs of
constructing and maintaining public buildings, money spent
in erecting fortifications, expenditures for public printing,
payments to the railroad companies for the transportation
of the mails, and purchases of supplies for the army, the
navy, the Post Office Department, and the other branches of
the federal government. It is impossible to estimate how
much of these expenditures was "pork" and it is equally
difficult to ascertain what was the share of the Empire State.
Only a few suggestions can be made. The scandals in connection with purchases made by the War Department in the
Spanish-American War denounced so vigorously by Roosevelt occurred under Secretary Alger, who was defended
and supported by Senator Platt. One authority upon our

[14] *Binghamton Press and Leader,* October 20, 1911. In 1909
Dunn was made receiver for the Hudson Valley Power Companies
by Judge Ray, one of his former political lieutenants.
[15] *New York Tribune,* December 28, 1893.

national government estimated that in 1908, the last year
that Senator Platt was chairman of the Committee on Printing, many millions of dollars could have been saved by
ordinary precautions against waste.[16] It is not here charged
that Senator Platt administered the affairs of this committee
in a corrupt manner,[17] but rather that the traditions of the
committee fostered inefficiency and extravagance. And so
with the other appropriations, each Republican congressman from New York was expected to "take care of his constituents," and if he failed to acquire facility in the art of
"log rolling" he was eliminated by that process commonly
called, the "survival of the fittest."

In 1903 several charges were made that frauds had been
committed in the Post Office Department during the McKinley administration. In a letter to Senator Lodge, under date
of September 30, 1903, President Roosevelt described one
of these alleged frauds as follows:

> I had a very ugly time over the indictment of a State Sen-
> ator of New York. He is a close personal, political and
> business friend of the Republican State Chairman, and of
> the State Comptroller. The Chairman is a heavy stockhold-
> er in the concern in behalf of which the crookedness was
> done, and he is very naturally bitter against me. Whether
> he himself was cognizant of the wrong-doing or not, I can-
> not say. It is greatly to be regretted that he is chairman of
> the state committee. The Comptroller came down to see
> me to explain that if the Senator were indicted it was his
> judgment that we should certainly lose the state next fall.[18]

The chairman of the state committee at this time was
George W. Dunn, the state senator from Dunn's district

[16] H. J. Ford, *The Cost of Our National Government* (New York
1910), p. 97.
[17] A. H. Lewis, "The Lesson of Platt," *Cosmopolitan Mag.*, XL
(1906), 644. Lewis accused Platt of attempted favoritism.
[18] Bishop, *op. cit.*, I, 254.

was George E. Green, former mayor of Binghamton, and the state comptroller was Nathan L. Miller, also from Dunn's senatorial district.[19]   The alleged fraud was "conspiracy" between the purchasing officer of the post office and a firm manufacturing time checkers. George E. Green was acquitted upon two indictments but he lost all in lawyers' fees and he also lost his health.[20] No insinuations are here intended, the simple purpose being to show that Platt's field marshals did have commercial relations with the federal government.

Platt also did not refuse to do business with the departments of the federal government. As the *Nation* cynically put it:

"Something equally as good" to Tom Platt as a seat in the Cabinet is a contract with the Treasury Department making the United States Express Company (T. C. Platt, president) the exclusive agent of the government for the transportation of all its moneys throughout the United States, and assigning to said express company rooms in the Treasury Department building at Washington for the transaction of their business.[1]

This contract was dated April 21, 1889, and it supplanted a contract which the department had made with the Adams Express Company during President Grant's administration. It was pointed out later by a magazine writer that this was an "exceedingly profitable contract" and that Platt enforced it whether or not he actually carried the money, but it was not shown that the United States Express Company re-

[19] *Legislative Manual*, 1903. Miller was appointed comptroller on November 12, 1903, vice Knight, resigned and elected Nov. 4, 1902.
[20] *New York Tribune*, Dec. 19, 1903.
[1] April 25, 1889, XLVIII, 335.

ceived any more than was customarily paid for such services.[2]

The analysis which has been given in this chapter of the spoils system in New York State during the time that Platt was manager of the Republican organization has set off the local, state, and federal patronage into separate compartments. This has been a convenient way to handle the material, but it does not give an accurate picture of the manner in which the system actually worked. Generally speaking, the office of the state committeeman in each one of the thirty-four congressional districts was a clearing house for all sorts of patronage. Thus, State Committeeman Barnes believed in "rotation in office" and any day the mayor of Albany might find himself in the postmastership of Albany or the state senator from Albany might land in the county clerkship.[3] Barnes, himself, did not refuse an appointment as surveyor of customs,[4] nor did he turn down any printing business because it was from the city of Albany and not the state of New York. The state committee, as a collegiate body, directed the entire process and sought Platt's advice upon questions of first importance. When state conventions assembled, this committee did not refuse to seat any delegate because he was only a local officer and not a state or federal employee; all office-holders alike were welcome. The delegates to the Republican State Convention at Saratoga in 1898 greeted the "old man" with just as prolonged cheers

[2] A. W. Atwood, "The Great Express Monopoly," *Amer. Mag.*, LXXI (1911), 758.

[3] *New York Evening Post*, September 17, 1910. Article signed W. T. A.

[4] *Barnes* v. *Roosevelt*, May 13, 1915, Barnes testifying as to the office which he held under Presidents McKinley and Roosevelt, p. 1888.

as they greeted the hero of San Juan.   Quigg said that they loved Platt because "age had mellowed him," but a more cynical observer said that they loved him on the old principle, "Blessed be the hand that gives." [5]   Roosevelt, himself, had not refused some favors from that hand.

[5] *Nation*, October 6, 1898.

CHAPTER X

"THE CORRUPT ALLIANCE"

In a campaign statement published on July 22, 1914, Roosevelt charged William Barnes with working through a corrupt alliance between crooked business and crooked politics.[1] On the basis of this statement, Barnes sued Roosevelt for libel. Roosevelt won the suit which indicated that the jury regarded his charges as true. Barnes was one of the successors to the system which Platt built up during the nineties. While Roosevelt was governor of the state, this system was in a particularly flourishing condition. The origin and development of the system came long before Roosevelt's official career. During the seventies and eighties, when the tone of the state legislature was rather low, many prominent business men grew especially fearful of "strike" bills. A "strike" bill was a bill introduced for the purpose of extorting money from those whose interests would be injuriously affected by the passage of the bill. "Strike" bills were made use of most frequently by the "Black Horse Cavalry," the "gang" or combination of legislators, Republicans and Democrats, which was ready to take money whenever it could. The "Black Horse Cavalry" found the giant public utility corporations and the great fiduciary institutions particularly vulnerable. To protect and further their interests these corporations maintained expensive lobbies at the state capitol.[2] In the early nineties when the Democrats

[1] *Barnes* v. *Roosevelt,* complaint.
[2] City Reform Club, *Annual Record of the Assemblymen and Senators from the City of New York,* (1891).

262

gained control of the state legislature, the professional lobbyists were superseded in a measure by a political boss who
undertook to deliver the party vote in the legislature in return for contributions or services to the party. There is
little doubt that the safety, security, convenience, and decor-
um of this new system appealed to Thomas C. Platt who, by
virtue of his strategic position, was able to apply it to his
own organization when the fortunes of his party revived.[3]

The habits and traditions of the members of the "Black
Horse Cavalry" were such that it was not possible to work
out this new system in any complete or thoroughgoing
fashion. The conditions revealed by the Allds investigation, cited above, are ample proof for this conclusion. It was
alleged by Benn Conger, the agent for the bridge companies,
that the bill which Allds and Nixon "put to sleep" for him
in the Rules Committee in return for bribes of $1,000 each
was a "strike" bill.[4] This bill was designed to put additional power into the hands of the state engineers and to
require towns to vote upon all outlays above the $500 limit,
a change which would have made it more difficult for the
bridge companies to secure contracts for a class of work
which had been a source of considerable profit. As one correspondent expressed it, "These bills, if passed, not only
would have added a great deal of red tape and complicated
the old fashioned method of dealing directly with local authorities, but went a long way toward eliminating the possibility of the bridge builders obtaining contracts by favoritism or bribery, rather than by open competition."[5] Alld's
attorneys contended that it was the bridge companies and
not their client who had been corrupt, and they introduced

[3] J. B. Bishop, "The Price of Peace," *Century Mag.,* XLVIII,
671 (1894).
[4] *Proceedings of the Senate,* p. 332.
[5] *New York Evening Post,* January 18, 1910.

evidence tending to show that a bridge "trust" had been formed which engaged in pernicious activities in several states.[6] It is difficult to see how this line of argument benefited Allds' case,[7] but it is equally difficult to defend the action of the bridge companies. The next year (1902) the bridge companies were more "proper," for they refused to "deal" with the individual legislators, turned their "contribution" over to the chairman of the Republican state committee, and "asked him to make this an organization matter and call off such strike legislation." As long as this newer system was adhered to, the measures hostile to the bridge companies were not passed.[8]

Of all corporations doing business in the state, the public utility corporations were perhaps the most sensitive to matters of legislation. The work of furnishing the additional transportation facilities demanded by the growing population of the great urban centers of the state was left to private enterprises, which, on their part, were powerless to make extensions without action upon the part of the government. After the privileges were granted which enabled the extensions to be made, it was the duty of the legislature to conserve the interests of the general public, a task which it found fraught with many temptations. Elihu Root, attorney during the eighties and nineties for one of the largest street railway combinations in New York City,[9] said of conditions:

[6] *Proceedings of the Senate*, pp. 1095, 2077. In summing up one of them referred to "the plunder and robbery of the municipalities of the state under the law as it then existed."

[7] They were trying to discredit Conger's testimony. Allds, they held, had "killed" the bill because he had been ordered to do so by Platt, who in turn had been hoodwinked by the bridge companies.

[8] *Proceedings of the Senate*, pp. 705ff.

[9] H. J. Carman, *The Street Surface Railway Franchises of New York City* (New York, 1919), chs. VI, VII, *passim*.

Many of us can now remember the dreadful days of the "Black Horse Cavalry" which came as an incident mainly, to the performance of this duty by the legislature. Further still, the fact that the great transportation companies were being attacked, the great public service corporations were being attacked in the legislature, justified them in their own minds in going into politics and electing, or furnishing the money to elect, members of the Senate and Assembly. Good men, good citizens, honest lawabiding men, justified themselves in the directorates of these railroads and other public service corporations in spending the money of the corporations to elect senators and assemblymen who would protect them against strike bills. The whole system became a scandal and a disgrace, and it was to remedy that here in New York and all over the country that this separate regulation by a commission created by law was established.[10]

In 1910 the State Superintendent of Insurance came into possession of some ledgers of a former New York stock brokerage firm, Ellingwood & Cunningham by name, which in the hands of a subsequent legislative investigating committee revealed many of the details of this "scandalous" and "disgraceful" system. It appeared that this firm had very close relations with one G. Tracy Rogers, who from 1894 to 1903 was president of the Street Railway Association of the state of New York, an association whose ostensible purpose was the acquisition and diffusion of scientific knowledge among its members. The membership of this association comprised nearly all the important street railway companies within the state, i. e., those in New York City, Buffalo, Rochester, Albany, Syracuse, Utica, and Binghamton.[11] The most important duty of the president of

[10] Addresses on Government and Citizenship, p. 188. Speech before the Constitutional Convention on August 25, 1915.

[11] Assembly Documents, 1911, No. 30, I, 8. (Report of the Joint Committee of the Senate and Assembly of the state of New York, appointed to investigate corrupt practices in connection with legislation, and the affairs of insurance companies, other than those

this association seems to have been the representation of the interests of the members in matters of legislation at Albany. To aid hirh in this work a fund was raised by levying assessments upon the various railroad companies which were members of the association in proportion to their gross earnings. Although the records of this association were either lost or destroyed, it is at least certain that a fund of not less than $25,000 was raised in this way in 1903. Of interest, perhaps, is the comment of the committee that "the distribution of this fund was wholly under the control of the president of the association and he was not called upon at any time to account, either to the executive committee or to the association, for the manner of its use." [12]

What were some of the "strike" bills that the "Rogers Trolley Trust" was interested in "putting to sleep"? Although Rogers admitted that "the best interest of the railroads" was a stronger actuating motive with him "the good of the public," [13] he claimed that "there was very little affirmative legislation desired, but there were a great many bills that would have made it impossible to have operated our roads." [14]   Mr. H. H. Vreeland, the president of the largest combination of surface lines in New York City, said that what they wanted was "uniformity of legislation throughout the state." [15] On the other hand, a letter written by the secretary of this association probably comes as near as anything to a definition of the "legislative interests" of the "trust." Among other bills of "considerable importance to railroad interests," was a bill extending the liabilities of employees for accidents to employees, a bill allowing any

doing life insurance business. Hereafter this will be cited as "Corrupt Practices Investigation").

[12] *Ibid.*, p. 9.
[13] *Ibid.*, p. 619.
[14] *Ibid.*, p. 179.
[15] *Ibid.*, p. 484.

citizen to commence an action to compel a corporation to comply with the terms of its franchise, a bill relative to injunction and labor disputes, and Senator Grady's bill to compel street railroads to furnish adequate capacity for all passengers at all times and under all circumstances, under a $50 penalty.[16] Undoubtedly several of the bills were introduced to badger the railroad corporations, but this does not necessarily hold true for all of them. It also appeared that Rogers had been interested in a bill, passed April 5, 1900, which made it possible for the New York Transportation Company, a public service corporation operating bus lines and other transfers in New York City, greatly to extend its franchise.[17] This was probably a little of that "affirmative legislation" that he sometimes desired.

Even so efficient an association as the Street Railway Association seems to have been did not escape the charges of the "Black Horse Cavalry." It appeared that the firm of Ellingwood & Cunningham was used by Rogers during the years that he was president of the association as a clearing house through which to transfer money from the treasuries of the various railroads belonging to the association to the individual accounts of certain members of the legislature whom they deemed "useful."[18] The favored members of the legislature were either upon the Committee on Railroads or upon the Committee on Rules. Thus, the names of Allds, Nixon, and Raines appeared upon the books of Ellingwood & Cunningham.[19] In addition to transfers of credit and stock, the firm furnished these men with valuable "tips" upon the stock market, one of which concerned the New

16 *Ibid.*, p. 545.
17 *Ibid.*, p. 11.
18 *Ibid.*, p. 12.
19 *Ibid.*, pp. 556, 560.

York Transportation Company, benefited by the legislation cited above.

Besides keeping on good terms with certain members of the legislature who occupied strategic positions, Rogers also employed the new system which called for campaign contributions to the party committees. In making the payments to the political parties, he had recourse to the same firm of Ellingwood & Cunningham because he didn't "think it would be wise to report campaign expenses for *both* parties." [20]   He said that he made payments to the state committees of the two political parties because through these committees he "wanted certain men helped." [1]   Then, too, he did not neglect the local committees although the amounts allotted to them were much smaller. The Broome County Republican Committee, his own local committee and also that of State Committeeman Dunn, received an annual contribution of $500 or more. Speaker Nixon's county was also upon his list. That the method of making contributions to the local organization was sometimes preferred to other expedients is shown by the following excerpt from a letter written by a traction man in Elmira to the secretary of the association:

MY DEAR MR. ALLEN: I return your letter enclosed, and I am surprised at the condition which the Cassidy bill has gotten into, for I have certainly been assured by the leading men of the district that if a donation were made to the party about which I have already spoken to you, that the bill would be put through. The whole thing at the present time is whether the donation on the lines already suggested can be raised, if so I would be willing to take the matter up

20 *Ibid.*, p. 602.
1 *Ibid.*, p. 604.

and push it. Otherwise, I am confident it would be thrown away and we can do nothing.[2]

There were some counties, so Mr. Rogers testified, that did not need any help from the association. One of these counties was the county of Albany. Theodore Roosevelt threw some light upon the reason for this particular exception when he said in effect that during the controversy over the franchise tax question Barnes came to him and protested against the measure on the ground that Mr. Robert Pruyn and Mr. Anthony N. Brady who were connected with street railways and electric power companies in Albany, had been very heavy contributors to the Republican campaign fund.[3] When Roosevelt expressed surprise and said that he had always understood that Brady was a very strong Democrat, Barnes answered that Brady had contributed, not as a matter of politics, but as a matter of business, because he could not have the great interests that he represented exposed to attacks by demagogues and scoundrels in the legislature.[4]

The Republican committee of New York County was another local committee that "didn't need any help." Chairman Lauterbach, an attorney and director of the Third Avenue Surface lines, had been quite close to the source of supplies. Lemuel Ely Quigg, his successor as head of the local organization, came into the employ of the Metropolitan Company as "general adviser" of H. H. Vreeland in

[2] *Ibid.*, p. 540. The Cassidy bill referred to in this letter was a bill which referred to the operation of electric lighting companies. The letter was written on April 26, 1905.

[3] *Barnes* v. *Roosevelt*, pp. 215–16.

[4] *Ibid.*, p. 649. Roosevelt added, "I believe that the expression he used was that it would be unjust to the widows and orphans who had invested in the concerns of which he was the head."

1899.[5] The leading luminaries in the Metropolitan Company were William C. Whitney, one of President Cleveland's cabinet officers and later his campaign manager, and Thomas F. Ryan, one of Tammany's main "contributors" and one of Alton B. Parker's chief backers in 1904.[6] It is quite obvious that there was no "politics" in Quigg's arrangement with the Metropolitan, his chief duties being, as he himself confessed, the representation of interests of his company in the lobby at Albany [7] and the manufacture of a public sentiment favorable to the schemes of his employers. This latter function Quigg called "accelerating public opinion," [8] and he admitted that he performed this duty very well even though it did cost the company over $150,000 for his services.[9] The Whitney-Ryan-Brady traction syndicate in New York City, according to its nominal head H. H. Vree-

[5] Public Service Commission, First District, *Investigation of the Interborough-Metropolitan Company and Brooklyn Rapid Transit Co.*, pp. 1397 ff.

[6] For a characterization of Ryan, see B. J. Hendrick, "Great American Fortunes and their Making," *McClure's Mag.* XXX, 246.

[7] *Investigation of the Interborough-Metropolitan, loc. cit.* In answer to a question as to why he was in Albany in 1903, Quigg replied: "I have no doubt that it was in connection with eithe: the promotion of legislation or the opposition to it." His work was done mainly in the committee room or with the chairman of committees and the speaker.

[8] *Ibid.*, p. 1485. Quigg said, "I accelerated their eagerness."

[9] *Ibid.*, p. 1411. Quigg said, "In their behalf, I caused to be organized in various parts of the city seven or eight, perhaps nine or ten, different associations of property owners and citizens whose property and business interests would be promoted by the adoption of the Metropolitan plans; caused them to appear from time to time before meetings of the commissions, before the Board of Estimate and Apportionment, before committees of the legislature and elsewhere, and to be represented by counsel." On p. 1412, Quigg explains how the money was spent to manufacture a giant petition, "I also caused to be prepared a petition which was circulated all over New York, and especially in the tenement districts, during the summer of 1904, and which cost well on to $50,000 I think

land, had contributed to the campaign funds of both the Democratic and Republican parties since 1893, and in 1903 Mr. Vreeland knew from his own personal knowledge that $20,000 had been turned over to the Republican organization through the medium of Quigg.[10] It may be that this action was necessary to drive off the charges of the "Black Horse Cavalry" but a careful student of the traction history of New York City has said, "The consolidation movement is a story featured with extravagant leases, rash expenditures, watered securities, and financial knavery, all of which have reacted detrimentally to public interests."[11]

That the management of other public utility corporations in New York City, those furnishing water and light to portions of the great populace, did not escape charges of similar "scandalous" conduct is evidenced by the preliminary report of the counsel of the "Mazet Committee" which appeared in the newspapers before it had been "properly edited." A portion of this "report" is given below:

The presence of prominent members of both parties in these companies, based directly on state legislation by special acts, and which are not designed to do business by themselves and without city support, causes public suspicion that combinations exist to secure public action on

. . . " The petition expressed opposition to Belmont's plans for a subway and endorsed the plans favored for the moment by the Ryan syndicate.

[10] This testimony first appeared in a Grand Jury investigation. See *New York Times*, April 23, 1908. It later appeared in the *Corrupt Practices Investigation, op. cit.*, pp. 489ff and in the Barnes-Roosevelt libel suit, *loc. cit.*, p. 921.

[11] Carman, *op. cit.*, p. 220. His chapter on the "Era of Consolidation" roughly covers the period when Platt was still influential. His conclusions are well documented. Quigg resigned the presidency of the New York County Committee in 1900 but he continued to be active in Republican politics.

both sides of the line of political division, and leads inevitably to scandal.[12]

The development and expansion of the steam railroad lines in New York during the two decades following 1890 could in no way compare with the expansion which took place in municipal traction systems during the same period,[13] but this does not mean that the directors of the steam railroads could relax the care with which they had watched affairs at Albany during the seventies and eighties when they had been active in making extensions. There were no scandals in the period under discussion like those which had occurred in the notorious "Erie war" of the seventies.[14] On the other hand, there were railroad men who were still interested in politics and one of these was Chauncey M. Depew, nominal head of the New York Central lines,[15] who said of his work as Republican campaign orator, "The position which this activity gave me in my own party, and the fact that unlike most employers, I protected the employees in their liberty of political action, gave me immense help in protecting the company from raids and raiders."[16] The New York Central Railroad was the most important single system in the state and therefore needed some sort of protection. Depew's relation to this railroad corporation and its affiliated lines changed from that of president to chairman of the board of trustees about the time that he was elected to the United States Senate. As United States senator and a member of the advisory committee of the state committee, Depew was at least in a position to see that

[12] *New York Tribune,* December 27, 1899. See to the same effect the minority report of the committee above, p. 170.
[13] See above p. 6.
[14] Sowers, *op. cit.,* pp. 88ff. See also C. F. Adams, *Chapters of Erie and Other Essays* (Boston, 1871).
[15] For summary of Depew's corporate relations see above p. 67.
[16] *Memories,* p. 249.

the Vanderbilt lines were not discriminated against by the political authorities.

Depew took part in the gubernatorial campaign of 1898. Whether he ever charged Roosevelt with ingratitude for the stand that the latter took as governor upon the franchise tax question is a matter of conjecture, but the following letter written by Platt to Roosevelt on May 5, 1900, is of interest in this connection:

Our friends of the New York Central are very anxious to have you sign Senate bill 763, exempting from the franchise tax grade crossing of steam railroads. I hope you can consistently do so. Senator Depew is very anxious.

To this Roosevelt replied by a telegram, dated May 7, 1900:

I received your telegram and one from Ford yesterday. It was too late for me to act, as I had already published a memorandum stating not merely that Ford was against the bill, but that the state tax commissioners opposed the bill.[17]

Besides attempting to obtain tax exemptions for the New York Central, Depew tried "to make the New York Central popular with the public without impairing its efficiency."[18] He granted a "great many passes" each year to politicians, editors and others of political importance.[19] He

[17] *Barnes* v. *Roosevelt*, p. 2481.
[18] *Memories*, p. 244.
[19] Before the constitutional amendment went into effect which prohibited the granting of passes to legislators, Depew said: "I should say that on the average every legislator got 10 passes from us during the session, besides his personal pass." *New York Tribune*, Nov. 15, 1894. Testifying in 1905, Depew said that no requests for passes came to him from members of the legislature and he added, "The New York Central grants a great many passes," *Testimony taken by Legislative Life Insurance Investigating Committee*, 1906, IV, 3187.

spoke at all sorts of political banquets, commercial gatherings, country fairs, and even workingmen's meetings. He made annual contributions to the campaign funds of the state committee and the New York County Committee.[20] At the same time he did not neglect to make recommendations regarding the appointment of a state superintendent of public works, the officer who had charge of a rival transportation system. In this and other ways he protected the interests of the greatest steam railroad system in the state.

As president of the United States Express Company, Thomas C. Platt was himself in fairly close touch with the big railroad directors. The principal business of his express company in 1900 was with the following railroads: Baltimore & Ohio; Chicago, Milwaukee & St. Paul; Chicago, Rock Island & Pacific; Delaware, Lackawanna & Western; and Lehigh.[1] The following letter shows that Platt as well as Depew was in the pass giving business:

August 22, 1894

MY DEAR SENATOR PLATT:
I have promised Manley to make four speeches in Mr. Reed's district on Sept. 5, 6, 7, and 8. I want to get transportation from New York to Boston and thence to Portland and return. Can you help me in this matter? I wish you would if you can.

Faithfully yours,
LEMUEL E. QUIGG.[2]

There was no law of Congress, enforced in such a way as to prevent the practice illustrated in the letter above, un-

[20] U. S. Sen., *Testimony before a Subcommittee of the Committee on Privileges and Elections*, Sixty-second Cong., Second Sess., p. 628 (The "Clapp" Committee on Campaign Expenditures).
[1] *Moody's Manual*, 1900. The directorates of these railroad interlock.
[2] L. E. Quigg, member of Congress, letter books relating to the affairs of his office and New York politics, April 15, 1894 to March 2, 1895 (Manuscript room, New York [City] Public Library).

til some twelve years later.[3] Several questions may be raised at this point. Why was Platt selected by the railroads as a dispenser of passes? Why did Depew ask Platt to intercede with Roosevelt in behalf of tax exemptions for the New York Central Railroad? Why was Platt so anxious to "call off" alleged "strike" legislation against the American Bridge Company?[4] It looks as though Platt was used as a political agent by certain corporations, especially utility corporations. This view is borne out by Roosevelt's testimony. At the time the franchise tax question was being discussed, Platt came to Roosevelt, so the latter claimed, and said that certain business men of great prominence in New York, who would be unfavorably affected by the passage of the bill, had been heavy contributors to the Republican campaign funds and that since the party could not afford to cut off such valuable pecuniary support the act should not be passed.[5] Who were some of these powerful financial men, "Democrats as well as Republicans," who were "irritated" by the franchise tax bill? The practice followed by the Metropolitan Street Railway Company and the New York Central Railroad has already been commented upon. When a similar question was asked of Theodore Roosevelt regarding the Republican campaign fund of 1904, he answered that E. H. Harriman's enormous contribution that year was made for state and not for national purposes.[6] Before 1904, Platt must have known of Harriman's interest in protecting certain railroads, express com-

---

[3] See II. George, Jr., *The Menace of Privilege* (New York, 1906), p. 245.

[4] Letter given above, p. 159.

[5] *Barnes* v. *Roosevelt*, pp. 215–16.

[6] Roosevelt's explanation of the letter he wrote to Harriman in which he said. "You and I are practical men." Harriman's contribution was $250,000. See Report of "Clapp" Committee on Campaign Contributions, pp. 181–82.

panies, and fiduciary institutions from the raids of fanatics and dishonest men in the national and state legislatures.[7]

Platt's "influence" with the governors gave him another way of insuring to the powerful financial men interested in public utilities the sort of "business man's" government that they desired. On December 18, 1896 Governor Morton appointed as one of the three railroad commissioners of the state, Frank M. Baker, of Owego, "the superintendent of a 'one-horse' railroad controlled by Mr. Platt."[8] On February 16 of the next year Governor Black appointed as railroad commissioner, George W. Dunn, of Binghamton, the president of the Binghamton General Electric Company and the vice-president of the Binghamton Railway.[9] The *New York Tribune* made the following remark upon this condition: "Mr. Platt thus has two of the three votes in the commission."[10] Inasmuch as the term of a member of this commission was five years, Governor Roosevelt was not in a position to disturb these "two votes," and even when Governor Odell, in a measure "broke" with Platt, State Chairman Dunn remained loyal to the "old man." The expenses of this board were borne by the railroads, a plan which Governor Hughes regarded as "wholly indefensible."[11] The Railroad Commission had the power to examine the books and affairs of all steam railroad and street surface railway corporations in the state. Did Commis-

---

[7] In 1901 Harriman was a director of the Baltimore & Ohio Railroad, the Brooklyn Rapid Transit Company and other utility corporations. It later came out that he owned a large block of stock in the U. S. Express Company. See *Commercial and Financial Chronicle*, LXXXIX (1909), 100. Regarding his insurance business, see below.

[8] *New York Tribune*, Jan. 24, 1898.

[9] W. S. Lawyer, *Binghamton* (Century Memorial Publishing Co., 1900), and *Binghamton Press*, October 18, 1911.

[10] *Loc. cit.*

[11] C. E. Hughes, *Addresses* (New York, 1908), p. 92.

sioner Dunn discover many irregularities? He might have known where to look, as his own name appeared upon the books of Ellingwood & Cunningham.[12] The commission also had the power to forbid the execution of mortgages, the increase or reduction of capital stock, and the construction of new lines. These were important duties, but as far as effectual regulation was concerned Governor Hughes found the scheme "inadequate." [13] The railroad corporations, however, were not known to be loud in their complaints.

In 1905 a quarrel between certain of these same railroad financiers for the control of the assets of the great life insurance companies precipitated an investigation which threw a flood of light upon the relations between business and politics in New York. As business men of great prominence, the contestants had for a long time realized that the huge accumulations of life insurance companies were "readily convertible into money and susceptible of application to varied uses" and therefore the struggle was a bitter one and the rending of the veil complete.[14] The legislative investigating committee, called the "Armstrong committee" from its chairman, was very fortunate in its selection of Charles E. Hughes as its counsel, for this brilliant lawyer conducted the inquiry with masterful skill.

The president of one of the three largest insurance companies declared upon the witness stand that the insurance companies had been badgered by the introduction of bad bills in the state legislature and that they had been com-

---

[12] *Corrupt Practices Investigation*, pp. 554–55.
[13] State of New York, *Public Papers of Governor Hughes*, 1907, p. 30.
[14] Heaton, *op. cit.*, chap. XVI "Equitable Corruption," gives the *New York World* credit for starting this investigation. See *Report of Legislative Life Insurance Investigation Committee* (1906), pp. 69, 278–79.

pelled to pay money to protect themselves against black-mailers. This plea sounds not unlike that made in defense of the public utility corporations. The following letter shows the sort of legislative matters in which the insurance companies were interested in:

Jan. 23, 1903.

Mr. A. C. Fields,
  C/o *Mutual Life Insurance Company,*
    32 Nassau Street, New York City.
  DEAR SIR—Referring to Albany matters during the present session, please note that we will be interested in all banking and insurance measures, taxation schemes and bills affecting particularly the following interests:
  Safe deposit companies, banks, trust companies, street railways and all measures affecting Suffolk County, New York franchises, water rights, land under water, transportation, etc.

Yours very truly,
(Signed) T. D. Jordan, COMPTROLLER.[15]

It is difficult to see how measures affecting some of these matters could be regarded as "strike" bills against insurance companies as such. Some of the specific measures referred to in other memoranda to A. C. Fields seem even more remote from the legitimate sphere of life insurance companies. Why should they oppose an act to provide greater security in hotels, inns, taverns, and tenement houses, a bill to safeguard the lives of patrons of amusement places, and a bill to cede to the Town of Islip certain water rights? The opposition to these bills becomes a little more intelligible when it is considered that bills endeavoring to protect the interests of the policy holders were even more violently opposed. The officers of the insurance companiess had become interested in a great variety of legislative matters because of

---

[15] *Ibid.,* p. 13. The other memoranda here referred to are given in the same place.

their connections with subsidiary companies, a relation which they felt necessary to protect in a surreptitious manner.[16]

A. C. Fields, it seems, represented both the Mutual and the Equitable in legislative matters and he maintained in Albany for this purpose a house which was jocosely styled the "House of Mirth." Fields was also at the head of the "Supply Department" of the Mutual which spent exorbitant sums each year for "stationery." The cost of maintaining his "House of Mirth" was charged to "legal expenses."[17] In his palatial abode he "entertained" the legislators with poker games and other pleasant pastimes. Listen to the way the Armstrong committee scored the body of which it was a part:

The pernicious activities of corporate agents in matters of legislation demand that the present freedom of lobbying should be restricted. They have brought suspicion upon important proceedings of the legislature, and have exposed its members to consequent assault. The legislature owes it to itself, as far as possible, to stop the practice of the lavish expenditure of moneys ostensibly for services in connection with the support of or opposition to bills, and generally believed to be used for corrupt purposes.[18]

Certain members of the legislature, however, were not the only organization Republicans involved in this investigation; there were some Republicans, higher up, who were also "exposed to assault." Among these was Senator Chauncey M. Depew, of railroad fame, who had received an annual retainer of $20,000 from the Equitable beginning about 1888 for "advisory services." During this time he had been a director and a member of the executive com-

[16] *Ibid.*, pp. 278–79.
[17] *Ibid.*, p. 9.
[18] *Ibid.*, p. 286.

mittee, and the report claimed that he was unable to describe any services that he had rendered to warrant his retainer which the society was not fairly entitled to receive from him as director.[19] In justice to Depew it should be said that he claimed his advice was worth many thousands of dollars to the company. Depew also made good his share of the "unfortunate" loan of $250,000 made by the society to the Depew Improvement Company. Since he was interested in both companies, he knew of this loan and when the reorganization scheme for the Equitable was hurried through he contributed his share to the reimbursement of the society.[20]

Governor Odell, the business man from Newburgh, was another one of Platt's friends and Roosevelt's advisers who faced the searching questions propounded by Charles E. Hughes. While governor of the state, Odell had seen no objection to the introduction of a bill repealing the charter of a company which owed him money. When it was publicly charged that the object of introducing this bill was to force the company to "settle up" with the governor, he informed the introducer that "as desirable as he believed the legislation to be," he feared his "unfortunate connection with the Shipbuilding matter" was of such a character that it would be better to "drop this legislation."[1] In its report the committee concluded that "it may be that the fact of its introduction was sufficient to induce a fear on the part of the officers of the trust company that proceedings inimical to its interests might be taken, if those who could initiate them were not appeased."[2] Odell could hope for no mercy at the hands of Mr. Hughes, but he might have expected bet-

[19] Ibid., p. 79.
[20] Ibid., p. 85.   See also D. G. Phillips, loc. cit.
[1] Ibid., p. 99.
[2] Ibid., p. 99.

ter treatment from his financial friend, E. H. Harriman. The most startling portion of Harriman's testimony is given below:

Q. Well, it has been openly charged that through your relations with Mr. Odell you have political influence. What would you say to that? A. Well, I should think that Mr. Odell had political influence because of his relations to me.[3]

It should not be supposed that the maintenance of a "House of Mirth" at Albany was the only precaution that the big insurance companies took against "improper and ill-advised" legislation. As in the case of the utility corporations, resort was had to the "new system" described at the beginning of this chapter. Thus, the usual contribution of the Mutual to the Republican state committee was $10,-000 [4] and that of the Equitable an annual contribution of the same amount,[5] to say nothing of much larger contributions made by these and other companies to the Republican national committee.[6] These payments were concealed by devious methods, some of which would rival the device of an Ellingwood & Cunningham. The following extract from the testimony taken before the committee shows how Senator Platt was taken off his guard and made a frank confession of what contributors expected of him:

Q. If you have any opinion, of course, we should be glad to have it, but the point that I want particularly to get at is this, what suggestion was there to the insurance companies of any quid pro quo, what was the insurance company to get out of the fact that they had made the contribution? A. There was not any suggestion of any sort.

[3] *Testimony*, VI, 5154. Harriman later tried to qualify this bald statement. Odell denied all its implications.
[4] *Report*, p. 15.
[5] *Ibid.*, p. 79.
[6] *Ibid.*, pp. 45, 239.

Q. What advantage really could they get? A. They get it through me being connected with the state committee.

Q. How could they get it through you? A. They would suppose that I would be very likely to defend them at any time when it was necessary, if I had occasion to do it.

Q. What would that extend to, what would you mean by defending them if occasion made it necessary? A. I don't know.

Q. What had you in mind in saying that? A. That they would expect me to support them naturally in anything that they naturally thought was right and that they were for.

. . . .

Q. To see that the legislature, for example, did not enact legislation which they thought hostile to their policy holders? A. That is what it would amount to.

Q. That is what it would amount to. How could you control that situation? A. I could not control it.

Q. How could you in any way influence it? A. I might have some influence.

Q. Through the disposition of the moneys in the election of legislators? A. Well, I could not say that.

Q. Is not that the way it really comes about, Senator, that the use of these contributions in the election of candidates to office puts the candidates under more or less of a moral obligation not to attack the interests supporting? A. That is what would naturally be involved.

Q. That is really what is involved, is it not? A. I should think so.

Q. And that is what you meant when you said that they would expect you, through your relations to the state committee, to defend them? A. Yes.[7]

Platt's relations with these corporations could hardly be revealed in a more striking manner. The committee regarded this practice as "wholly unjustifiable" and said that those who had engaged in it were open to "severe and just condemnation."[8] The money was evidently paid to Platt

[7] *Testimony*, IV, 3396–97.
[8] *Report*, p. 284.

in cash; there were no express promises, there was no talk
of special favors, for no pledges were needed; it was all a
"moral obligation," a "gentlemen's understanding." [9]   The
aged Senator said that he did not know of the activities of
the insurance company lobbyists; his influence in the matter
was through his "being connected with the state committee,"
through his relations with Chairmen Hackett, Odell, and
Dunn.

If the actual operation of the Insurance Department can
be taken as any criterion, this branch of the state government was also under implied "obligation" to defend the insurance companies.   The committee through its counsel Mr.
Hughes found that the superintendent had had ample power
to perform his duty of exposing abuses and assuring correct administration, but year after year the superintendent
had certified to false statements which concealed the enormous salaries paid to the officers of the societies, which covered up the enormous syndicate profits which men like Harriman [10] and Morgan [11] were able to make through the use
of the policy holders' money, and which gave no clue as to
the amount of money "improperly spent" to influence legislation through lobbyists and party committees.[12]   The superintendent also failed to discover the "unique situation"
which operated beneficially for the officers of an up-state
insurance company [13] of which Colonel Dunn was vice-presi-

[9] Roosevelt, *op. cit.*, p. 275.
[10] *Report*, pp. 87, 101.   The Equitable subscribed to $2,500,000
worth of stock in one of Harriman's railroad syndicates in a surreptitious fashion.
[11] *Report*, pp. 39, 51, 54, 57-58.   Through G. W. Perkins, vice-
president of the New York Life and a member of J. P. Morgan &
Co., the New York Life participated in the Morgan steel, railroad,
and navigation syndicates.
[12] *Ibid.*, pp. 246 ff.   The committee's indictment of the department.
[13] *Ibid.*, pp. 177-78.

dent.[14] Superintendent Hendricks tried to defend himself by saying that his duty did not extend beyond ascertaining whether the companies were solvent or not. Such things as the continuation of Fields' clerk as examiner in the department, the failure to make any examination at all of certain companies for long periods of time, the lax interpretation of the rules that the department made, and the making of an examination which the committee called "plainly a farce," escaped the superintendent's attention. It will be remembered that Platt was very anxious that Roosevelt "consult" him regarding the appointment of "Lou" Payn's successor as state superintendent of insurance. Hendricks was an old man, and even Hughes treated him gently. It was the system that was at fault.[15]

So far only the services that the state government was made to perform for the benefit of the directors of the great corporations have been discussed. It should be kept in mind that the insurance societies and the railroad corporations made contributions to the Republican national committee as well as to the state committee.[16] The insurance companies also maintained lobbyists at Washington.[17] The money collected by the national committee was sometimes

[14] *Testimony,* V, 4415.

[15] *Report,* pp. 14, 86, 145, 151, 247, 253.

[16] President McCall and Vice-President Perkins of the New York Life and President McCurdy of the Mutual boasted about the contributions they had made out of the policy holders' money to the Republican national campaign funds in 1896, 1900, and 1904. See *Testimony,* I, 751, 826; II, 1851. Harriman understood that for the money he raised in 1904 Senator Depew was to be made ambassador and that he (Harriman) was to be consulted upon railroad matters touched in the President's message. When these arrangements were not carried out he asked Webster, "Where do I stand." See "Clapp" Committee on Campaign Contributions, pp. 183, 245.

[17] *Report,* p. 37.

used to aid the election of certain congressmen.[18] What was "expected of" the New York senators and representatives and of the departments of the federal government? The "politics" of sugar industry will be taken as a typical illustration of the relations between big business and the members of the Republican state organization enjoying the federal patronage.

As far back as 1894, Henry O. Havemeyer, president of the American Sugar Refining Company, testified that his company was in the habit of contributing to the campaign funds of both the Republican and Democratic parties in New York, and he added that whichever party won, "We expect protection from the police and fire department, and anything that the state and local organization can give." The "Sugar Trust" had no politics but "only the politics of business."[19] What were some of the things that the state organization could "give"? The giant "Sugar Trust" was not concerned with small "game" like the bounty granted by the state legislature during the years 1897 to 1908 to the struggling up-state beet sugar refineries which amounted altogether to only some $500,000;[20] it was after the big "gifts" at the disposal of the federal government. Although Havemeyer called the tariff "the mother of all trusts," he made one exception and that exception was the sugar refining industry.[1] The New York congressmen in 1897 voted "regular" upon the tariff schedule and thus did

[18] "Clapp" committee, p. 626 (Depew's contribution to congressional campaign committee).

[19] *Senate Reports,* Fifty-third Congress, Second Sess., No. 606, X, 655ff.

[20] Located at Lyons and Binghamton. These refineries were charged with trying to corrupt legislators. See Corrupt Practices Investigation, p. 846.

[1] *Industrial Commission,* I, 101.

their part toward enabling the "Sugar Trust" speculators to net millions of dollars. The indirect benefits of this tariff were perhaps even greater, for until 1913 the duties on sugar restrained foreign competition and thus made it easier for the trust to maintain monopoly prices.[2] Not satisfied with practically writing the sugar schedule of the tariff, the "Sugar Trust" officials connived with the New York customs officers to defraud the government of millions of dollars due in the form of duties on raw sugar.[3] At the trial of the culprits instigated by President Roosevelt in 1907, it was shown that the practice of underweighing shipments of raw sugar had begun at least as early as 1901, that the company's superintendent exercised a large amount of influence in the New York Custom-house and that the company often procured the removal of "obnoxious" weighers.[4] While Platt was not implicated in this matter, some of his "henchmen" were and the Secretary of the Treasury made the following diagnosis:

The study of the causes of the demoralization which has been revealed is still incomplete, but the main causes are evident. It is clear, for instance, that the influence of local politics and politicians upon the customs service has been most deleterious, and has promoted that laxity and low tone which prepare and furnish an inviting soil for dishonesty and fraud. Unless the customs service can be released from the payment of political debts and exactions, and from meeting the supposed exigencies of political organizations,

[2] F. W. Taussig, *Tariff History of the United States* (New York, 1914), pp. 305-314.

[3] Over $2,000,000 was recovered by the government. See *Annual Reports of the Attorney General*, 1910, p. 2; 1911, p. 20; 1913, p. 27.

[4] *House Reports,* Sixty-first Congress, Second Sess., Doc. No. 901, p. 8.

big and little, it will be impossible to have an honest service for any length of time.[5]

The evidence which has been adduced so far to illustrate the relations between the political managers and the directors of the great business and industrial corporations has been of a more or less definite character. As Platt confessed before the Armstrong committee it was not part of the code of politics to make these things definite, so the fact that there is any concrete information available at all on this topic must be explained by the existence of internal maladjustments. To describe the complete working of the system is, of course, impossible, but in view of what has been revealed it is significant that Thomas C. Platt was president of the United States Express Company throughout the entire period of his political domination and his senatorship. In 1880 a special committee of the New York legislature was investigating the subject of railroads and in its report it mentioned very casually the express companies, whose "rates to the public were not for want of time inquired into."[6] The express business was extremely profitable and a practical monopoly was enjoyed by four big companies: the Adams, the American, Wells-Fargo, and the United States Express Company. Platt's company was the smallest of these four companies, but it was important enough to be considered by the great financiers who were interested in transportation matters.[7] In 1891, John Wanamaker, postmaster general under President Harrison, said in

[5] *Annual Report of the Secretary of Treasury,* 1919, p. 8.

[6] *Report,* p. 13.

[7] Interstate Commerce Commission, *First Annual Report on Statistics of Express Companies in the United States for the year ending June 30, 1909.* See also A. W. Atwood, "The Great Express Monopoly," *American Mag.,* LXXI (1911), 764.

his annual report, "In point of fact there are but four strong objections to the parcels post and they are the four great express companies." [8]   They continued to be "objections" as long as Platt remained a power in politics. In fact, not only was there no parcel post until after Platt's death, but the express companies were not even subject to investigation by the Interstate Commerce Commission until 1906 when Platt's power as a political manager had been broken and Roosevelt was securely in the saddle. In 1909 a suit brought against Platt by one of the stockholers of his company showed that for half a dozen years or so his company had violated both the state and federal anti-trust laws.[9] Was there any prosecution by state or federal officers during this time? When this condition was revealed by the report of the Interstate Commerce Commission and the attorney general of the state (who was a Democrat) threatened to bring a suit against the three companies which had pooled their interests, appearances were mended.[10] Needless to say this event occurred long after Platt's political power had begun to wane.

Senator Platt proudly dubbed himself the "Begging Chief" and asserted that, inasmuch as he had only a limited income, "it was therefore a duty and a pleasure, when party exigencies arose, to solicit donations from men abundantly able to give, and to whose vital interest it was that the party supremacy be sustained." [11] There were none of Platt's field marshals who showed any inclinations to dispute this dis-

[8] P. 114.
[9] *Dudley* v. *Platt,* 118 New York Sup. 1058.
[10] A. W. Atwood. *loc. cit.*
[11] *Op. cit.,* p. 532.

tinction claimed by their chief; in fact, upon several occasions Odell made it emphatic that up to 1904 Senator Platt had always gathered the great bulk of the campaign funds together.[12] In describing his governorship, Roosevelt said:

In New York State, United States Senator Platt was the absolute boss of the Republican party. "Big Business" was back of him; yet at the time this, the most important element in his strength, was only imperfectly understood. It was not until I was elected governor that I myself came to understand it. . . . But big business men contributed to him large sums of money, which enabled him to keep his grip on the machine and secured for them the help of the machine if they were threatened with adverse legislation. The contributions were given in the guise of contributions for campaign purposes, of money for the good of the party; when the money was contributed there was rarely talk of special favors in return. It was simply put into Mr. Platt's hands and treated by him as in the campaign chest. Then he distributed it in the districts where it was most needed by the candidates and the organization leaders. Ordinarily no pledge was required from the latter to the bosses, any more than it was required by the business men from Mr. Platt or his lieutenants.[13]

On the one hand stood the government with favors to grant and with burdens to impose, while on the other stood the corporations anxious for favors and not averse to escaping burdens. The government and the corporations were both forms of social organization in which the few tended to dominate. The temptations which confronted the leaders in politics and industry were many, especially considering the secrecy and freedom from restrain with which their

[12] Legislative life insurance investigation, *Testimony*, IV. 3154; *Barnes* v. *Roosevelt*, p. 1836.
[13] *Op. cit.*, pp. 274–75.

powers were exercised.[14]   Platt frankly defended the system throughout his entire public career.   Roosevelt himself admitted that he did not understand the inner workings of the system in the early part of his career but in his later years he denounced it upon several occasions as the "corrupt alliance."

[14] F. J. Goodnow, *Politics and Administration* (New York, 1900), 252; Fuller,* *op. cit.,* p. 139; H. Croly, *The Promise of American Life* (New York, 1909), pp. 117 ff.

CHAPTER XI

PLATT'S DECLINE AND ROOSEVELT'S CAPTURE OF THE ORGANIZATION

In the closing weeks of the year 1900 Thomas C. Platt must have looked with some satisfaction upon his achievements as leader of the Republican organization in the state of New York. Had not the troublesome Roosevelt been "shelved" in the vice-presidency? Had not Odell, an organization man, been elected governor of the state? Had not McKinley, the "most tender-hearted man in politics," been re elected president of the United States for another term of four years? Were there not three years left to his own term as United States senator and did he not have the amiable companionship of Depew at Washington? Was not his tried and trusted friend, Colonel Dunn, who from his work as railroad commissioner knew every corner of the state, chairman of the Republican state committee?[1] Had not his friend at Albany, Speaker Nixon, demonstrated his superior ability as a parliamentarian? Were not his friends in New York, who were "abundantly able to give," making money faster than ever? Apparently he had no cause for worry about state or federal appointments, about legislation at Washington or Albany, about party primaries or the state committee, about campaign funds or election workers. What other matters concerned him as a manager of a state party? Like Hill in 1892 and like other "bosses" of his own day, Platt thought in terms of his organization and failed to realize that his organization might defeat itself.

[1] Dunn was elected chairman in Odell's place on November 17, 1900.

Platt had had his difficulties with Governor Roosevelt, but in December, 1900, little did he dream that Odell, the first "organization" governor that he had ever "elected," would cause him more trouble than any man he ever had in the governor's chair. Platt had "breakfasted" with the Governor-elect Odell before his inauguration and evidently thought that matters would run smoothly.[2] Since he was getting on in years, he had turned over many things to Odell. Imagine his surprise when Governor Odell, in one of his first official acts, asserted his "independence" in unmistakable terms. Platt had understood that he would be "consulted" with reference to the selection of a superintendent of public works, but the governor appointed to this office, Charles S. Boyd, a personal friend of his, without a word to Platt beforehand. Even Roosevelt had not done anything like this. While Platt covered up this blow, he was unable to hide the damaging effect of the next. One of his "favorite" measures had always been a metropolitan police measure which vested the control of the New York Police Department in the state government, and in 1901 the scandals of "Deveryism" seemed to give an excuse for the passage of such a drastic act. Unlike Governor Roosevelt, Governor Odell refused even to "confer" over the matter and issued a public statement announcing that he would veto such a measure.[3] Although the break was unmistakable, Platt kept on insisting that there was no "dissension" between him and the Governor.[4]

When Platt thought that he had "shelved" Roosevelt in the vice-presidency, he had evidently neglected for the mo-

[2] Platt, *op. cit.*, p. 423.

[3] *New York Tribune*, March 22, 23, 1901; *Nation*, March 28, 1901, LXXII, 249; Platt, *op. cit.*, pp. 424-30.

[4] *New York Tribune*, December 29, 1901.

ment the possibilities of that office. Although the assassination of Garfield some twenty years before had caused him great embarrassment and grief, it is hard to see how the assassination of McKinley caused him any less. Theodore Roosevelt, president of the United States! What would happen to the federal patronage in New York? To federal legislation affecting corporations and big business? Platt was not kept in suspense very long, for he and the new president soon clashed over the perennial source of factional controversy, the New York Custom-house. The President informed the Senator that he had decided to let Collector Bidwell go. When Platt and Depew perceived that the president was determined, they did not appeal to "senatorial courtesy" nor did they threaten to resign. Platt had learned much in twenty years, and besides he was "consulted" with reference to Bidwell's successor. The cases were "different." [5] Shortly after this incident another disagreement occurred over the reorganization of the immigration office in New York. The commissioner in charge of the station in Ellis Island and his deputy got into a quarrel with the commissioner general of immigration. Roosevelt resolved to make a clean sweep of both offices. Platt objected, but Roosevelt was again firm and the Senator's "leadership" received another set-back.[6] Less spectacular than these assaults upon Platt's organization but nevertheless of great importance to him were the extensions of the competitive system, the changes in the civil service rules, and the improved efficiency in the execution of the Civil Service

[5] Bidwell was retained until the expiration of his vacation appointment on April 1, 1902. See New York Tribune, November 16, 1901 and F. E. Leupp, The Man Roosevelt (New York, 1904), p. 130.

[6] Leupp, op. cit., p. 134 and New York Tribune, Mar. 15, Apr. 13, 1902.

Law brought about by the new president.[7] These inroads into the federal patronage so weakened the Senator's position in the city of New York that at the "suggestion" of President Roosevelt, he co-operated with the other anti-Tammany elements in 1901 to bring about the election of Seth Low as mayor of Greater New York,[8] thus repudiating in part the position taken by the Republican organization in 1897. The new president, himself a New Yorker, began to wield a powerful influence in state affairs. As Platt said, Roosevelt in some of his methods of dealing with public problems was the "direct antithesis of McKinley." [9]

At the State Convention held in September, 1902, Platt, for the first time in fourteen years, failed to live up to Barnes' definition of a state leader. He was not nor did he claim to be the "most active operating force" in that convention. About two and a half weeks before the convention met, it was announced in the papers that Platt and Odell had agreed upon the state ticket and that their choice for lieutenant-governor was George R. Sheldon, a New York banker.[10] There was no question as to Odell's renomination for governor. On the eve of the convention certain newspapers made comments upon Sheldon's career as a "trust" promoter which tended to imperil his "availability." Alarmed by the popular disproval of trusts that Roosevelt helped to foster, Odell let it be known that he would not run with Sheldon. But Platt held fast to the prearranged ticket and said to Sheldon, "If he (Odell) wants to get off the ticket, let him." [11] Odell was willing enough to confer with Platt,

---

[7] Foulke, op. cit., chap. xii.

[8] Barnes v. Roosevelt, p. 756, Roosevelt's testimony with reference to conferences that he brought about between Low, Platt, and Odell with reference to the affairs of Greater New York.

[9] Op. cit., p. 402.

[10] New York Herald, September 6, 1902.

[11] New York Herald, September 24, 1902.

and it was said that he showed great tact in doing so. On the other hand, Platt did not show that command of himself which had been one of his striking characteristics, and when he saw that Odell had the upper hand, he became petulant. The newspapers said that Platt was forced to request Sheldon to withdraw; in his *Autobiography*, Platt maintained that he was "loyal" to Sheldon to the 'end and never made any such request. Whichever account is true, the central fact remained that Platt had been beaten openly upon the floor of the convention and had left no avenue for retreat. The federal and the state patronage had turned the tide against "the old man." In the following election it was alleged that Platt and those who clung to him "knifed" the Republican ticket,[12] but this seems improbable to the writer. Although Odell was elected by a very narrow margin of less than 8,000 votes, the Republican candidate for the Court of Appeals was defeated, an event which the *Nation* regarded as a "direct slap" in Platt's face.[13] Besides, Platt could not have afforded to cut the head of the ticket without endangering the state legislature which was to elect a United States senator at the expiration of his term the following year.

At the beginning of year 1903, Platt could still say that he had some "influence." He had had a conference with the Governor regarding the annual message to the legislature. With reference to the senatorship, State Chairman Dunn had said, "There is a tremendous sentiment in the Republican organization, which Mr. Platt will not resist when he realizes its magnitude."[14] A year and a half before the

[12] Platt, *op. cit.*, p. 440. In support of this claim it can be cited that Odell took charge of his own campaign a few days before the election and that certain Platt organs in New York published scare stories regarding the outcome of the election.
[13] Nov. 6, 1902, LXXV, 253.
[14] *New York Tribune,* December 9, 1902.

Senator had admitted that he was tired of his duties at
Washington partly because of advancing age,[15] but when he
saw a chance to reassert his "leadership" by a re-election in
1903, he fulfilled Chairman Dunn's prophesy and responded
to that "tremendous sentiment." If there was any such
"sentiment," it failed to find expression in the caucus which
selected him, for in that solemn meeting no speeches were
given and a funeral atmosphere pervaded as if most of the
legislators expected their nominee to die soon.[16] Platt was
not, as he claimed, the unanimous choice of all the Republicans when the final vote was taken in the legislature.[17] The
fact that he was re-elected at all may be explained upon the
ground that he was still in a position to "help certain men
out" around election time. Then, too, Roosevelt and Odell
did not wish as yet to make a complete break with the man
who had been so intimately connected with their political
beginnings.

If Platt thought that his re-election would be a vindication, he was soon disappointed. The very legislature which
had elected him turned around three months later and dealt
him a "mortal blow." When the term of Platt's railroad
commissioner, Frank M. Baker, expired in April, Odell sent
Baker's name to the state Senate for a reappointment, according to his agreement with Platt. The rejection of the
nomination by the Senate was regarded by some as "conclusive proof of the ending of the domination of the old Republican machine," in that the governor had beaten Platt at his
own game.[18] At any rate, Platt was not immediately successful in covering the wound, and he could not conceal the

[15] Ibid., June 16, 1901.
[16] New York Herald, January 20, 1903.
[17] Of the Republicans 111 voted for Platt and 3 for Root; the
78 Democrats all voted for Stanchfield. For Platt's assertion, see
op. cit., p. 441.
[18] Nation, April 23, 1903, LXXVI, 325.

damaging effect that some of Odell's appointments had upon his prestige.[19]

When the "vindicated" senator took up his senatorial duties again, he found a few more surprises in store for him. Among other things of a discouraging nature, he received a "letter of regrets" from President Roosevelt on the subject of a judicial appointment in New York, which ran in part as follows:

You say that "if Mr. H.'s appointment follows this protest, I shall view it with absolute disgust. I shall, moreover, experience a diminuation of that interest in public affairs that has been for so many years a vital element of my life.'

This, my dear Senator, seems hardly worthy of you. I cannot believe that you seriously mean that if I should, after careful and conscientious thought, conclude to nominate a man recommended as Mr. H. is recommended, and standing as high as I know him to stand, you would feel like losing interest in public affairs. My life has been much shorter than yours, yet I have seen a good many appointments made to federal position, during the last twenty years, of which I by no means approve. But it never occurred to me, on account of any or all of those appointments, to refuse longer to take an interest in public affairs. . . .

Finally, my dear Senator, you say: "If you cherish the belief that Mr. H. will be able to accomplish the political results that you have in mind, I simply wish to express the opinion that he cannot, and, moreover, will not, meet your expectations."

I am wholly at a loss to know what you mean by this sentence. The political results I shall have in mind if I appoint Mr. H. are those that I hope will follow the appointment of a first class man whom the community in general and the bar in particular will accept as a first class man in

---

[19] An Odell adherent took Baker's place. McCullagh, Platt's head of the New York Bureau of Elections also failed to receive a reappointment. Later on Baker was again nominated and his nomination was confirmed.

point of character and ability, and whose appointment they will feel reflects credit upon the bench. . . .[20]

One can imagine Platt saying, *"Governor* Roosevelt would never have written such a letter." To which an impartial observer might have rejoined, "Nor would you, Senator Platt, in those days have shown yourself so querulous and peevish, nor would you have talked so openly of the 'political results' of a judicial appointment." Things had changed. In connection with this very appointment Roosevelt wrote to another congressman, saying that he wanted to support both Platt and Odell and take the advice of both, but when he was convinced that the advice of both was wrong, he acted as he pleased.[1] What constitutional right had a governor to be "consulted" with reference to federal appointments? Senator Platt may have mused over this point when he thought that the federal patronage was used against him.

Shortly after the letter cited above was written, another incident occurred which must have raised doubts in Platt's mind as to whether he really was the senior senator from New York. In March, 1903, Platt persuaded Roosevelt to send in the name of William H. Plimley for the assistant treasureship at New York. The President later admitted that he knew nothing about Plimley until the Senator proposed his name. At the time this nomination was passed upon favorably by the Finance Committee, Aldrich, of Rhode Island, the chairman of the committee, was in New York. When he came back to Washington, he moved that the nomination be recommitted. Entirely off their guard, Platt and Depew agreed; whereupon, to their amazement, charges were filed against Plimley. Aldrich, of course, knew all the time this would happen. The adverse com-

[20] Bishop, *op. cit.,* I, 235–36.
[1] Roosevelt, *op. cit.,* p. 359.

BOTTLED UP

(Cartoon by C. G. Bush, *New York World*, 1904)

ment was so strong that Roosevelt withdrew Plimley's name, and Platt had another reason for losing "that interest he had shown in public affairs." [2]

In 1904 the collapse of Platt's "leadership" was well-nigh complete. As step by step he lost control of important elements in his old state organization, he tried desperately to cover up his humiliation. Thus, when Governor Odell supplanted Colonel Dunn as chairman of the state committee, Depew and other extorted from the "Governor-Chairman" an acknowledgment of Platt's "active" leadership.[3] This acknowledgment did not conceal the fact that President Roosevelt "recognized" Odell as the new head of the New York organization nor did it cover up the fact that the Senator had lost "influence" at Albany.[4] Similarly the New York delegation to the Republican National Convention of 1904 was willing to choose Platt as its "head" and to applaud him as the "peerless leader," but, when it came to choose its national committeeman, it selected a man who was close to Odell.[5] These and other inroads into the Senator's powers account in part for the sweeping victory scored by the Roosevelt-Odell forces in the state convention held in September. Platt had declared himself in favor of the nomination of Root for governor. Root declined to allow his name to be considered, and Platt then came out for Woodruff, one of the few remaining field-marshals of the old régime who had not been "dragooned" into Odell's camp. As if to make the issue more clearly defined; Platt declared that any candidate with "an Odell tag" on his was foredoomed to defeat.[6] After consulting Hendricks, President

[2] Leupp, *op. cit.*, p. 128; Thompson, *op. cit.*, pp. 120ff; *New York Tribune*, Mar. 11, 17, 15, 18 and 19, 1903.
[3] *New York Tribune*, Mar. 21, 1904; Platt, *op. cit.*, p. 450.
[4] Thompson, *op. cit.*, pp. 104–5.
[5] Platt, *op. cit.*, p. 454; *Nation*, December 22, 1904.
[6] *Nation*, Sept. 22, 1904, LXXIX, 227.

Roosevelt's trusted adviser in New York affairs, Odell picked as his candidate Lieutenant-Governor Frank W. Higgins, who, according to Platt's account, had stood long under Odell "without hitching." Odell suggested a conference and asked Platt to attend, but the Senator hotly replied, "Not by a damned sight," [7] so the two carried their struggle into the convention where all could see the old man's "leadership" torn up by the roots. What chance had Platt against the "entire influence" of the national administration? In the campaign, that followed, Odell assumed full charge of everything from the collecting of the funds to the making of a card index of the voters, and when his candidate was elected, he declared that he had been "vindicated" in spite of the fact that the election turned largely upon the popularity of Roosevelt.[8]

When Odell was about to lay down his duties as governor, his political power seemed invincible; he was chairman of the state committee, he had "influence" in the state legislature, and he had shown his mastery of two state conventions. What else did he need to establish his prowess as a political manager? A United States senator. Already he discovered a "tremendous sentiment" in favor of former Governor Black as Depew's successor.[9] At this point Platt attempted his last display of his old time power. He began working for Depew by issuing interviews in his old style, seeing legislators, and reviving his "Sunday-school." How much his activities actually influenced the situation, it is difficult to say. The great financial powers were almost solidly behind Depew. When someone convinced Odell that he must

[7] Platt, *op. cit.*, pp. 454–59.
[8] *Nation*, November 17, 1904. Although Higgins had a plurality of 80,560 he was nearly 100,000 votes behind Roosevelt. The figures were: Roosevelt 859,533; Parker, 683,981; Higgins, 813,264; Herrick, 732,704.
[9] *Nation*, December 22, 1904.

retreat and come out for Depew, Platt was in a position to assert some of his former claims to glory. Harriman, Roosevelt, and Higgins have each been held responsible for Odell's ignominious retreat upon the senatorship.[10] There is evidence that indicates that Roosevelt was one of those who made a sudden shift on this question.[11] Whatever the "active operating force," it was soon obvious that Odell's retreat did not mean Platt's advance, and the Senator openly declared that he had lost that interest in "public affairs" which had been such a vital element in his life.

Odell assumed the leadership of the Republican state organization under much more difficult circumstances than had confronted his predecessor. The party had been in power long enough to accumulate a record which was very vulnerable in many spots. Of even more significance was the fact that Republican voters no longer viewed with complacency the claims and activities of the "organization." Odell was stigmatized as the "Governor-Chairman" and placed by some in a category along side of David B. Hill. The charges made regarding campaign funds aroused grave suspicions. Moreover, the outcome of the struggle between Platt and Odell had left some bitter resentments. These feelings and suspicions furnished a fruitful soil for the growth of that popular revolt which followed the revelations of the life insurance investigation begun in the latter part of 1905. The confessions of Senators Platt and Depew and of Chairman Odell before the Armstrong Committee disillusioned many, even in the most rock-ribbed Republican communities, as to the real nature of the system which their

[10] Platt claimed that Harriman was responsible, *op. cit.*, pp. 460ff; but see the letter that Harriman wrote to Webster, *loc. cit.* The *Nation* claimed that Higgins was responsible, Jan. 5, 1905. See also Thompson, *op. cit.*, p. 107.

[11] George Kennan, *E. H. Harriman: A Biography* (New York, 1922), II, 181–97.

votes had supported for so long. This material was seized upon eagerly by the type of journal which had already increased its circulation during Roosevelt's administration by digging up exposures of other unsightly practices in business and politics.[12] While the Republican editors did not go as far in their denunciations of the old régime as some of the writers in *McClure's,* they could not escape commenting upon uncontrovertible evidence. There were even demands that Senators Platt and Depew resign. President Roosevelt was not the one to ignore such an upheaval in public sentiment, and he therefore broke with Odell and chose as his representatives in the state, Governor Higgins, whom Odell had not found to be "subservient," and Herbert Parsons, the newly elected congressman from New York City, who owed nothing to the old organization except the support that he had gained by coming out against it.[13]

The completeness of the change wrought by the events of 1905 was revealed in the Republican caucus of 1906 which chose a successor to Speaker Nixon, who had died the previous fall. Nixon's death was one of the causes of Odell's decline in politics.[14] Odell's candidate for Nixon's place received just fourteen votes. The election of Wadsworth as speaker was sufficient to convince men like Woodruff, Dunn, Barnes, and Fassett, who had once gone to the Fifth Avenue Hotel for instructions, to go thereafter to the White House or to Higgins for "advice."[15] The legislative session of

[12] See the article by Phillips in the *Cosmopolitan, loc. cit.,* B. J. Hendrick, "The Story of Life Insurance," *McClure's Mag.,* XXVII, 36. For the attitude of the *New York World,* see Heaton, *op. cit.,* chap. XIV, "Equitable Corruption."   ffl
[13] *New York Tribune,* July 11, 13, Nov. 17, 22, 26, 30, Dec. 7, 22, 29, 1905.
[14] Interview with Professor R. C. E. Brown.
[15] *New York Tribune,* Jan. 3, 14, 22; May 6, 1906; Thompson, *op. cit.,* pp. 400–401. Wadsworth turned out to be an organization man.

1906 passed several notable bills which were in themselves indications of a changing order. The way for the eighty-cent gas bill, the insurance reform laws, and the corrupt practices act had been carefully prepared by Charles E. Hughes, the able counsel for two legislative investigating committees. Under these laws, greater protection was extended to policy holders, corporations were prohibited from making political contributions, and the activities of lobbyists were curtailed.

Insurance reform not only marked Odell for defeat but it also made Hughes the logical candidate for governor. In his *Autobiography* Platt denies that he had any connection with the events which took place at Saratoga in September, 1906. Contemporary accounts, however, give evidence of an Odell-Platt alliance in the months immediately preceding the memorable convention.[16] The primary elections clearly indicated that Odell and Platt were playing a losing game. As one Republican editor expressed it, "The Republican primaries held in the large cities Tuesday resulted in a sweeping victory for Governor Higgins and President Roosevelt and a crushing defeat for Chairman Benjamin B. Odell and his followers throughout the state." [17] In New York, Herbert Parsons, the new chairman of the county committee, won a decisive victory over Quigg, backed by Odell and by what was commonly known as the "corporation pirates." [18] In Kings County, Woodruff, leading the Higgins forces, administered a stinging defeat to Dady who led the fight for Odell. The victorious Roosevelt-Higgins forces in other parts of the state were led by men like Butler

---

[16] *New York Tribune,* July 12, 13, 20, 1906; Platt, *op. cit.,* p. 462; *Independent,* August 9, 1906, LXI, 340.

[17] *Lyons Republican,* Sept. 21, 1906. Charles H. Betts, the editor, denounced Odell in a meeting of the state committee, *New York Tribune,* Aug. 16, 1906.

[18] *Buffalo Evening News,* Sept. 10, 1906.

and Greiner of Buffalo,[19]   Barnes of Albany, Hendricks of Syracuse, and Aldridge of Rochester.   While the primaries made it plain that one of these leaders would supplant Odell, it was not so clear that they would nominate Hughes until at the end of an all night deadlock Parsons brought a message from Roosevelt to the effect that in Roosevelt's judgment Hughes should be nominated for governor.   The influence of the national administration was decisive.   The next morning Hughes was nominated by the convention, and the new state committee elected Woodruff as its chairman in place of the discredited Odell.[20]

The campaign of 1906 was somewhat different from the kind to which the organization Republicans had grown accustomed and it is probable that they viewed it with some misgivings.   Hughes started out by promising a discussion of state issues only.   He declared that the supreme issue of the campaign was not an issue of Republican principles or of Democratic principles, but "the vital issue of decent government, an issue which should array on one side all lovers of truth, of sobriety, and of honest reform, whether they were Republicans, Democrats, or Independents" and that his only ambition was to give the state a "sane, efficient and honorable administration free from taint of bossism or of servitude to any private interests." [1]   The politicians who had been accustomed to hide behind national issues in a state campaign could get little comfort from such words as these.   Another innovation in this campaign was the direct appeal to the voters for funds to take the place of the con-

[19] Butler was the editor of the *Buffalo Evening News*. For his attacks upon Committeeman Warren, editor of the *Buffalo Commercial*, who supported Odell, see issues of September 17, 22, 1906. Greiner was the Postmaster of Buffalo.

[20] *New York Tribune*, September 25, 27, 1906; Platt, *op. cit.*, p. 462.

[1] *Addresses*, pp. 14–15; *New York Tribune*, October 3, 1906.

tributions obtained from corporations in previous campaigns.[2] The climax of this strange campaign came when President Roosevelt sent Elihu Root, his chief cabinet officer, to attack William R. Hearst, the Democratic candidate, in a bitter speech at Utica.[3] Thus aided by the power of the President, who was then at the summit of his popularity, Hughes was elected, but his Republican colleagues upon the state ticket, largely organization men, fell by the wayside.[4]

The sort of campaigning that Hughes believed in did not end with election day. He was no sooner inaugurated than he started to make speeches in various parts of the state upon the subject of adequate regulation of public utility corporations, agitation concerning which had been started in Governor Roosevelt's administration. Hughes' aim was to arouse the public consciousness so that the people would bring pressure to bear upon their representatives to pass such laws as would "remove the causes of unrest which lie in the abuse of public privilege."[5] This method of making direct appeal to the people over the heads of the legislators was called "tyrannical" and "dictatorial" by Platt who had been accustomed to less obtrusive practices.[6] "Dictatorial" or not, the Hughes tactics secured the passage of several thoroughgoing laws which placed the regulation of public service companies in New York upon a new basis. The first function performed by one of the commissions created by those laws was a detailed investigation of the New York

[2] *New York Tribune*, September 29, 1906.

[3] *New York Tribune*, November 2, 1906; *Independent*, November 8, 1906, LXI, 1075.

[4] Hughes 749,002; Hearst 673,268; Hughes' plurality 75,734. The Democratic candidate for lieutenant-governor won by a plurality of 5,574 votes.

[5] *Addresses*, p. 101 *et passim*.

[6] *Op. cit.*, pp. 464-65.

traction system, in which Quigg was brought forward as an "accelerator of public opinion." Quigg's methods, however, like those of his employers, could not stand the kind of publicity that Hughes, aided by the muckrakers, was giving them. In fact, Quigg admitted that profits were not what they once had been.[7]

The next outstanding victory that Governor Hughes won by his "dictatorial" methods was the passage of the anti-race-track gambling laws. It will be remembered that the laws passed during Governor Morton's administration ostensibly to carry out the constitutional mandate upon this question had failed to provide for penalties. Governors Black, Roosevelt, and Odell had done nothing to change this situation. The race track gamblers had become thoroughly entrenched through an alliance with the agricultural societies and with certain organization legislators, but many did not approve of the arrangement and a considerable number responded to the Governor's ringing messages and speeches calling for action. Legislators were deluged with letters, some were denounced in public meetings, and some were made to see what they would fail of re-election if they did not uphold the reform program.[8] Against the bitter opposition of both the old-line Republicans and Democrats, the bills were finally passed.

The events of Governor Hughes' first administration so jolted the "Old-Guard" Republican organization that in the State Convention of 1908 there was no one who was a "most active operating force" in the sense that Odell and Platt had been. Instead there was a league of minor "bosses" who seemed unable to unite upon any common policy or to with-

[7] See above p. 270.

[8] J. O. Hammitt, "An Awakening in New York State," *Independent*, Oct. 1, 1908, LXV, 758.

stand pressure from the national administration. As one of them put it a week before the convention:

In the old days, I would go down to New York and see Senator Platt and find out what was going to happen. Then I would come back and get the boys in line. But now I go to New York and I learn nothing. I ask the man who, according to the old system, ought to know and he tells me something. When I get on the train I find myself thinking it over, and likely as not when I am an hour out of New York I have made up my mind that the big man has told me wrong.[9]

Some of the "big men" of the party had boasted before the state convention that they would "turn Hughes down" as they had in the national convention, but when they came to the test, they stood up one after another and voted for Hughes. What did they fear? There had been post card canvasses before the convention, the people were aroused, and again, Roosevelt's endorsement of Hughes had exerted great influence.[10] Roosevelt had preferred Taft to Hughes for the presidential nomination, but he was too shrewd a politician to let the "bosses" shelve so popular a candidate. In the election of 1908 more people in the state voted in the gubernatorial than in the presidential contest. Hughes' plurality was considerably less than Taft's, but Roosevelt could claim that he had had a part in preventing the "Old Guard" from doing to Hughes what it had done to him in 1900.[11]

The next year the official careers of Platt and Roosevelt ended. When Roosevelt retired from the presidency on March 3, 1909, he was at the peak of his popularity. The

---

[9] *Ibid.,* p. 760.
[10] Heaton, *op. cit.,* pp. 234, 237.
[11] President—Taft, R. 870,770   plurality 202,602
        Bryan, D. ... 667,468
    Governor—Hughes, R. .. 804,651   plurality 69,462
        Chandler, D. 735,189.

tremendous Taft majority was, in part, an endorsement of his policies. On the other hand, Platt's retirement from the United States Senate was practically unnoticed. For more than three years, Senator Platt had been a pathetic figure at Washington, old, infirm, unable to walk without assistance, neglected, without influence or prestige, an unwilling witness of the first stages of disintegration and decay in the organization which had been the pride of his former days.[12] As the aged Senator stepped down to make way for Elihu Root, he had to take what comfort he could in the memories revived by the *Albany Evening Journal*.[13] The papers which praised Roosevelt were hostile to the things which Platt represented.

About the same time that Platt and Roosevelt were making their exit from American official life, Governor Hughes levied a vigorous attack upon the old convention system. The "dictatorial" Governor was pointing out the dangers of the game "on the political chess board" which Platt had played and Roosevelt had, up to that time, tolerated. He said in part:

But the most serious consequences is to the people at large. To the extent that party machinery can be dominated by the few, the opportunity for special interests which desires to control the administration of government, to shape the laws to prevent the passage of laws, or to break the laws with impunity, is increased. These interests are ever at work stealthily and persistently endeavoring to pervert the government to the service of their own ends. All that is worst in our public life finds its readiest means of access to power through the control of the nominating machinery of parties. Party organization needs constantly to defend itself from these encroachments, and the people for

[12] Wheeler, *op. cit.*, p. 124.
[13] March 4, 1909.

their proper security must see that the defenses are built as strongly as possible.[14]

While Governor Hughes was waging a disheartening fight with the "Old Guard" in order to secure the passage of a direct primary law, ex-President Roosevelt was abroad hunting wild animals and courting European royalties. When Roosevelt returned to America, he was persuaded to join the fight for the direct primary in the state. The law was not passed, but Roosevelt was committed to a struggle with the old order of party affairs which later led to the spectacular events of 1912.[15]

There were several events in 1910 which hastened the progress of party reform largely by way of discrediting the old style of party management of governmental affairs. The first of these was the investigation demanded by Senator Jotham P. Allds. The charges against Allds developed out of the struggle in the state Senate over the selection of a successor to Temporary President John Raines, who had died the previous fall. Allds, who had been in the state legislature continuously since 1895, was selected as the organization candidate for this place. There were murmurs against this choice and loudest among the objectors was Senator Benn Conger, who after the caucus, told a select group that he had seen Allds solicit and receive a bribe in 1901 for staving off legislation adverse to certain bridge companies. On January 18, 1910, Conger reluctantly authorized a public statement of these charges, and thereupon Senator Allds demanded an investigation.[16] The Senate sat as a body to consider the charges and on March 29 voted,

[14] State of New York, *Public Papers of Governor Hughes* (1909), p. 37.

[15] *Buffalo Commercial,* October 30, 1909, furnishes an illustration of the suspicions that were aroused.

[16] *New York Evening Post.*

forty to nine, to brand as a blackmailer the very man whom
it had elevated to its highest honor two months before.
Allds resigned, but he had been convicted before the bar of
public opinion long before his resignation. In commenting
upon the testimony a month before, the *Independent* had
said:

> Both men have testified fully and without contradiction,
> and everyone believes he has told the truth. To one man,
> now dead, $4,000 was given for distribution. To the speak-
> er of the house, Mr. Nixon, as testified to, $1,000 was paid,
> and as much to Mr. Allds. And this continued year after
> year and men chosen, in theory to make wise laws for the
> state, made trade of their office, and amassed fortunes.
> What worse crime, what more shameful perversion of a
> trust could be conceived.[17]

Thomas C. Platt died on March 6, 1910, while the Allds
trial was in progress. A few days before Platt's death,
Allds' attorneys had been defending their client upon the
basis of some letters that Platt had written urging that the
bills adverse to the bridge companies be held in the Rules
Committee.[18] As one newspaper put it, "It is a strange and
nothing less than tragic circumstance, that within a few
days of Mr. Platt's death the Republican machine, driven at
bay by charges of civic betrayal, with cowardly coldblooded-
ness sought to shift the blame on Platt. 'He made me do it'
—he, the frail, worn-out old man, with 'none so poor to do
him reverence!' "[19]   Tragic or not, the Allds affair was
coupled with Platt's obituaries.[20]   Editorials on Platt's
career were used as indictments of the old system.

Shortly after Platt's death and while the Allds investiga-

[17] February 24, 1910, LXVIII. 424, "Yellow Dogs."
[18] See above, p. 159.
[19] *Buffalo Commercial*, March 7, 1910.
[20] See the *New York Tribune* for March 7, 1910 and *New York
Evening Post, New York Times, New York Sun,* for the same date.

tion was still pending, the "Old Guard" received a jolt from another quarter. The State Superintendent of Insurance began to inquire into the methods used by the representatives of the fire insurance companies to stave off "strike" bills, and he soon discovered that they, like the life insurance companies, had had "legal expenses" at Albany. In particular, he found that a bill had passed the legislature in 1901 which cost the New York Board of Fire Underwriters some $13,311, of which $5,000 was given to the Republican state committee, while the remainder went to influential politicians. One of these influential politicians was State Committeeman Aldridge who had accepted a check of $1,000 for the "benefit of the Monroe County organization."[1] This disclosure did not deter Aldridge from nominating himself as the Republican candidate for the special congressional election which was held one month later. Flushed with a local victory that he had won the previous fall, Aldridge thought that his organization was invincible. The campaign that followed was one of unusual bitterness and heat and attracted nation-wide attention. At the polls, Aldridge, the "Old Guard" régime in the state, and the Republican tariff received a crushing rebuke.[2]

Following the revelations made in the Allds affair and in the investigation started by the Superintendent of Insurance, Governor Hughes made a recommendation to the legislature that a wide sweeping investigation be made by a legislative committee into corrupt practices in the state past and present. Upon May 24 such an investigation committee was appointed and testimony was quickly brought forward showing that the Street Railway Association of the state

[1] New York newspapers, March 20, 1910.
[2] *New York Sun*, April 21, 1910; *Owego Times*, April 21, 1910; *Independent*, April 28, 1910, LXVIII, 938.

of New York had maintained its "isles of privilege" by "debauching" Republican legislators and politicians.[3]

Although the accumulative effect of these disclosures was to greatly weaken the "Old-Guard" Republican leaders, it seemed impossible to dislodge them from their control of the governmental and the party machinery. The appointment of Governor Hughes to the Supreme Court Bench in April, 1910, to be effective the following October, gave them renewed courage and they successfully blocked the Governor's last fight for a direct primary bill. The organization leaders who had selected Allds for temporary president of the state Senate were still not without "influence" at Albany. Had not Thomas C. Platt said that Woodruff would have made a "splendid governor" and that there was "no cleverer politician in the state" than Barnes? It was Woodruff, chairman of the state committee, and Barnes, chairman of the executive committee, who led the battle against the "dictatorship" of Hughes.[4]

In his last struggle with the legislature over the reform of the nomination system, Governor Hughes had enlisted the powerful aid of ex-President Roosevelt.[5] Roosevelt had let it be known that he was in favor of direct nominations, and once in a fight, he was not the one to back down. If the "bosses" were not willing to put through the direct primary,

[3] See above p. 265.

[4] W. T. A. (Arnt) in the *New York Evening Post,* September 24, 1910, said of Barnes: "His hostility to the Governor, which some people believe is monomania with him, reached its climax at the dinner of the Legislative Correspondents' Association last winter, when he openly insulted Mr. Hughes in his presence, drawing from the Governor in reply the most remarkable speech he ever uttered, and one which is credited with doing more to shake the Old Guard control in the Republican party than anything that has happened."

[5] On June 29th, Roosevelt was in Cambridge as president of the Harvard Alumni Association and he there met Hughes who requested his aid in the fight for primary reform.

Roosevelt was willing to meet them upon their own ground, the state convention. It was widely proposed that Roosevelt be made temporary chairman of the Saratoga Convention which was to nominate a Republican candidate for governor. When Barnes and Woodruff heard this, it is said that they chuckled and set the wheels of the state committee in operation to select Vice-President Sherman for the position of temporary chairman. President Taft's assent to this program was given on the express condition that Roosevelt's agreement to it should be secured in advance. Roosevelt, however, was not consulted in advance and the state committee selected Sherman. "To the floor of the convention," was then the cry of the Roosevelt supporters,[6] for it was known that Sherman was not only opposed to direct nominations and kindred reforms, but he was constantly quoted as saying contemptuously that all the sentiment for primary election reform in the state of New York had been elevated to the United States Supreme Court Bench.

Upon the eve of the convention, Roosevelt issued the following statement:

"The men, who, by trickery, kept control of the state committee, and who now come here in the effort to dominate the convention, are the very men who are responsible for the corruption which produced Allds, and for all that has been discreditable in the party management, and now these deeply discredited bosses resent the effort of the people, the effort of the plain people who make up the great bulk of the Republican party, to rescue that party from the factions which have used it only to further their own base and selfish purposes.[7]

Chairman Woodruff, according to the time honored custom, opened the convention and amid scenes of disorder presented the name of James S. Sherman for temporary

[6] *Review of Reviews*, XLII (1910), 516.
[7] New York newspapers, September 27, 1910.

chairman. During the period of Platt's domination of Republican politics in the state, the selection of the state committee for this position had invariably been the choice of the convention. This precedent was broken in 1910, for Roosevent was nominated from the floor and elected by a vote of 568 to 443. While in this struggle Roosevelt had the aid of some federal office holders and a few former followers of Platt, the bulk of the "Old-Guard" leaders, the natural "heirs" of the "leadership" that had once been Platt's, were opposed to him.[8] In his "key-note" speech, Roosevelt sounded the battle cry against "the degrading alliance of crooked business and crooked politics."

The vanquished, thus assailed by Roosevelt, did not bolt the convention, but, as they expressed it "laid down cold" and let the "new boss" run his own course. While Roosevelt was making the "key-note" speech, while he was defending the majority report of the committee on resolutions, and while he was advocating the nomination of Henry L. Stimson for governor, the "Old-Guard" sat in silence and "sneered."[9] This "wrecker of parties," let him win without their help if he could. What profited it a politician to win an election, if he had lost control of the nominating machinery?

The "Old-Guard" Republican leaders probably took some grim satisfaction in the Republican defeat at the polls that fall. Theodore Roosevelt had assumed the "responsibility" for the first Republican disaster in the state for sixteen years. He had captured the organization, but he had not

[8] *Ibid.*, September 28, 1910.

[9] One of the Old Guard leaders remarked: "Colonel Roosevelt was the star performer at every session of the convention. He forced his election as temporary chairman, he mixed it up over the platform, he used the steam roller and the big stick when it came to the nomination. Roosevelt is written all over the convention," *New York Times*, September 29, 1910.

won over the Republican voters. Some of the Republican voters stayed away from the polls because it rained, some because there were no carriages to "take them out," and others because they disliked "Rooseveltism." Roosevelt's policies alarmed the business men. There were also voters who remembered the "fearful story of Republican wrong-doing at Albany," who remembered the "shameful details" of the corrupt practices investigation, the fire insurance investigation, the Allds investigation, the investigation of municipal accounts, the investigation of the New York traction system, and the life insurance investigation. Even Roosevelt could not blot out the memory of the stories that had involved influential Republicans like Allds, Conger, Aldridge, Raines, Nixon, Quigg, Depew, Odell, and Platt. The Republican ranks were split. For the first time since 1891 a Democratic legislature and a Democratic governor were elected in the state of New York.[10]

With the election of 1910, it may properly be said that a political cycle closed in the state of New York. In the early nineties the Republicans came into power in the state largely because of the popular upheaval against the excesses and blunders of the Democratic leaders; in 1910, the Republicans went out of power largely because of their own indiscretions and dissentions. The political organization in New York which Thomas C. Platt brought so near to perfection in the late nineties was founded upon a complacent local sentiment. As Roosevelt put it, "the conscience of the people was in no way or shape aroused." "Big business" was back of Platt; yet at the time this, the most important element in his strength, was only imperfectly understood.[11] Gradually by such appeals as Governor Roosevelt made

[10] Dix, D. .... 689,700 plurality 67,401.
Stimson, R. .... 622,299.
[11] *Op. cit.*, pp. 274, 279.

upon the franchise tax question, by such exposures as were made in the insurance investigation, by such speeches as Governor Hughes made upon the regulation of public utilities, by the fight which both Roosevelt and Hughes made for the direct primary and by the publicity given to all these matters in the press, "the people began to wake up more and more to the fact that the machine politicians were not giving them the kind of government which they wished." Tax reform laws were passed, campaign funds were made public, the public utility corporations were brought under stricter governmental supervision, and the "isles of privilege" became less numerous. While leadership of the managerial type is indispensable for any kind of political organization, the particular methods which Platt employed became discredited. Platt's reputation as a political manager is therefore likely to be short-lived. Roosevelt, on the other hand, although somewhat of a political manager himself, used methods that were frank and open. His championship of the cause of honesty in politics is already one of the prized heritages of the American people.

CHAPTER XII

PERSONAL QUALITIES OF PLATT AND ROOSEVELT

There can be little question that Thomas Collier Platt was the established leader of the unofficial government of the state of New York during Roosevelt's official headship of that government. As governor, Roosevelt's duties were for the most part set forth in the constitution, the statutes, and the judicial decisions of the state, but Platt's duties as manager of the Republican party of the state depended merely upon party custom and upon personal connections with the members of the party hierarchy. Though less ostensible and less clearly defined than Roosevelt's leadership, Platt's leadership was nevertheless real. Did a local politician want to know the program of the next state convention? He went to Platt rather than to Roosevelt. Did a factional leader wish to have the stamp of "regularity" put upon his organization? He laid his case before Platt. Did a local committeeman desire some money to run a primary or to conduct an election campaign? Was the chairman of the state committee pressed for funds? Platt handled such matters without requiring vouchers or even receipts. Did a county chairman wish to place some of his influential constituents in state or federal offices? Did the editor of a party organ wish a diplomatic post? These men got in touch with Platt as well as with the official heads of the government who nominally made the appointments. Governmental officials as well as party workers were among those who saw Platt. A legislator who wanted to get upon a certain committee, who had certain bills which he wished to see passed, or who wanted money for his campaign, made his needs and aspirations known to Platt. When Governor Roosevelt wanted to know the qualifications of certain men for certain administrative and judicial positions, when he was interested in finding out in advance how certain parts of his annual message would be received, when he was concerned about the confirmation of a certain appointment which he wished to make, he, the chief executive of the state, saw Platt. Outside the governmental and the party machinery, there came to see Platt, representatives of various associations and societies who wanted to see the party adopt certain policies or pass certain laws. Directors of corporations who wanted to suppress certain adverse legislation, or to secure exemption from certain sorts of taxation, or to obtain certain valuable privileges, or to enjoy immunity from annoying enforcement of the law, were among this number. The men who came to see Platt at the Fifth Avenue Hotel or at No. 49 Broadway did not always go away satisfied. Neither did those who went to see the governor at the state capitol. However, during the late nineties, many people kept on coming to see both.

Why was it that county and state committeemen, assemblymen, state senators, congressmen, state and federal executive officers, governors, secretaries of business men's associations, reformers, ministers, prominent attorneys, directors of large corporations, and all those seeking to achieve certain ends involving the use of the governmental machinery, came to see Platt, a man whose position with reference to that machinery was in no place set down in definite and concrete fashion? It may be well to consider first what there was in Platt's personality and in his general behavior that led men to see him as well as Governor Roosevelt about things that were ostensibly in the hands of the popularly elective officials.

Washington correspondents of McKinley's time have said that visitors, coming to the capitol for the first time, have exclaimed, when Senator Platt of New York was pointed out to them: "That Tom Platt? Why, he looks very ordinary. He must be smarter than he looks!" Platt's parchment-like skin and delicate looking figure presented a striking contrast to the ruggedness of Theodore Roosevelt. The Senator did not make a very prepossessing appearance as he hunched over his seat in the United States Senate chamber. He looked more like a New England college professor or a retired clergyman than he did like a seasoned political warrior.[1] Lemuel Ely Quigg, his faithful New York lieutenant, said that he was so little magnetic that even the act of shaking hands he performed listlessly.[2] And yet this was the man who was successful for a while in directing some of the activities of the vigorous, the fascinating, the magnetic, Roosevelt.

In dealing with persons important to his plans, Platt was usually courteous, quiet, conciliatory, diplomatic and careful to avoid giving offense. Although seemingly indifferent to the impression that he made, he was always neat in his dress and smooth in his manner. When he talked, it was in a "soft and easy tone" and his voice was low. When conferring with his party leaders, it was his custom to ask them what they wanted and then to quietly request them to indicate what they really expected to get, pointing out the

[1] J. M. Rogers, "Thomas Collier Platt: A Study of the Easy Boss," *Booklovers Mag.*, IV (1904), 331; *New York Sun*, March 7, 1910; *New York Herald*, March 25, 1896; E. G. Riggs, "Thomas C. Platt" in Stealey, *Twenty Years in the Press Gallery* (1906), p. 392.

[2] *Op. cit.*, p. 668.

danger there might be in demanding too much.[3]   William
Barnes admired Platt because "his dealings with men were
as man to man, on the level of equals, never as between one
who arrogates to himself a superior plane and arbitrarily
places others below."[4]   An admiring writer upon the *New
York Sun* said that Platt's "natural kindness enabled him to
grant a reasonable request without humiliating him who
asked, and to refuse an unreasonable one without offending
him who was denied."[5]   As he grew older he was sometimes peremptory and irritable upon little matters, but on
big occasions he was diplomatic and open to any suggestion
that did not embarrass the ultimate at which he was aiming.
Andrew Dickson White wrote of the interview in which
Platt sounded him out on the governorship as follows:
"Mr. Platt's frankness in reply increased my respect for him.
. . . Mr. Platt was from the first to the last perfectly
straighforward."[6]   Theodore Roosevelt, the aggressive,
energetic, fighting executive, although often engaged in
active warfare with the Senator, found him "always most
kind and friendly in his personal relations."[7]   In Platt's
non-resisting attitude is found one of the secrets of his success.   He realized that he could not win in an open fight
with a man like Roosevelt.

    Another reason for Platt's success as a political manager
is summed up in Roosevelt's dry comment that he could not
find that Platt had "any tastes at all except for politics, and
on rare occasions for a very dry theology wholly divorced

[3] H. C. Hansbrough, *The Wreck* (New York, 1913), p. 23.
[4] *Albany Evening Journal,* March 7, 1910.
[5] January 14, 1897.
[6] *Autobiography,* I, 232.
[7] *Op. cit.,* p. 284. Mrs. Robinson, Roosevelt's sister, who attended
many of the Platt-Roosevelt conferences said Platt was "a most
interesting and unusual personality," C. R. Robinson, *My Brother
Roosevelt* (New York, 1921), p. 81.

from moral implications."[8] Platt's personal interests were narrow and his habits for the most part conformed to the mores of his native village, Owego, a small backward country town situated in central New York. His religious interests did not interfere with his political aspirations. While in New York City, Platt attended Dr. Charles H. Parkhurst's church until that worthy crusader against Tammany delivered a sermon one Sunday in which he made the startling announcement that one Platt was worse than five Crokers. Platt indignantly changed his church affiliations.[9] In Washington as in New York, Platt lived in hotels, went out rarely into society, and spent most of his time on politics. While Roosevelt with his varied interests, his versatile tastes and exuberant spirits was finding a dozen different occupations all interesting, Platt was absorbed by a single interest, his passion for politics. Platt's narrow outlook enabled him to concentrate his efforts upon the details of New York politics without pining for other diversions and this quality made him the master of routine matters that Roosevelt found boresome.

To keep at the political game as long as Platt did required some enduring qualities. His friends said that he was energetic, industrious, punctual, unyielding, tenacious, patient, persistent, and persevering. A hostile critic has called him an immovable, inexorable, grinding, persistent "machine."[10] Platt knew his political chess-board; he spent an enormous amount of time and energy in studying the exact capacities of all his minor leaders,[11] the size of the vote which they could deliver, the various factional quarrels that cropped out now and then within the organization, the

[8] *Op. cit.,* p. 274.
[9] *Nation,* Jan. 17, 1895, LX, 4.
[10] W. A. White, "Platt," *McClures Mag.,* XVIII (1901), 152.
[11] Thompson, *op. cit.,* p. 103.

chances for dicker and intrigue, the relative purchasing power of the dollar in the rural and the urban districts, and the various ways of supporting the rural press and other branches of the organization. This knowledge, so essential to his continued ascendancy, could not be obtained without a large amount of patient work and watchful waiting. Following the famous "Me-Too" episode of 1881 in which he and Roscoe Conkling went down in disgraceful defeat, he put in sixteen years of hard, gruelling, discouraging work in order to secure a re-election to the United States Senate. Platt's patience and persistency were often utilized by the impatient Roosevelt, who was prone to play the game which brought immediate results and who showed on many occasions an inability to stand through years of defeat for a success far distant in the future.[12]

Besides his patience, another one of the "natural elements" of Platt's character was a "trait which led him to consider that the retention of an enmity, the harboring of a grudge, the keeping alive of a resentment after the incident in which it had originated had passed and gone, was scarcely worth his while." [13] For instance, he did not always remain hostile to all the state legislators who voted against his return to the United States Senate in 1881. Fourteen years after the memorable contest, he endorsed the appointment of one of them to an important state position.[14]   In 1889

---

[12] After his defeat in 1886 Roosevelt went out West, but Platt remained on the job in New York.

[13] Quigg, *op. cit.*, p. 673.

[14] "Although I had voted against the return of Senator Platt nearly fifty times, and there was no reason why he should favor me, he proved a friend . . . I was ambitious to be superintendent (of public instruction) and I had no hesitation in consulting Senator Platt. His prompt reply was: 'Of course, I will support you,' and he also favored my re-election in 1898 and 1901." —C. R. Skinner, "A Memorable Senatorial Contest," *State Service*, IV (1920), 30.

Platt found it convenient to forget his former animosity toward Elihu Root, his "consistent opponent in New York state political affairs," and he made no objections to Root's appointment as secretary of war in place of Russell A. Alger.[15] There were many occasions upon which Platt overlooked Roosevelt's past hostilities. In 1886 when Roosevelt was nominated for mayor of New York, Platt swallowed his resentment at Roosevelt's course in the national convention of 1884 and his irritation at Roosevelt's opposition to Levi P. Morton's senatorial candidacy in 1885. In 1897 Senator Platt mollified his wrath at Roosevelt's course as New York police commissioner and consented to his appointment as first assistant secretary of the navy. The supreme test came in 1898 when Platt was willing to relegate to the background all the grievances he had had with the annoying young reformer in order to save the state ticket. Roosevelt, himself, was not always able to be as magnanimous as Platt. Roosevelt was hostile toward his critics and tended to class all who opposed his policies as personal opponents.[16]

Although he sometimes seemed to be generous toward his foes, Platt was not precisely of a forgiving disposition. The letter which he wrote to President McKinley arguing against the appointment of Whitelaw Reid as ambassador to Great Britain is extremely bitter and vindicative.[17] Platt never seemed to forget the vigorous attacks which Reid made upon him in the editorial columns of the *New York Tribune* during the early nineties. It was said that he carried one of these editorials around in his pocket and that he produced it when he found someone before whom he could vent

[15] Alger was one of Platt's close friends and advisers.
[16] See the article entitled "Mr. Roosevelt" in *Atlantic Monthly*, CIX (1912), 577.
[17] See above p. 132.

his wrath against Reid. William Allen White said that Platt was not charitable but "made the virtue of generosity out of his impotence." [18] While vindictive toward a few, Platt did not engage in as many personal controversies as did the combative Roosevelt.

One of the qualities usually associated with leaders of both the official and unofficial type is courage.[19] The kind of courage that Platt displayed was of entirely different sort than that manifested by Roosevelt. Roosevelt was aggressive, pugnacious, venturesome, daring, and audacious; Platt was unyielding, tenacious, and dogged. One editorial writer said that Platt had shown himself to be an indomitable unyielding, and veritable tiger.[20] Platt's courage was of the feline variety rather than that of a full grown bull moose. In the Republican National Convention of 1896 Platt fought for the gold standard and against McKinley's candidacy persistently although the odds against him were overwhelming. For a politician this course was "courageous," because it involved the danger of falling outside the breast works, but it is likely that Platt had some sly ulterior purpose in view.[1] In election campaigns and in conventions, Platt was essentially a defensive fighter as opposed to the aggressive, offensive Rooseveltian type.

In describing the American "boss," M. Ostrogorski wrote: "Cultivated or without culture, the boss is, in any event a man of superior intelligence, but of an altogether special kind of superiority which shows itself in a very deli-

[18] Loc. cit.

[19] C. E. Merriam, The American Party System (New York, 1922), p. 48 and Introduction.

[20] New York Sun, January 11, 1897.

[1] See above p. 114. Platt wanted to create the impression that McKinley could not carry New York on election day unless he had the co-operation of the Platt organization.

cate appreciation of particular situations." [2]   Platt had little
of the mental energy and the mental exuberance possessed
by Roosevelt.   On the other hand, he was said to have a
keen mind, clear judgment, admirable powers of concentration, a good memory for names and faces, and to be alert,
sane, shrewd, and cunning.[3]   Quigg referred to his "unfail-
ing good judgment at critical moment and in things of
highest importance."   In party conferences he was plausible,
persuasive, and resourceful.   As one of the party committeemen put it: "He did not dictate the policy of the party, but
in the committee meetings he listened to everyone's opinion
and if a better plan than his was presented he accepted it.
If he thought that his plan was the best, he had a way of
putting it up to the committeemen so logically, tersely and
clearly that they were soon convinced that he had the best
plan and went along with him." [4]   He had a genius for
bringing together men of the most diverse ambitions and
temperaments and conforming them to his own principal
ends.   In concrete situations, he was able to turn the talents
of others to account.   Roosevelt had all these qualities with
the possible qualification that he was not as cautions, and in
addition Roosevelt had a marvelous sensitiveness to political
issues that would have a wide appeal.[5]   Quigg wrote that
Platt had "no very clear conception of the trend of public
sentiment on the issues of the day" and "no very keen respect for popular opinion even when he recognized its
strength."   Roosevelt could not only formulate new principles and policies that showed unusual appreciation of
social and industrial tendencies, but he could also combine
widely varying groups of men in a movement to carry out

[2] *Democracy and the Party System*, p. 253.
[3] Rogers, Hansbrough, White, Thompson and Barnes, *loc. cit.*
[4] Interview with Hon. Charles H. Betts of Lyons, New York.
[5] S. P. Sherman, *Americans* (New York, 1922), chap. X, "Roosevelt and the National Psychology."

those policies. Roosevelt's "news sense" and his love of the
dramatic constantly brought him on to the front part of the
stage while Platt stayed behind the scenes and played the
part of a wire puller, a diplomatic "gumshoer," an intriguer,
and a manipulator, a part for which his mental equipment
fitted him.

Regarding Platt's ability as a political manager, Theodore
Roosevelt wrote: "Senator Platt had the same inborn
capacity for the kind of politics which he liked that many
big Wall Street men have known for not wholly dissimilar
types of finance." [6] Senator Depew was slightly more eulogistic in his expression of the same sentiment: "Senator
Platt gave his whole life to politics and to the party his marvelous talent for organization. If he had devoted the same
time and energy to business, with his skill in the handling of
men, he would have been one of the foremost business men
in the United States." [7] Senator Platt did devote part of
his time and energy to the management of the United States
Express Company, of which he was president from 1880
until the time of his death in 1910. Judged by the standards of his time, he was not a successful business man. In a
time of great profits, his company did not pay high dividends
nor give high salaries.[8] In the early eighties when Platt
was "out of politics" and devoting his energies to his busi-

[6] *Op. cit.*, p. 277.

[7] *Owego Times*, March 10, 1910.

[8] The details of his management of this company came out in
an unsuccessful suit which one of the stockholders brought against
him in 1909. *Dudley* v. *Platt*, 118 New York Supp., 1058. In 1909
the company had an accumulated surplus of about $10,000,000 which
was equal to the par value of the stock as it had stood since 1887.
One half of the accumulated net earnings of the company accrued
during the eight years when its interests were pooled with those of
the other express companies, years when Platt was broken down in
health and scarcely able to attend to his duties in the United States
Senate. In the nineties the company's dividends averaged less than
3 per cent.

ness, the fortunes of his company were at their lowest ebb. The company did not achieve a recognized position in the financial world until 1901, when, in flagrant violation of the charter and the laws of the state, the heads of the great rival express companies gained control of its directorate.[9] In the nineties, Platt's salary as the president of this company was only $18,000 a year, and when he died, his total estate was estimated to be not more than $200,000.[10] In the days when "money was king," he was numbered among the comparatively poor. He was not versatile enough to win fame along more than one line. Roosevelt attained success along many lines. Business might well have been one of them.

Another criterion by which a leader may be judged is his powers of expression. Platt was not a masterful advocate like Roosevelt. He could not make a speech, for one could hardly call the essays which he read from time to time speeches. Unlike Roosevelt, he was not a brilliant conversationalist although he could keep the reporters amused by telling odd stories and could now and then "scorch" his enemies by telling phrases. He called Carl Schurz a "lively German peddler of apples of discord and a retailer in vinegar, manufactured from the juice of sour apples." There is nothing, however, in this diatribe to compare with some of Roosevelt's immortal phrases like "the muckrakers," "the malefactors of great wealth," "the lunatic fringe," and "a cootie on the body politic." During the seventies Platt did some political writing and throughout his life he was constantly writing letters, some of which show considerable force and vigor, but none of which would compare favorably

---

[9] James C. Fargo, president of the American Express Company; Levi C. Weir, president of the Adams Express Company, and Francis L. Stetson, counsel for the firm of J. P. Morgan.

[10] New York newspapers, March 8, 1910.

with a random sample of the two hundred thousand epistles which Roosevelt left behind him. Both Platt and Roosevelt wrote autobiographies. There is more excuse for an official leader to write a defense of his life than there is for an unofficial leader. At the height of his power Platt realized the value of secrecy, for he made the remark to some reporters: "If I ever become reminiscent please go to the nearest drug shop, get an ounce of cyanide of potassium, and I'll swallow it at a gulp." [11]   Platt had been a druggist, so he knew what this meant. The Senator's autobiography is not entirely the product of his own efforts.[12]   It was written in his dotage, and the fact that he favored its production indicates that his judgment was failing. The book is full of inaccuracies because he and his editor put too much trust upon a memory which had begun to weaken and it naively reveals a philosophy and outlook which many of his contemporaries were condemning. In contrast to Platt's curious jumble of fact, fable, and diatribe is Roosevelt's masterful defense of his public career, a defense which is now constantly repeated in biographies and histories of the period in which he lived.

As to the moral qualities which the two leaders possessed, there is naturally great difference of opinion. Platt clearly believed in the philosophy that the end justified the means. There are some who say that Roosevelt did also.[13]   Be this as it may, there was a vast difference between the moral fibre of the two men. Platt's *Autobiography* gives many examples of the brand of opportunistic politics which he practiced. The account of President-elect Harrison's selection

[11] Riggs, *loc. cit.*

[12] It was edited by Louis J. Lang, now a political reporter and correspondent on the staff of the *New York American*. Mr. Livingston Platt, Platt's grandson, informed the writer on September 27, 1922 that the *Autobiography* was not satisfactory to the family.

[13] E. S. in the *Atlantic Monthly, loc. cit.*

of a secretary of treasury is one.[14] Platt was willing to give credence to a story which related the use of duplicity and deceit on the part of his followers. One reason why Platt was called the "Easy Boss" was the fact that he never questioned the methods employed by his subordinates. These methods might be corrupt, mercenary, and ruthless, but as long as they got results, he was satisfied. Platt, himself, was not above sly, stealthy "moves," as the way in which he thwarted Governor Roosevelt's desire to appoint Judge Daly to the state judgeship demonstrates.[15] He seemed incapable of using the frank, open fighting tactics which Roosevelt employed so effectively.

The integrity of men in political life in America is always brought into question sooner or later. Roosevelt's evident sincerity has disarmed most of his foes on this point. As to Platt's integrity it can be said that no critic has accused him of being dishonest in the sense of openly robbing the public treasury or appropriating campaign contributions to his own use.[16] It is true that his express company obtained a lucrative contract from the United States Treasury Department in 1889, but it does not appear that he charged any more for the services rendered than the other express companies had been charging for similar services to the government.[17] How should the "pulls" which Platt exercised in order to obtain government business for the "Platt family law firm" and the "Platt family bonding concern" be judged? These pulls were not much different from the sort of influences

[14] Pp. 207–8. Alexander in his *Four Famous New Yorkers*, p. 132, discredits the truth of this story, but the fact that Platt repeats it is significant.

[15] See above p. 207.

[16] This claim is made by Roosevelt, *op. cit.*, p. 274; Thompson, *op. cit.*, p. 95; W. A. White, *loc. cit.*; Quigg, *loc. cit.*; and by Platt himself, *op. cit.*, p. 533.

[17] See above p. 259.

which business men in general were accustomed to exercise in behalf of their sons. Did not the insurance investigation show that the presidents of the three great life insurance companies of New York had been taking care of their sons and relatives?[18] Persons closely connected with the game of business and politics in the state of New York during the late nineties hesitated to throw stones at Platt. Roosevelt, himself, probably remembering some of the embarrassing questions that he had been asked about campaign contributions, stated in his *Autobiography* that Platt was recognized by the business men, the big contributors, as an "honorable" man; not only a man of his word, but a man who, whenever he received a favor, could be trusted to do his best to repay it on any occasion that arose.[19] Platt's field marshals made a feature of his "personal intergrity."[20] By personal integrity they simply meant integrity in money affairs. Not being a candidate for popular elective office after his second election to Congress in 1874, Platt did not need in his work of political management such a spotless record of domestic tranquility as Roosevelt possessed. However, Platt's reputation and political standing were somewhat damaged by the circulation of reports which indicated certain irregularities in his domestic life.[1]

It is difficult to find any man in public life who is not said to be loyal to some particular group. There are many testimonials as to Platt's loyalty to his party and to his "organization." Andrew Dickson White wrote of him: "His pride and his really sincere devotion to the interests of the Republican party, as he understood them, led him to desire

[18] *Report*, pp. 12, 47.
[19] P. 275.
[20] Colonel Dunn's interview, *New York Tribune*, December 9, 1901.
[1] See above p. 28, and also see the *Nation*, November 22, 1906. Platt separated from his second wife whom he married late in life.

above all things, a triumph over the Democratic forces, and the only question in his mind was, who could best secure the victory?"[2] According to Quigg, "Mr. Platt's third important characteristic was his loyalty. . . . What he said he meant, and he went on meaning it, no matter how greatly the conditions changed nor how difficult it became to give effect."[3] Platt and Roosevelt both possessed the quality of loyalty. Platt's loyalty differed from Roosevelt's loyalty in its breadth and comprehensiveness. Roosevelt was loyal to many, Platt to a few; Roosevelt's sympathies were so broad that he felt called upon to preach his ideals to the nation, Platt took a narrow view toward his duty to the public and assumed a cynical attitude toward idealists. William Barnes once wrote that Platt was staunchly loyal to all who trusted him and were his friends.[4] There were many persons, Roosevelt included, who disagreed with what Platt regarded as the essentials of friendship.

It is hard to make an objective analysis of men in public life whether they belong to the official or the unofficial government because as soon as they become of any importance a group of myths grow up about them which tend to obscure their real character. To those who opposed him, Platt became the symbol of an evil system, a modern Machiavelli, who grew out of a sinister alliance between corrupt business and corrupt politics. To those who made use of him, he was the personification of party loyalty, the head of an "efficient organization," the manager of a "business man's government." After Platt's death there were not many legends which grew up about him and his name tended to fall into obscurity, but Roosevelt's death was the signal for a myriad of myth makers to begin their work constructing

[2] *Op. cit.*, p. 232.
[3] *Loc. cit.*
[4] *Albany Evening Journal,* March 7, 1910.

phantasies about "the typical American." Another obstacle
in the way of any accurate analysis of the behavior of Platt
and Roosevelt is the fact that both men wrote autobiographies. Historians and others are prone to judge men by
what they say about themselves. Roosevelt's *Autobiography*
is in large part an elaborate defense of positions which he assumed during his public career. Platt's *Autobiography* is
also in the form of a defense reaction, a rather crudely constructed one in places. Platt came to believe with the *Albany Evening Journal* that the word "Platt" did not mean
Thomas C. Platt, the man who lived at the Fifth Avenue
Hotel, but a "combination of the most active, earnest, and
aggressive Republicans in every city, village, and hamlet in
the state." His *Autobiography* shows that he thought that
his power to unite and organize contending men and conflicting interests and bring them to work together with a common purpose for mutual benefit was probably not "possessed
in like degree by any other politician in America." [5] Even
the unfavorable publicity which he received from certain
metropolitan newspapers increased the public impression
and his own impression that he was a man of importance
and he could say, "One day everybody, friend and foe, began
to call me 'boss.' " [6] He was a "disinterested" politician,
but he had great love for power, he took great satisfaction
in thinking himself an "autocrat," and he had a passionate
fondness for the game of politics. He was quite willing to
admit that he wrote his *Autobiography* because the great
pride that he took in his "leadership" had been wounded.
Nothing hurt him more deeply than the failure of his old acquaintances to do homage to his "leadership" when his actual power was gone. [7] He had the sincere conviction that

[5] Quotations cited in the *New York Tribune*, February 16, 1895,
January 14, 1897 and January 15, 1897.
[6] Quigg, *loc. cit.*
[7] *Op. cit.*, pp. 519, 531.

the Republican party of the state of New York could not get along without him. When broken in health and scarcely able to move around, he sought a re-election to the United States Senate. He then clung to his seat in that august body for the full six year term in spite of the fact that he could hardly attend to the routine duties of his office. He could not let go of this one remaining cachet of respectability. Needless to say, Roosevelt also did not lack in self-esteem. It was his ability to advertise himself and his works that has been in part responsible for the creation of a large and enthusiastic band of admirers. If Platt had been a little more skillful advertiser, his name might stand higher in the hall of notable New Yorkers to-day.

Roosevelt's reputation as a statesman is largely dependent upon that portion of his life that comes after 1901, a portion which has been scarcely touched upon in this book because Platt's influence upon it was practically negligible. Platt will be known as one of the state bosses and senator-managers of the McKinley era. Although Platt did not have the intellectual acumen and the speaking ability of David Bennett Hill, although he lacked the cleverness of Mathew Stanley Quay, although he did not possess the aggressiveness and the energy which characterized Marcus Alonzo Hanna, and although did not have that ability to master all sorts of men possessed by Nelson W. Aldrich, he will be classed with these men because he was the manager of the Republican organization in the largest state of the Union where resources and men were plentiful.

CHAPTER XIII

THE TECHNIQUE OF PARTY MANAGEMENT

The problem of the efficient management of the Republican party of New York was what brought Platt and Roosevelt together. Roosevelt's talents were such that he could make himself felt in public life without having any "organization," but Platt never could have achieved distinction as a political manager if he had not gathered about him an able band of politicians to carry out his orders and to advise him on important matters. He could not make a speech himself, but when there was need for some public speaking to be done he could rely upon the oratorical abilities of the mellifluent Depew or one of the many other "spellbinders" who belonged to the organization. Platt did not drink, but there were several of his field marshals who felt very much at home in a hilarious and bibulous company. Platt did not have a great deal of physical energy, but his chief of staff, "Ben" Odell was commanding, pushing, and aggressive. Platt did not understand the arts of publicity, but Quigg was known as an "accelerator of public opinion." Because of his confining work in New York and Washington, Platt could not visit the up-state regions very often so he was practically compelled to delegate many important functions to his division chiefs. In Monroe County he was fortunate in being able to rely upon Committeeman Aldridge, who was noted for his loyalty to the party, his "generosity," his industry, and his great skill in organizing men.[1] William Barnes,

[1] C. E. Fitch, *Encyclopedia of Biography of New York* (New York, 1916).

the feudal lord of Albany, was unquestionably a man of great physical and mental force; big, brazen, florid, over-bearing, he looked like the bullying sort of "boss" that he was said to be.[2] Across the Hudson river, there was "Lou" Payn, with a political experience about equal to Platt's and a "genius" for "handling things" in the state legislature. In the legislature itself, there was Senator "Uncle" John Raines who, according to Elihu Root, "would rather go to hell with the Republican party than dwell with other in tents of righteousness."[3] In the lower house, there were Assem-blymen Allds and Nixon, both of whom were huge men with loud voices, quite capable of over-awing any noviates who happened to venture to the state capitol. The gover-nor's chair was occupied successively by men of high stand-ing who put their prestige and abilities at the service of the organization. The oratorical abilities of Black and all the dramatic qualities of Roosevelt were used by Platt to main-tain his position. Roosevelt, on the other hand, used Platt as long as Platt held the reins of the party organization. Although these two men had widely divergent aims and methods, both put into practice the principle of the division of labor, so important in the complexity of modern society.

Why was it that among so many able Republicans it was Platt "whose advice was taken quite largely, pretty largely, by the men of the political party with whom he was as-sociated?"[4] Platt was a man of superior organizing ability, and besides he was a man of superior knowledge. Because of his long training and experience, he was the natural heir of the corporate tradition which had known up around Roscoe Conkling. In the fifties and sixties, Platt had been

[2] B. J. Hendrick, "Governor Hughes and the Albany Gang," *Mc-Clure's Mag.*, XXXV, 507.
[3] *Lyons Republican*, August 3, 1921, p. 24.
[4] Barnes' definition of a leader before the Bayne Committee, see *Report*, p. 120.

a minor cog in the organization built up by that master
strategist, Thurlow Weed. In the seventies he had blos-
somed out as Conkling's chief of staff after he had held
every conceivable position in his party's committee hierarchy
ranging from the chairmanship of his county committee to
a place upon the state, the congressional and the national
committees. During his long period of service, he had attended some sort of Republican convention nearly every
year and since around 1870 there never had been a year
when he was not "interested in the election of a Republican
legislature." He knew every local politician of any importance, he knew the dangers of factional quarrels, he knew
all the party precedents that governed the conduct of
primaries and conventions, he knew the strength of party
custom, he knew the weaknesses of the sort of men who
were attracted by the game of politics, and he knew how
many voters there were who could be counted upon as
"regular." In the later eighties, Platt's wealth of political
information must have been very impressive to the younger
men like Roosevelt, Aldridge, Barnes, Odell, Fassett, and
Woodruff, but what can be said about "Lou" Payn, Chauncey Depew, and some of the other old political war-horses?
Why did not one of these become the manager-in-chief of
the Republican organization in the state of New York instead of Platt? Depew was very "popular" and Payn was
very "skillful." The only explanation seems to be that they
were interested in other things. Depew, as president of the
New York Central Railroad, was interested in making
money for the Vanderbilts and in making a name for himself in the financial world.[5] Payn put in most of his time
in the lobby of the legislature and in the stock exchange,
working for certain "undisclosed principals." Why did not
one of the governors use the state patronage to build up a

[5] Depew, *Memories*, pp. 15, 227.

machine of his own? Governor Black made a beginning, but his attempt failed. Governor Roosevelt was more interested in writing books, in learning how to box, and in campaigning in the West than he was in the details of party management. As Quigg put it, Platt was the man who had the "interest" and he combined this interest with the requisite knowledge.

Platt's long experience had taught him that the first law of any political organization is self-preservation. He did not originate the methods which he used to preserve the Republican organization of his state. Platt was no innovator like Roosevelt. Besides the lessons which he learned from his former chief, Roscoe Conkling, and the technique that he had picked up as a member of Congress, sitting under Speaker James G. Blaine, Platt acquired many "tricks of the trade" and received many "warning lessons" from his political enemies. He was in New York City shortly after the downfall of the notorious Tweed. He studied the methods employed by Samuel J. Tilden, Daniel Manning, and David B. Hill, all well-known managers of successful Democratic campaigns. When he came to the great metropolis, there he found much to admire in the ways of Kelly and Croker, his Tammany Hall contemporaries. Upon the national field, Platt availed himself of the experience and wisdom of Mathew S. Quay who in the neighboring state of Pennsylvania was solving problems of a sort very similar to those that arose in New York. As in business, it was difficult for any politician to keep a "trade secret" to himself. The political heritage which was indispensable to Platt was accessory to Roosevelt.

Political patronage was the cement that Platt saw was commonly used to keep political "organizations" together and he spent the greater part of his political career trying to control and protect its sources of supply. Even the men at the top like Roosevelt, Black, Aldridge, Barnes, Dunn, Odell, and Depew were "loyal" to the organization in part because the organization had helped to elevate them to public office. As superintendent of public works, Aldridge enjoyed a comfortable salary and considerable "influence." The same could be said for Dunn, as railroad commissioner. Depew undoubtedly enjoyed the distinction of being a United States senator. It would be hard to find a governor of New York who was not ambitious. Before these men were actually "placed" in public office, they had "expectations." There were, of course, other reasons why the "big men" in the party remained loyal to Platt and his organization. Barnes admired Platt because he thought that the Senator was like his grandfather, and then Barnes was grateful because in a close primary fight the faction which he led had been recognized as "regular" by the state committee. Field marshals, who were loyal, could "get things done" at Albany and received pecuniary aid in hotly-contested primary and election campaigns. And then, these "higher-ups" had the satisfaction of wielding political power and the joy of winning elections, a joy not unlike that which comes to the champion sportsman or the victorious warrior after a successful contest. To Platt the distribution of the spoils of office was a serious business. Roosevelt, although he thoroughly understood the cohesive power of political patronage, often treated the allotment of offices as an amusing game.

Field marshals who were "disloyal" or "insubordinate" were disciplined. As Platt put it:

A political organization should be conducted upon the simplest principles of business. Merit and devotion should be rewarded. Demerit and treachery should be condemned and examples made of those guilty of them. I have always

maintained that a majority rather than a minority of an
organization should control the party and its policy. . . .
    During an experience of over fifty years in politics, I
have learned that obedience to instructions and gratitude
are about as scarce as snow in the dog-days. In choosing
my lieutenants and candidates, I invariably insisted upon
the qualification that the man must know enough to "stand
when hitched." The list of those who have ignored or defied
this rule would fill a large volume. And that has made it
necessary for me, as an organization chief, to reluctantly
and sometimes mercilessly administer punishment to a subordinate. Only in this way can the discipline of any body
of men be enforced.[6]

    Reduced to other terms, the problem of discipline was,
How could a local leader's "majority" be turned into a
"minority?" Because of J. Sloat Fassett's refusal to withdraw from the preconventional gubernatorial campaign of
1894, Platt "placed Colonel Archie E. Baxter in charge of
the regular organization forces in the Chemung District,
and for a number of years Fassett was an inconsequential
factor in politics, where he had been a power." Because
Jacob Worth, "boss" of the King's County organization,
supported Low for mayor of New York in 1897, "the state
organization concluded to deputize Timothy L. Woodruff
to 'cut the ground under Worth's feet.' " And so on, Platt
gives examples of other "Holier than Thou's" who were
"punished."[7] It seems that an unruly leader was disciplined
by having the patronage, local, state, and national thrown
against him and by having his primaries drenched with
money in behalf of the new man who had been "deputized."[8]
The state committee then recognized the faction which had
been created to oppose him and it seems that this body did
not always have that love for "majority rule" that Platt

[6] *Op. cit.*, pp. 501–3.
[7] *Op. cit.*, chap. xxv, *passim*.
[8] *New York Tribune*, December 2, 4, 1897.

professed.[9]   When Fassett saw the men that he had "made"
turn against him, he probably agreed with Platt that gratitude" in politics was "about as scarce as snow in dog-
days." [10]   As Platt admitted, the system was "military."
When President Roosevelt began to "discipline" him, Platt
tasted some of his own bitter medicine.

When a sufficient number of the local leaders were "loyal"
the state leader did not have to worry much about state
conventions.   The delegates to these party assemblages were
for the most part local office holders or other individuals
who had been "handpicked" for the occasion by the state
committeemen or some other local leader.[11]   For many
years the employees of the New York Custom-house had
been very "influential" in state conventions.[12]   President
Roosevelt did not ignore the fact in 1906, 1908, and 1910.
The state conventions which met in these years were controlled by the delegates from the great cities of the state,
principally from New York.   Needless to say "reliable
delegates" could be found among those who had done some
work upon the canal.[13]   The reason why it was always easy
for the state leader to "get the Albany delegates" is indicated by the following statement, reputed to have been
made by Committeeman Barnes in answer to a request made
by a prominent citizen of Albany regarding a certain appointment:

I don't want any person who wears a high hat and has
his shoes blacked, and who could obtain pretty nearly what
he wants.   I want a candidate for this office who is down

[9] *Ibid.,* August 26, 27, 1896.

[10] Alexander, *Four Famous New Yorkers,* p. 238.

[11] *Rochester Herald,* September 30, 1898.

[12] *Nation,* May 5, 1892, LIV, 332.

[13] *New York Tribune,* September 28, 1896.   Aldridge was the
highest candidate for several ballots.

and out, on his uppers, and has fringed clothes, then I can hoist him into office and he will be mine.[14]

The preliminaries of the convention, the temporary officers, the platform, and the "slate," were all agreed upon in advance by Platt and his field marshals in a "Sunday school" session at the Fifth Avenue Hotel. When the convention met, it only remained for the "will of the party" to be expressed upon the decisions of the leaders. Even if the delegates had not been for the most part of the "hand-picked" variety, there was little danger that the "program" of the few would be rejected because the customs and traditions which governed the procedure of the conventions discouraged any assertion of "independence." The state committee made up the temporary roll and thereby practically determined how the contests would be settled; it also "recommended" the appointment of the temporary chairman, the officer who "made up" the committees of the convention upon the basis of the "suggestions" made by the local organizations. Nothing made Committeeman Barnes more angry than the way Theodore Roosevelt "smashed these time-honored and "sacred" traditions in the State Convention of September, 1910[15] Roosevelt's tactics in 1906 and 1908 had also upset the program of the pre-convention conference. In the late nineties, when Platt was at the height of his power, such violations of party precedents would have been inconceivable.

The principal function of state conventions during Platt's time was to arouse enthusiasm among the party workers. The way in which Platt acted during a convention showed

14 *Barnes* v. *Roosevelt*, p. 173.

15 *Barnes* v. *Roosevelt*, May 13, 1915, p. 1919, Barnes testified that "Mr. Roosevelt, in appointing the Committee on Resolutions did not accept, in every case, the man recommended by the delegation from the congressional district, which had been the custom for many years."

that he had a good deal of understanding of crowd psychology. He always endeavored to make things run off smoothly and "harmoniously" so that the delegates would get the impression that the organization was being "efficiently" managed. In 1896 when Warner Miller who had been ruthlessly ruled out by the state committee, was being "howled down" by a portion of the delegates, Platt rose in his seat and requested that Miller be given a chance to speak.[16] This show of "fair play" immediately won the admiration of the "boys." Usually, however, Platt remained silent and let his most popular "spell-binders" do their work. It is interesting to note that Roosevelt used exactly the opposite tactics in the State Convention of 1910. Platt endeavored to iron out all differences quietly behind the scenes, but Roosevelt fought openly for his platform and candidate.

Platt carried with him to national conventions the same "little band of able politicians" that ran his state conventions for him. He also had the close co-operation of Mathew S. Quay and a few of the other "manager-senators." His style of tactics in national conventions called for the raising of a big "rumpus," which in the nineties meant that he was dissatisfied with the way that the pre-convention campaign had been running and wanted to make it plain that he must be "propitiated." Since he controlled a portion of the election machinery which was very crucial in presidential campaigns, this sort of strategy was more successful than it appeared upon the surface. Thus in 1896, although the fifty-five votes that he held in line for Morton did not count for much, his actions in the convention led Mark Hanna to "come around" during the campaign. In 1900, Platt's organization made a good deal of the way that "Roosevelt had been kicked up-stairs." In the Republican National Conventions of 1904 and 1908, Roosevelt had **no**

[16] See above p. 105.

trouble with the organization which had "shelved him." While he was president of the United States, he made the best of the imperfect national nominating system and effectively prevented the delegates from New York from using guerrilla tactics.

The state legislature was so "organized" that Platt could influence its work through a clique of half a dozen men or so in each house. This legislative clique worked in secret and it practically determined the course of legislation except when it was forestalled by vigorous action on the part of the governor. In maintaining his legislative control, Platt was greatly aided by the cult of party regularity. Legislators who "bolted" the caucus were marked for "discipline." William Barnes once said to Roosevelt:

> You know yourself, Mr. Roosevelt, the Senator (or Mr. Platt) does not bully. He does not have to. That the man who went into politics and wanted to go ahead found out for himself that he could not get ahead if he didn't do what the organization, what the leader, what the boss wished. That it was not necessary to give orders; it was quite sufficient to have it understood by example that the man that stood by the organization benefited because the organization stood by him and that if he did not stand by the organization he got punished and that the ordinary man found this out for himself. If he declined to learn, then he got dropped; he failed to make a record, he could not satisfy his constituents, that his bills were not passed or his work failed in other ways, and that he did not get a renomination and he was eliminated.[17]

The Allds investigation of 1910 showed that in Platt's time the Assembly was controlled autocratically by a few men, who in themselves constituted a "corrupt clique for the selling of legislation." Fred Nixon, who was first elected speaker at the beginning of Governor Roosevelt's

[17] *Barnes v. Roosevelt*, p. 1316.

administration, appointed all the committees and was himself the head of the Rules Committee which took complete
charge of all legislation during the last weeks of every
session. His chief aid was Floor Leader Allds. These two
men took orders, of course, from Platt and his "Sunday
school," for there were state committeemen who "wanted
things done" at Albany, but they also "levied blackmail"
upon the side. When an election came around, the "organization stood by them" by contributing to their campaign
expenses. The corrupt practices investigation of 1910–11
showed that this system had also crept into the state Senate.
If the organization leaders themselves threatened to revolt,
Platt drove them into line by threatening wholesale bribery
prosecutions. As in party conventions, he ruled by appealing to custom, gratitude and fear. Governor Roosevelt
worked with Platt in legislative matters when he could and
against him when he felt he must. In fighting for his legislative policies, Roosevelt employed all the arts of newspaper
publicity and the popular appeal.

At Washington where Roosevelt's star shone brightest,
Platt was eclipsed. To be sure the large Republican delegation from New York in the House of Representatives
received ample recognition in the allotment of committees,
and in 1899 one of its numbers became the floor leader of
the House, but Platt was never more than the nominal
leader of this delegation. He and Depew were in the United
States Senate by virtue of the efficient "organization" which
had been set up in the state legislature. New York congressmen had to engage in "log-rolling" and had to struggle
for their "patronage rights" pretty much the same as other
congressmen. They were part of a national "system."
During his "Easy-Boss-ship" as well as at the time of the
"Me-Too" episode, Platt's chief concern at Washington was
the strength of the time-honored custom of "senatorial

courtesy," and a president who failed to "consult" him upon New York matters was warned about the next presidential campaign. President Roosevelt, however, repeatedly ignored these warnings.

"Senatorial courtesy" at Albany meant that the governor should "consult" Manager Platt, or as it was euphemistically put, the "organization," before any important appointment or gubernatorial message was sent to the legislative chambers for action. Governor Roosevelt paid his respects to this custom when he authorized his secretary to send a letter to the state committeemen welcoming suggestions regarding appointments and other matters,[18] when he had "breakfast conferences" with Platt regarding the more important appointments, and when he sent Platt an advance copy of the message which he planned to send to the legislature. One of the causes of Committeeman Barnes' bitter hostility to Governor Hughes was the latter's failure to observe party custom in the matter of appointments.

It was much harder for Platt to "discipline" a governor when he became "unruly" than it was for him to discipline any other state officer. The governor was a conspicuous figure; he worked in the open, he had important powers, and in case Platt "affronted" him, he could "fire back" at the organization by a skillful use of the patronage, the special message, or the veto power. On the other hand, Platt was not without his weapons in dealing with the governor. Did a governor want to make a "record" by the passage of some laws "demanded by the people?" He could see Platt, who was for some purposes a "majority of the legislature." Did he wish the state Senate to confirm some appointment which would "raise the tone of the administration?" He could see Platt, who had an "iron-clad" arrangement with that body. Did he care anything about his political future?

[18] *New York Tribune,* January 18, 1899.

Platt was a man to be reckoned with. There is no doubt that Platt played upon the ambitions of every governor with whom he had "relations." Governor Morton had presidential aspirations, Governor Black wanted a renomination, and no one can deny that Governor Roosevelt was ambitious. In the second year of his governorship, Roosevelt was more enthusiastic about party harmony than he was about reform. As long as Platt controlled the primary and election machinery, Roosevelt thought it wise to stand in his good graces.

Platt's control over the finances of the party made him valuable to candidates for all state offices, especially the gubernatorial candidates. The appeals that Platt made for campaign funds to those "who were abundantly able to give" were of a very obvious sort. In fact, they were so clear that there was no need for spoken or written words between them. Platt learned the "system" by carefully observing the way the Democratic organization in the state raised money in the early nineties. There were some corporations, like the public utility companies and the fiduciary institutions, which were constantly in touch with the legislative and administrative branches of the state government. Platt had a "mania for political organization;" the directors of these corporations had the "money craze." The latter found that they could make money by obtaining certain exemptions and privileges from the various governmental agencies which were charged with the protection of the interests of the stockholders and the public. They went to Platt, they made huge contributions to the Republican campaign funds, and Platt supported them "naturally in anything that they naturally thought was right and that they were for" through his "being connected with the state committee." What was more "naturally right" than that they should make money? Platt took their cash contribu-

tions and distributed it among the local leaders and legislators who "needed help" around election time. These legislators were then "under moral obligations not to attack the
interests supporting them," and the administrative officers
also felt bound by the same rule. It was "matter of business not of politics" which led many corporation directors
to see Platt. Roosevelt took part in many a campaign that
was financed in this way.

While Roosevelt had great confidence in his own abilities
to win votes, he did not sneer at Platt who, like other
political managers, put great faith in the organization as a
vote-getter. With a "loyal" organization behind him and
with plenty of money, Platt was well equipped during the
late nineties to battle with the Democratic organization for
votes upon election day. Platt tried to create an attitude
in the voters' minds which was favorable to his organization as well as toward the party candidates. He did this
by liberally subsidizing newspaper editors and proprietors
with offices, public printing, government advertising, and
other "favors." The up-state Republican newspapers, the
city dailies as well as the country weeklies, kept up a steady
stream of party propaganda which undoubtedly had its
effect. The great mass of up-state voters, many of whom
were born and raised in the atmosphere of Republicanism,
were given to believe that there was nothing wrong with
the Grand Old Party. As a primary day or an election day
drew near, Platt speeded up the work of his literary bureau.
Country editors were given "boiler-plate" editorials or were
paid out right to circularize their paper free to the voters.
This and the other activities of Platt and his organization
around election time centered upon the building up of that
narrow margin which was necessary for success. Platt
could count upon a huge block of "loyal" Republican voters
in the up-state; it was the stragglers who caused him trouble.

To gather them in he selected candidates who represented different regional, religious, racial, social, and economic groups, and his party workers utilized all the well-known devices to interest these groups in the candidates and the campaign. Upon election day the heavy power of the money bag was brought into play; thousands of party "workers" were hired for the day; thousands of farmers were paid for their time and the use of their teams in bringing voters to the polls; and there were thousands who did not bother with subterfuges in getting their "pay." This machinery was much more essential for state than for national campaigns as Roosevelt discovered in the gubernatorial contests of 1898 and 1910.

The sources of Platt's political power and Roosevelt's political influence were quite different. The mechanical elements of Platt's autocratic power were: first, control over the nomination and the election machinery through his co-operation with the state committee; second, control over the state legislature through his relations with the oligarchy ruling that body; third, control over the patronage through whatever influence he had with the president, the governor, and the federal, state, and local administrative officers; fourth, his control over the party campaign funds through the relations which he maintained with the directors of certain corporations who were high in financial circles; and lastly, control over the minds of the voters through his intimate relations with party editors and men of influence in the business and political worlds. By checking off these levers one against the other he was able to play upon the habits, customs, traditions, ambitions, rivalries, gratitudes, greeds, and fears of those with whom he had dealings. He was a fit leader for a rivalrous, egotistic organization like the Republican machine in New York during the late nineties. Roosevelt, on the other hand, owed his political influence to his fearless use of the various official positions which he held. As governor of New York, he consulted the party organization, but he made it clear to the public that he was not afraid to make independent use of the governor's message power, the governor's appointing power, and the governor's position as the official leader of the state government. When Roosevelt became president of the United States, he went much farther in exalting the importance of the executive, and he assumed a position of leadership in the Republican organization, state and national. In state affairs he intervened in the selection of the chairman of the state committee, he made suggestions to the state nominating conventions, he used his influence in legislative matters, and he recognized his friends in the distribution of the federal patronage in New York. Roosevelt's interference in these matters ended for a time the control of the state government by any single unofficial leader of Platt's type, thus showing the importance of these elements to that kind of party management. Against such usurpations of party powers and against the direct appeals that Roosevelt made for popular support, the old régime had not constructed any adequate defensive armor.

CHAPTER XIV

CONCLUSION

Theodore Roosevelt began to exalt the importance of the official leadership of the state government at a time when Platt's power as the unofficial leader of the state government seemed to be complete and arbitrary. Each of these men became very powerful in his own way, but neither could control the affairs of government outside the limits imposed upon them by the social and economic conditions of the period. The party organization which they led was a delicate mechanism, and the parts were so interrelated that the slightest disarrangement in one of them was liable to wreck the others. The larger society in which the party organization functioned was infinitely more complex and finely adjusted than the party itself. Only as long as the political leaders of New York during the nineties fitted into their time and place situation did they retain their position of ascendency.

One of the conditions of political control over a large area is the existence of local political organizations whose leaders come more or less as a matter of habit to look to the central organization for advice. A state party manager like Platt could discipline some of the local political leaders who did not listen to his advice, but there were others so firmly entrenched in their social situations that he realized it would be useless for him to try to root them out. Successful local chieftains like Barnes or Aldridge were factors with which the central leaders had to reckon at all times. Their contacts with local business men, local labor leaders, and local groups having political influence were such that they could not be easily severed by one working from the outside. When some of the local leaders began to look to Odell and Roosevelt for advice, Platt's days as a political manager were numbered.

Beyond the inner group of party managers, stood the great body of active party workers whose loyalty to the organization depended in part upon the existence of a large number of public offices available for their use. Neither Platt nor Roosevelt created the thousands of elective and appointive positions in the government services which came to be looked upon as the spoils of party victory. On the contrary, both men had something to do with the movement which made the sources of patronage more inaccessible for partisan uses. Platt's resignation from the United States Senate with Conkling in 1881 in order to vindicate the spoils principle not only gave him the title, "Me-Too," but it also gave an impetus to civil service reform in both the state and the nation. When he began to regain power in the nineties, he felt the pinch of this reform. Theodore Roosevelt as one of President Harrison's civil service commissioners lessened the amount of federal patronage available, and the new state constitution of 1894 gave Governor Roosevelt a chance to protect the merit system in the state civil service. One saving element in the situation from the point of view of the organization was the great increase in the number of executive appointments due to the expansion of the social and economic functions of the government. The organization was recognized in most of the appointments made by Governors Morton, Black, and Roosevelt. Roosevelt, however, staged several dramatic fights before certain important state positions were filled and thus brought the organization to name the man whom he regarded as its best candidate. Roosevelt also had a part in the independent movement in municipal politics which threatened the bipartisan system

which had been established in the cities of the state for the
purpose of dividing local spoils between the two party
machines. In national affairs, President Roosevelt was not
as "kind hearted" as McKinley had been. With the aid of
Governor Odell he made great inroads into the body of
Platt's friends among the state and federal services. In
endeavoring to control primaries and nominating conventions, Roosevelt as well as Platt relied upon the support of
an active body of party workers.

In election campaigns the chief reliance of both Platt and
Roosevelt was the great block of habitual Republican voters
in the state. As manager of the party organization, one of
Platt's chief concerns was the delivery of this vote upon
election day. It was his duty to see that the confirmed
Republican voters came to the polls and voted. Considering
the blind allegiance of the great mass of up-state farmers
and shop-keepers to the Republican tradition, this was an
important function. There were hundreds of thousands of
voters who, because of their early training and environment,
their anti-urban prejudices, or their business and social connections, could be counted upon to vote the Republican
ticket if they voted at all. These voters constituted perhaps
the most essential basis of Platt's political power. Their
unquestioning loyalty to the candidates and issues bearing
the Republican label was the *sine qua non* of Republican
successes. In campaigns for the control of the state legislature, Platt found their prejudices together with the constitutional gerrymander an almost unbeatable combination.
In his campaign for the governorship, Roosevelt made a
wide appeal for votes, but he addressed himself primarily to
the native American, up-state Republicans.

Large as the habitual Republican vote was in New York,
it could not be relied upon alone for state-wide victories.
The state contained an equally numerous and immovable

block of Democratic voters located for the most part in New York City. In state elections the Republican organization vote was largely offset by the machine vote of the Democrats, and the result was likely to turn upon the attitude of the independent voters. The overwhelming Republican victories of the middle nineties were brought about by those who broke away from the old party traditions. After 1896 the Republican leaders had an up-hill fight in state-wide elections that were not overshadowed by national issues. The decline of the rural population and the rapid growth of the population of New York City made inroads into the Republican strength. In order to limit the Democratic vote, the Republican managers secured the adoption of drastic ballot reform laws for the great metropolis, but in order to increase their own vote they were compelled to make appeals to the independent voters. It was the necessity of combining both the Republican and the independent vote that brought Platt and Roosevelt together. Platt knew that the man who had rigorously enforced the Sunday closing law in New York City and who had been a champion of civil service reform at Washington would not be a subservient governor. Roosevelt knew that the organization which Platt represented did not always practice the kind of political morality that he preached. In order to produce a vote winning combination, these two men entered into a makeshift partnership which had its drawbacks on both sides. Both defended this partnership on the ground that the exigencies of the political situation demanded it.

In legislative matters, the power of the official and also the unofficial leader depended largely upon the strength of the social groups that could be lined up in favor of particular measures. Platt was by no means an arbitrary law-maker. In the face of the governor's vote, the opposition of the press and the hostility of several civic associations, he was unable to force through the legislature two of his favorite measures, an anti-caricature bill and a metropolitan police bill. The passage of the Raines Liquor Tax bill was looked upon as one of the great accomplishments of Platt and his organization. However, the bill passed largely because more powerful interest groups were marshalled in its favor than were marshalled against it. A majority of the organization men favored the bill because of its patronage features, and the up-state farmers were pleased with the revenue raising provisions which rested more heavily upon the urban than upon the rural communities, but it is also true that the moralists, the preachers, the temperance men, and the prohibitionists favored the bill because it lessened the number of saloons and weakened the saloon power of Tammany Hall. In like fashion, the Greater New York bill was passed because a sufficient number of people were interested enough either in the patronage possibilities, in the commercial opportunities, or in the civic potentialities that would be created by the formation of the greater city to get behind the bill and override those who were opposed. The limitations of the control which the organization exercised over the lawmaking process came out very clearly during Roosevelt's administration as governor. When Governor Roosevelt aroused the farmers, the market gardeners, the mechanics, and tradesmen having small holdings, and the real estate associations to the full realization of the fact that they were paying an improper and excessive portion of the general taxes, Platt and his legislative cabal did not dare block the passage of the Franchise Tax Law. Roosevelt was also able to persuade the legislature to enact much social and economic legislation which was opposed by the large corporations. The growing power of the labor unions, the increasing number of civic associations, and the development of reform societies were factors which the Republican organization could not afford to ignore. Roosevelt learned to marshal these groups much more effectively than did the organization leaders.

The politico-industrial system with which Platt was identified was working so smoothly during the McKinley administration that even Roosevelt was not fully aware of some of its unfortunate by-products. Platt did not try to initiate any great policies but was content to act as the agent for any social or economic group which was powerful enough to make itself felt in a political way. When the interests of several powerful groups conflicted, he brought about the best sort of a compromise that he could. The financiers or capitalists, the most highly organized industrial group, got in the main what they wanted from Platt but not always, because Platt sometimes saw that their demands, if carried out, would alienate a sufficient number of voters to endanger his position. Several financiers were disappointed when the Franchise Tax Law was passed. The directors of the utility corporations were opposed to the law, but Platt felt that he could not openly adopt their view without undermining his own political power. That his power as a political manager was something worth conserving seemed to be the opinion of the most influential capitalists. At least they were willing to trust him with the enormous campaign contributions that were so necessary to the smooth working of the Republican organization. The New York Republican organization rendered valuable service to the financiers in advocating the gold standard in 1896 and in supporting the Dingley Tariff Bill of 1897. These general services as well as many other less conspicuous special services deserved their reward. The insurance investigations showed that the directors of the great corporations did not regard it as improper for them to use the corporate funds to help out both of the two major parties. The period of the Platt régime was one of great lavishness in all directions. The rapidly growing population of the Empire State created an ever growing need for better means of transportation, communication, and marketing, and for newer and more specialized types of work. Great investments of capital were required to meet these needs. The investment bankers were therefore in a strategic position, and they made the best of the traditional philosophy that the public interest was promoted by stimulating individual economic activity. As long as this situation continued, Platt could rely upon huge campaign funds provided also that his charges for favors were not too high and that the services which he rendered were reasonably efficient. He himself was wholly in sympathy with the view which postulated the "right of a man to run his own business in his own way, with due respect of course to the Ten Commandments and the Penal Code." He, like the financiers, was inclined to take a rather narrow view as to what the Ten Commandments meant and as to what should go into the Penal Code. It was difficult for him and the money kings who used him to realize that their activities were injuring others. Roosevelt delivered few attacks against the evils of this system before he became president of the United States. The Franchise Tax bill which he pushed through the legislature in such dramatic fashion was not as revolutionary a measure as Platt tried to make it appear. A similar law had been upon the statute books before. When Roosevelt laid down his tasks at Albany, he admitted that he was leaving many ragged edges behind.

The insurance investigation was one of the events which helped to lift the fog which had surrounded the old individualistic system. The corporation heads then sensed the anger of the policy-holders and the stock-holders who felt that they had been robbed. The public which had formerly admired, respected and idolized the successful business man now purchased eagerly the magazines and papers which pictured some of the great millionaires as "malefactors of great wealth." The growing scarcity of natural and artificial opportunities tended to increase the discontent that was felt with the traditional alliance between big business and politics. It was this discontent that Roosevelt capitalized so successfully as president. When he preached executive reponsibility and the need for a government which would do things, the people went along with him.

In the election of 1896 the voters of the United States were presented with a more clearly defined issue than they had had in thirty-six years. In the state of New York, for various reasons, Platt's candidates, McKinley's personality, and the Republican policies and traditions appeared more attractive to a majority of the voters than did the Hill-Croker candidates, Bryan's policies, and the Democratic traditions. The momentum of this election helped to continue Platt's organization in power for fourteen years. During this time the monetary question ceased to be a live issue, and the seeds of corruption began to grow in parts of the Republican organization. Until the extent of this corruption was revealed by several investigations, the voters in the upstate regions were fairly complaisant. They had no means of knowing what was going on within the government. As long as their own interests were not directly affected, they were indifferent to political issues and events. The upward trend of the business cycle tended to create a feeling of satisfaction with existing arrangements among all classes. While the farmers did not gain a proportionate share of this prosperity, the prices of their products did rise and they could boast of a semblance of good times. In such an era, who was willing to keep alert day and night in order to hold the many headed government to account for the charges committed to it? There was Platt busily engaged behind the scenes doing his part to bring about some sort of continuity out of a disintegrated administrative system, to choose the least objectionable of the office-seekers, and to secure the co-operation of the governor and a two-chambered legislature made up of two hundred localists. Until Roosevelt and others tried to do some of these things openly, the Easy Boss was able to cling to his place as an agent of the properties classes, a retailer of franchises, government contracts, and special legislation.

INDEX

INDEX

Albany Argus, on Odell as a legislative agent, 165–66; on Platt's withdrawal from the senatorial contest, 28.

Albany, investigation of the county and city of, 224–29, 244–45.

Albany Evening Journal, Barnes, editor of, 63–64, 100, 136, 228, 308; Weed, editor of, 15.

Aldrich, Nelson, United States senator, 178–79, 298–99, 333.

Aldridge, George Washington, "boss" of the city of Rochester, 62, 76, 96, 110, 161–62, 221, 311, 334, 350; state superintendent of public works, 205–6, 208, 216, 238–40, 244, 338.

Alexander, De Alva S., congressman, 174.

Alger, Russel A., on Platt, 257, 323; on Platt and Dana, 134.

Allds, Jotham P., floor leader of Assembly, 157–59, 198, 267, 335, 344, state senator, investigation demanded by, 245–46, 263–64, 309–10, 343.

Allds investigation. *See* J. P. Allds.

"Amen Corner," significance of, 57–58.

Appointments, made by governor, 205.

Armstrong insurance investigation. *See* Insurance investigation.

Arthur, Chester A., nomination to vice-presidency, 24; and Platt, 26, 28; removal from collectorship, 23.

Assembly, organization of leadership in, 154 ff. *See* state legislature.

Astor House, meeting place for Weed conferences, 15; 56.

Astoria Gas Company, 247.

"Availability," 95–97.

Baker, Frank M., railroad commissioner, 276, 296.

Barnes, Thurlow Weed, 63, 103.

Barnes, William, Jr., "boss" of Albany, 63–64, 76, 82, 107, 139, 162, 224–29, 244–45, 260–62, 269, 302–4, 312, 331, 334–35, 338, 340–43, 350; relations with Roosevelt, 244–45, 262, 304, 341.

Barnes-Roosevelt libel suit, 245, 262.

Bayne Committee, 226–29, 244. *See* Albany.

Bidwell, George R., collector of port of New York, 253, 293.

Binghamton Leader, on Platt's convention leadership in 1898, 100–101.

Binghamton Republican, Dunn manager of, 61, 135.

Bipartisan system in New York cities, 225, 352.

Black, Frank S., governor, 94–98, 184; relations with Platt, 188–89, 194–96, 202–4, 206–7, 216–17, 235, 238, 276, 346; senatorial candidate, 300–301.

Black Horse Cavalry, 262–65, 267, 271.

Blackmail. *See* "strike" bills.

361